PE 3102.
N42
AFR

AFRICAN AMERICAN ENGLISH SPEAKERS AND THEIR PARTICIPATION IN LOCAL SOUND CHANGES: A COMPARATIVE STUDY

AFRICAN AMERICAN ENGLISH SPEAKERS AND THEIR PARTICIPATION IN LOCAL SOUND CHANGES: A COMPARATIVE STUDY

Edited by

MALCAH YAEGER-DROR

University of Arizona

and

ERIK R. THOMAS

North Carolina State University

Publication of the
American Dialect Society

•

Number 94

•

Published by Duke University Press
for the American Dialect Society

Supplement to American Speech, *Volume 84*

PUBLICATION OF THE AMERICAN DIALECT SOCIETY

Editor: ROBERT BAYLEY, *University of California, Davis*
Managing Editor: CHARLES E. CARSON, *Duke University*

Number 94
Copyright 2010
American Dialect Society
ISBN: 978-0-8223-6732-1

Library of Congress Cataloging-in-Publication Data

African American English speakers and their participation in local sound
  changes : a comparative study / edited by Malcah Yaeger-Dror and Erik
  R. Thomas.
    p. cm. — (Publication of the American Dialect Society ; no. 94)
  Includes bibliographical references and index.
  ISBN 978-0-8223-6732-1 (cloth : alk. paper)
    1. Black English—Phonology. 2. English language—Dialects—United
  States. 3. Sociolinguistics—United States. I. Yaeger-Dror, Malcah.
  II. Thomas, Erik R. III. Series: Publication of the American Dialect
  Society ; no. 94.
PE3102.N42.A37 2010
427'.97308996073–dc22   2010003605

British Library Cataloguing-in-Publication Data available

CONTENTS

ACKNOWLEDGMENTS

This book would never have been possible without funding from the National Science Foundation extended to several of these projects. Nor would it have been possible without the cooperation of the individual authors in our endeavor to provide as direct a comparison as possible of the corpora developed. To make this book possible, the authors had to carry out their corpus collection following a single protocol, with speakers interviewed in each location using the same interactive style. The speakers from the African American community had to be matched with local "predominant vernacular" speakers with more or less the same demographic background, and interviewed in the same style. Consequently, this took a great deal of cooperation among the participants and a great deal of consultation. All of the authors who made it to the finish line have been truly remarkable team players. They also agreed to follow a single protocol for acoustic analysis so that the results from various cities can be compared, and they all took advantage of the NORM protocol developed by Erik Thomas and Tyler Kendall to normalize their data. Consequently, while direct statistical comparisons have not been made here, the vowel diagrams are all comparable and reflect similarities and differences available to the naked eye. The unified protocol—for demographics, for interview style, and for the analysis itself—would not have been possible without the work of William Labov; the methods used to compare speakers of different groups within society are based both on the work of Labov and his students, and on early and more recent work spearheaded by Walt Wolfram. We might add that the authors worked without any overarching funding for this project. That the papers are comparable is primarily thanks to the assiduous work and communication among all the participants. The results have proven quite as groundbreaking as we had projected, and we hope the participants and other local researchers can continue to work in this vein, permitting the narrowed focus and demographically sophisticated comparisons called for by Labov, Wolfram, and others.

1. INTRODUCTION

ERIK R. THOMAS   MALCAH YAEGER-DROR
North Carolina State University   *University of Arizona*

THIS PADS VOLUME has been a long time in the works. It was initially envisioned as a book dedicated to Walt Wolfram, who has initiated so much work on African American English (AAE), first in Detroit (1969), then in Mississippi (1974), and since 1992 in North Carolina. The studies presented here were first introduced in two Linguistic Society of America symposia (Yaeger-Dror and Thomas 2007, 2008). Papers that were offshoots of those symposia were then delivered at the New Ways of Analyzing Variation conference or the International Conference on Language and Social Psychology and the results incorporated into the subsequent articles in this volume and in a forthcoming volume on interdialectal accommodation to be published in the *Journal of English Linguistics* in 2010 (Yaeger-Dror and Purnell forthcoming).

We address variation within African American English here—not the variation related to social class and gender that previous studies have examined, but geographical variation. AFRICAN AMERICAN ENGLISH (AAE), in this text, will be used for the dialects spoken by African Americans who are citizens of the United States. For the most part, we are referring to speakers whose ancestors were living in the United States before the end of the Civil War in 1865. We will try to avoid the impression that we are including speakers who are from other parts of the New World (e.g., Guyana, the Dominican Republic, and Haiti) or are African immigrants themselves. The extent to which blacks who have immigrated to the United States since 1865 (much less 1965!) have assimilated into this African American culture and dialect is a much more complicated question that will be left to future studies.

We use PREDOMINANT VERNACULAR ENGLISH (PVE) where previous studies have referred to European American English. The speakers of what is determined to be the predominant dialect, or local PVE, of a given locale are (in each study) non–African

Americans who speak the local KOINÉ—often referred to as the RE-GIONAL DIALECT of the area. This locution has been chosen both to emphasize that in each city studied there is a locally predominant vernacular norm which differs from city to city, as Labov, Ash, and Boberg (2006) have now reconfirmed, and to avoid the impression that the speakers of this dialect are all of European descent. This is an important point in a research environment where there is a great deal of evidence that Latinos (e.g., Thomas 2001; Fought 2003; Konopka and Pierrehumbert 2008; Roeder forthcoming) do not necessarily speak this dialect, although they certainly are in-fluenced by it, and that Asian Americans (Wong 2007; Chun 2009; Hall-Lew 2009) generally do and may in fact have influenced the regional PVE.

AAE has generated several controversies, a fact which is not sur-prising for the most extensively studied single group of dialects in North America. During the 1960s, there was debate about whether vernacular forms of AAE (or AAVE) were "adequate" as linguistic systems. This debate was resolved by the early work of Labov, Wol-fram, and their colleagues: AAVE certainly is a complete linguistic system (see, e.g., Labov 1972).

There were also debates about whether AAVE is consistently distinct from the predominant local vernacular in a given area. This debate emerged because the important early studies of AAVE (Labov et al. 1968; Wolfram 1969; Fasold 1972; Labov 1972; Rick-ford and McNair-Knox 1994) were conducted in Northern or semi-Northern cities of the diaspora, where AAVE was found to differ quite extensively from the local speech and was found to share many of the same patterns from city to city. However, AAVE had been transplanted from the South only a generation or two before these studies, and it was unclear to what extent it differed from Southern White Vernacular English (SWVE). Studies such as Wol-fram's (1974) examination of speech in Mississippi demonstrated that it did, though other studies suggested that most differences were more quantitative than qualitative (e.g., Bailey and Bassett 1986; Dorrill 1986; Pederson et al. 1986–92; Thomas 1989a, 2001; Bernstein 1993).

Questions about the origins of AAE have attracted debate continuously since the 1960s. This debate has centered around two opposing positions: the Anglicist (e.g., McDavid and McDavid 1951) and neo-Anglicist (e.g., Poplack 2000) position that AAE features originated from dialects of the British Isles, and the Creolist position (e.g., Dillard 1972) that AAE originated from a creole that was once widely spoken on plantations across the South. However, there are other positions, such as a view that early AAE exhibited substrate features from western African languages without coalescing into a true creole and a hybrid view that AAE combined features from British Isles dialects and from creoles, since, after all, many slaves were brought from the West Indies to the American South.

Other issues have concerned the continuing development of AAE with respect to specific local vernaculars. The first was the Divergence/Convergence Controversy, which flared up during the 1980s, based at first on data that had been collected during the 1960s and early 1970s. It began when Labov and Harris (1986) reported that AAVE and the local PVE in Philadelphia were diverging, not converging as had been assumed for AAVE and PVEs across the country up until that point. Considerable debate ensued (Fasold et al. 1987; Bailey and Maynor 1987, 1989; Butters 1989), but it was short-lived. Quite recently, a new controversy, the "Uniformity Controversy," has appeared (Thomas 2007). This controversy involves a number of related questions:

a. Is there a set of norms for AAE throughout the country to which many or most African Americans are oriented (even if not all African Americans acquire the normative forms)?
b. What degree of geographical uniformity does AAE exhibit?
c. How dependent or independent is geographical variation in AAE from geographical variation in the white vernaculars of the same region?

In earlier years, researchers tended to assume that AAE was geographically uniform and that the principal differentiations within it fell along social class and gender lines. As Thomas (2007) notes, when a researcher encountered a difference between his or her own results and those of another researcher elsewhere, the difference was generally attributed to variations in corpus design or analysis methods. Earlier researchers assumed implicitly that there was a widespread set of norms for which AAVE speakers aimed. In fact, following Labov's earlier discussion of "group members" versus "Lames" (Labov et al. 1968; Labov 1972), studies often discounted speakers who did not converge toward those norms, based on the assumption that their behavior was, as Harlem preteen group members referred to them, "Lame" (Labov 1972).

However, even preceding the results from those early studies in the Northern diaspora, other studies had already shown there were regional variations within AAE in the South. Dialect geography revealed a rather complex picture, one that even the dialect geographers themselves were prone to oversimplifying. For example, Kurath (1949, 6) asserted that "by and large the Southern Negro speaks the language of the white man of his locality or area and of his education." However, Dorrill (1986), who compared African American and white speakers from the same communities using data from Kurath's own Linguistic Atlas of the Middle and South Atlantic States, found that the situation was more complex than Kurath had suggested. Dorrill's analysis showed that African Americans in these states shared numerous local features with nearby whites, such as the allophonic variations of the BITE and BOUT vowels that used to predominate in Virginia. Nonetheless, he also showed that African Americans tended to exhibit more monophthongal forms of the BOAT, BAIT, and BOUGHT vowels than whites in a given area. Data from the Linguistic Atlas of the Gulf States (LAGS) (Pederson et al. 1986–92) also showed the same sort of mixed picture: AAE is far from geographically uniform in LAGS, but not identical to white speech, either. The clearest exemplification of the geographical heterogeneity is the Mississippi Delta region, in which African Americans (and whites) used numerous phonological and lexical forms seldom found elsewhere in the LAGS territory. However, African Americans also exhibited some general trends that set them off from whites, such as showing significantly less fronting of the BOUT nucleus than whites in LAGS.

More recent studies have also uncovered pockets illustrating the great diversity within Southern AAE. Wolfram and Thomas (2002), for example, found that African Americans in remote Hyde County, North Carolina, showed several features infrequent in AAE elsewhere. Among these were morphosyntactic features, such as leveled *weren't* (e.g., *it weren't cold*) and plural -*s* (*the cars goes too fast*), and vocalic features, such as fronted forms of the BOAT vowel and front-gliding forms of the BOUT diphthong. Nevertheless, younger African Americans were losing many of these features, and even older African Americans showed subtle differences from local whites. To the west, Fridland (2003) and Fridland and Bartlett (2006) have noted that African Americans in Memphis share some vowel developments with local whites, such as fronting of the BOAT vowel and a switch in the relative positions of the BAIT and BET nuclei (both associated with the Southern Shift proposed by Labov 1994). Nevertheless, they also found that African Americans were adopting the fronting of BOAT more slowly than whites.

The diversity of patterns reflects the diversity of communities across the South. Hyde County had a long history of isolation. For most of its history, it was much easier to reach by boat than by land, and its African Americans were particularly cut off from African Americans elsewhere. Similar kinds of situations occurred in many parts of the South, such as the Appalachians, where tiny African American communities existed in scattered locations; the Sea Islands off the coast of South Carolina and Georgia, where African Americans constituted the majority and have maintained the creole Gullah to this day; and the swampy hinterlands of southern Louisiana, where French was long the main medium of communication. Conversely, the more central areas where the plantation culture flourished in antebellum days had large African American populations but were not isolated. The growth of Southern cities with the rise of mill towns starting during the 1870s and continuing during the twentieth century (Woodward 1951; Cobb 1984; Feagin 2004; McNair 2005) created new and substantial communities of African Americans who had close contacts with other African American communities.

Outside the South, the Great Migration, the movement of African Americans to large Northern and Western cities, created a new situation for African Americans. This arrangement consisted of dense communities of African Americans in inner-city neighborhoods surrounded by white Anglo, Hispanic, or less often Asian American communities, which in turn were surrounded by rural areas with almost no African Americans. African Americans in these new urban neighborhoods lacked the kinship ties to nearby rural communities that had existed in the South. Economically, they were tied to factories and other industry and had left behind agriculture, exemplified by the old sharecropping system. Linguistically, African Americans from different parts of the South found themselves living side by side. This situation likely created the mixing of dialectal forms and subsequent leveling of regional differences that make up KOINEIZATION, as Trudgill (1986) defines it. (See also Payne 1976, 1980; Kerswill 2002; and Auer, Hinskens, and Kerswill 2004.)

As will be discussed in this volume, the Great Migration of African American speakers to the North occurred relatively recently, peaking during World War I, the Great Depression, and World War II. This had not left a great deal of time for geographic differences to develop when data were gathered in the 1960s. In addition, movement of African Americans between cities may also have encouraged the development of widespread norms for AAE at the expense of local norms, as has the prestige of musical styles like hip hop (Alim and Baugh 2007; Alim, Ibrahim, and Pennycook 2008; Alim 2009; Blake, Fix, and Shousterman 2009), which has even led to the "crossing" of white speakers (e.g., Bucholtz and Skapoulli 2009; Guy and Cutler forthcoming), providing further motivation for a supraregional norm. Much of the morphosyntactic evidence, as well as some lexical (Smitherman 2000) and vocalic evidence, suggests that widespread AAE norms emerged. However, the dialect contact that African Americans experienced with surrounding non–African Americans differed from what they had known in the South. The dialects with which they found themselves in contact differed from city to city, too. In building new communities, they were free to create new linguistic norms that might differ from one city to another. While evidence emerged for widespread AAE norms, there is also evidence that AAE phonology and sometimes morphosyntax varies in different cities, even while their phonology remains (at least quantitatively) distinct from that of other ethnic groups (Thomas 1989b; Deser 1990; Henderson 1996; Pollock and Berni 1997; Hinton and Pollock 2000; Anderson 2002; Flood 2002; Jones 2003; Nguyen 2006; Bloomquist 2009). Evidence to be presented here will demonstrate that there is also convergence toward the local phonology.

A problem that follows from this evidence is that we should be just as careful not to imply hegemony of regional PVEs over African American varieties as we are to avoid the simplistic assumption that there is a single iconic AAVE.

While many forms of AAE retain their distinctiveness from neighboring varieties, an unanswered question is how much independence they show. Has AAE developed regional differentiation from a supraregional norm that did not result from accommodation to regional dominant dialects? The few previous papers addressing regional variation in AAE have discussed features, such as rhoticity and fronting of the BOAT vowel, that clearly represent accommodation to local varieties (Pollack and Berni 1997; Hinton and Pollock 2000; Flood 2002; Fridland and Bartlett 2006). This potential bias mirrors earlier reports by dialect geographers, such as the above-mentioned quotation from Kurath (1949).

In the reported cases in which accommodation to dominant varieties has been attested, whites outnumbered African Americans considerably, and the relative population sizes alone seem to account for the direction of assimilation. For one region in which African Americans vastly outnumbered whites at one time—the Low Country of coastal South Carolina and Georgia—it has been suggested that monophthongal forms of the BAIT and BOAT vowels spread from African American speech to white speech (Thomas and Bailey 1998) rather than vice versa. Other studies have suggested that the limited amount of copula deletion found in SWVE spread from AAE (Wolfram 1974) and have revived an old theory that nonrhoticity in Southern white English may have been promoted by nonrhoticity in AAE (Feagin 1997).

Another factor the studies in this volume consider is the degree of interaction that exists between different communities within the urban setting: the degree to which a given AAE accommodates to the local PVE norms is theoretically also influenced by the degree of actual face-to-face contact that occurs between members of each group in any given locale. Presumably, the greater the degree of segregation that exists in a given locale, the smaller the opportunity for assimilation or accommodation in either direction. Of course, the factors of power and prestige also play a role in the direction of assimilation, and their precise effects with regard to the transfer of features between AAE and local varieties remain to be worked out.

The number of studies that provide evidence for geographical diversity within AAE, especially outside of dialect geography, remains small, however. The previously mentioned studies do not provide anything close to a broad geographical picture of AAE phonology. Moreover, they either explore a small subset of phonological variables or focus on syntax. Nevertheless, this preliminary work has provided a tantalizing taste of how much geographical variation might exist in AAE now that there are large numbers of adult speakers native to each area. It can be used to provide a historical perspective on the work to be presented here. We have attempted to address this part of the Uniformity Controversy—the degree of geographical variation in AAE—in this collection. To facilitate comparability, each research group followed the same protocol, analyzing both African American and local PVE speakers. Each speaker's vowel system was analyzed to permit the comparison of the local AAE and "General American" vowel phonology, as compared with that of the archetype for a supralocal AAE, as well as with the local PVE's idiosyncrasies. Each research group also considered the available evidence on the degree to which speakers from one group actually are in contact with the other group. Some of these studies also considered the degree to which an individual AAE speaker interacts with local PVE speakers—either by considering where they live and what their own relationships are, or by self-reports of the individual speakers.

In fact, aside from our unifying the protocol for these studies so that the works are comparable, we also found that it would be helpful to formulate a convention to unify the text and simplify the reader's task; with that thought in mind, we have suggested that authors use neither a phonological / / nor a variable ( ) presentation, both of which differ in conventions from author to author. We have chosen instead to refer to a given vowel class using keywords, following the principle behind Wells (1982). To further simplify, we turned to Ladefoged's (2005) choice of keyword paradigm, which uses words that are as untrammeled by their consonantal environment as possible. To obtain these keywords, he chose an H_D frame, to have his speakers "Say HEED again."

To minimize the need for varying the "carrier" environment, in each case, the vowel being focused on here will be a B_T paradigm (see table 1.1). Where the environment requires a more specific formulation, the paradigm word will be chosen to reflect that change. For example, most instances of BITE in the volume refer to the diphthong /aɪ/ in all contexts; however, where the following

TABLE 1.1
Keywords Used to Represent Vowel Classes

IPA	Keyword	[_r]	[_l]	Specific Formulations
/i/	BEET	BEER	PEEL	
/ɪ/	BIT		BILL	BIN [_N]
/e/	BAIT	BEAR	BAIL	
/ɛ/	BET		BELL	BEN [_N]; BEG [_g]
/æ/	BAT			BACK [_k]; BAG [_g]; BAN [_N]; TAP [_p]; TAB [_b]; BAD, for Milwaukee [_d], for New York see p. 109
/ɑ/	BOT	BAR		
/ɔ/	BOUGHT	BORder	BALL	
/o/	BOAT	BOAR	BOWL	
/ʌ/	BUT		CULL	
/ʊ/	BOOK	BOOR	PULL	
/u/	BOOT		POOL	TOOT [C_{coronal−}]
/aɪ/	BITE	PYRE	BILE	BIDE [_C_{vd}]; BUY [_#]; PINE [_N]
/aʊ/	BOUT	HOUR	HOWL	BOUGH [_#]
/oɪ/	BOY		BOIL	
/ɚ/	BIRD			BURR [_#]; bothER [−stress]

phonetic environment is pertinent, BITE, BIDE, PINE, and BUY are used to indicate /aɪ/ followed by a voiceless obstruent, followed by a voiceless obstruent, followed by a nasal, and in word-final position, respectively. Pre-/r/ and pre-/l/ vowels are differentiated with their own keywords. We hope that this convention will permit the reader to follow all the authors without difficult transitioning between chapters.

The communities included here represent strikingly diverse contact situations. First, there are two studies of communities in what might be called the "Old South"—rural, relatively isolated locales. These two chapters describe communities that are otherwise dissimilar. The first, by Childs, Mallinson, and Carpenter, examines two locales at the eastern end of North Carolina and two at the western end, all of which were surveyed in research initiated by Wolfram. One of the eastern locations is Hyde County, the same one studied by Wolfram and Thomas (2002) and Wolfram, Thomas, and Green (2000). In all four locales, African Americans formed fairly small communities that were isolated from other African Americans for long periods. The dominant dialects were the Pamlico Sound dialect in the east and the southern Appalachian dialect in the west, and African Americans showed considerable—if not complete—accommodation to them. The second study, by Wroblewski, Strand, and Dubois, examines AAE in three parishes in rural southern Louisiana. In striking contrast to the North Carolina locales, many African Americans in southern Louisiana, who often identify themselves as Creoles, have a long tradition of French language use. Like their white neighbors, the Cajuns, they exhibit dialectal features in a mixture not found elsewhere. They share features such as monophthongal forms of the BOAT and BAIT vowels with the Cajuns. Yet they show evidence of some older features as well.

Next is Andres and Votta's study of a "New South" community: Roswell, Georgia, an exurb of Atlanta. This community is as close to the mainstream of AAE as any surveyed in this volume. Even in Roswell, though, AAE appears to show some influence from the speech of the neighboring PVE. Andres and Votta examine some features associated with the "Southern Shift" (e.g., Labov 1994), a series of vowel shifts that occur in Southern white speech, and the merger of the BOT and BOUGHT vowels. These processes seem to have spilled over from the PVE to AAE, but the details are more complicated. Andres and Votta's results are similar to those from Memphis that appeared in Fridland (2003) and Fridland and Bartlett (2006). It is notable that evidence for both convergence and dialect maintenance occurring together was not found in earlier studies, when most of the parents of the AAE speakers were not from the local community, but is more likely to be found in these newer studies based on more settled communities. After the urban South, we move to the urban Northeast. Here we examine two cities with strikingly different PVEs as well as different settlement histories: New York and Pittsburgh.

An intricate interethnic relationship appears in Pittsburgh in the chapter by Eberhardt. African Americans came to Pittsburgh even before the Great Migration, to work in the steel mills; they have adopted the local BOT-BOUGHT merger and fronting of the BOAT vowel from Pittsburgh's PVE. However, they have not adopted monophthongization of the BOUT diphthong, which they self-report as a feature indexing "white" identity rather than local identity and which Eberhardt finds is not being retained by younger white speakers either. At the same time, they have retained two widespread AAE features that are not common in Pittsburgh's PVE, the BIN-BEN merger and monophthongization of BIDE.

In New York, Coggshall and Becker also find that AAE and the PVE reveal a complex relationship. African Americans have lost some typical AAE features that were documented in Labov's earlier work, while accommodating to locally salient features, such as the complex offglide of the BOUGHT vowel; at the same time, they have retained other AAE features.

Finally, we have two studies of cities in the Midwest: Columbus, Ohio, and Milwaukee, Wisconsin. However, like our featured Northeastern cities, the PVEs in these two cities differ substantially. Columbus lies in the Midland dialect region, typified by fronting of the BOAT and BOOT vowels and various mergers, including ongoing merger of the BOT and BOUGHT vowels. Milwaukee, meanwhile, lies in the Northern dialect area, where the series of vowel changes called the Northern Cities Shift (Labov 1994) occurs. Milwaukee was largely settled by African Americans after the Great Migration was past.

The Northern Cities Shift includes, among other shifts, the raising and ingliding/downgliding of the BAT vowel in all contexts, fronting of the BOT vowel, and lowering or retraction of the BET vowel. The AAE speakers in the sample appear to share some of these local features, though they eschew Canadian Raising of BITE-BIDE (in which the nucleus is higher for BITE than for BIDE), which also occurs locally, and they retain the BIN-BEN merger. Purnell takes a closer look at the amount of contact a particular African American has with local PVE speakers and whether accommodation to an interviewer's speech occurs. He finds that certain variables—especially fronting of the BOOT vowel, the weakness of the BIDE glide, and the height of the BET vowel—are strongly affected by those factors in Milwaukee.

For Columbus, Durian, Dodsworth, and Schumacher find, once again, that African Americans converge toward the local PVE for some features but not others. They have adopted fronting of the BOAT and BOOT vowels but differ from whites in their environmentally influenced realizations of the BOT and BOUGHT vowels. They also show a raising and fronting shift of the BUT vowel that is not reported in the PVE, but which Thomas (2001) suggested would be more advanced in AAE than in most PVE speech.

These studies should be considered as preliminary evidence for the early years of the twenty-first century. The evidence described in these studies reflects a much more nuanced assessment, linguistically speaking, than was possible in the late 1960s or even in the 1980s. Certainly, the evidence presented here from the South (in the papers by Childs et al., Andres and Votta, and Strand et al.) supports Wolfram's (2007) assertion that the hypothesis (or, as he now refers to it, the "myth") of a uniform AAE cannot be maintained.

However, perhaps the theory was never intended to be relevant for communities in which AAE and local vernacular speakers had been in consistent contact for 200 years. Maybe it reflected the "new town" situation that arose during the Great Migration—with the parents of the speakers, as well as most of the speakers themselves, new to the area and interacting primarily with other speakers whose roots were in various regions of the South rather than with African American OR with white speakers who were from the local area. It may pertain primarily to settings where AAE speakers—like people in the situations discussed in Trudgill (1986), the mostly white children in King of Prussia, Pennsylvania (Payne 1976, 1980), families in mill communities such as Anniston, Alabama (Feagin 2004), and Griffin, Georgia (McNair 2005), or the "new towns" of Milton Keynes, England (Kerswill and Williams 2000), and the suburbs of Texas (Thomas 1997)—had relatively limited contact with speakers from outside the nonlocal, nonnative, segregated community.

Thus, while the more insular Southern communities provide a sense of perspective on what members of the parent generation may have had as a linguistic background, evidence from non-Southern communities 20–50 years further on provides crucial points for comparison as well. In the Northeastern and Midwestern cities discussed here, we find a great deal of regional diversity, even while certain characteristic features of AAE appear repeatedly. As discussed above, it appears that each local AAE community has incorporated features of the local predominant vernacular, while maintaining some nonlocal features, presumably to index social identity.

Is there some consensus by these authors that this increased accommodation to a given locally predominant vernacular is caused by increasing integration into the local community? Unfortunately, the studies are fairly clear that actual integration has been reduced since the 1970s, so the degree of face-to-face interaction with local vernacular speakers has perhaps even decreased since the studies that were carried out in the 1960s. On the other hand, we would be wise to consider the results in the light of earlier theoretical work: the work of Milroy (1980) and Sankoff (Sankoff and Laberge 1978) is particularly helpful. The interaction of social network and Linguistic Marketplace (developed on the basis of Bourdieu's early theories) may weight the importance of local vernacular features so the speakers in the workforce are more prone to accommodate to them.

Thus, the picture this text paints is more nuanced than earlier studies, but it also leads to new questions about AAE that will have to be resolved in future work. Is there a way to determine which local features will be used to index local identity? How can we determine which AAE features will be used to index racial identity? Exactly what role does the level of contact with non–African Americans play in a speaker's vowel configuration? While some communities seem to favor, for example, the BIN-BEN merger as a marker of ethnicity, that is not universally the case. There seems to be a suite of variants that are widespread in AAE, but in a given community, African Americans keep some of those features, discard others, and adopt selected features from the local PVE. The studies included in this volume demonstrate clearly and importantly the direction future research needs to go. The next steps will be to examine whether and how the local situation determines the development of local AAE, whether contact with African Americans from other regions reinforces the variants that are widespread in AAE, whether—even in the absence of extensive supraregional AAE contacts—the speakers in a given place will focus on the same AAE features to index/demonstrate their ethnic/racial affiliation, and the degree to which the use of such indexical features is contingent on processes similar to those that cause "crossing" among the white fans of rap and hip hop.

Initial studies of the importance of various factors on Speech Accommodation (Giles 1973, 1984; Coupland 2007) are already providing preliminary analyses of "accommodative" tendencies in different communities (e.g., Bucholtz and Skapoulli 2009; Harwood and Pitts 2009; Yaeger-Dror and Purnell forthcoming). However, very little of that work has addressed the issue of the degree to which AAE speakers accommodate to the national "General American" norm, to the locally dominant norm, or neither, and whether the degree to which they may do so is influenced by the degree of actual face-to-face contact that occurs between African Americans and PVE speakers; future research will also focus on the importance of indexical weighting (Yaeger and Feagin 2005) of favored and disfavored realizations.

REFERENCES

Alim, H. Samy. 2009. "Translocal Style Communities: Hip Hop Youth as Cultural Theorists of Style, Language, and Globalization." In Bucholtz and Skapoulli 2009, 103–28.

Alim, H. Samy, and John Baugh, eds. 2007. *Talkin Black Talk: Language, Education, and Social Change.* New York: Teachers College Press.

Alim, H. Samy, Awad Ibrahim, and Alastair Pennycook, eds. 2008. *Global Linguistic Flows: Hip Hop Cultures, Youth Identities, and the Politics of Language.* London: Routledge.

Anderson, Bridget L. 2002. "Dialect Leveling and /ai/ Monophthongization among African American Detroiters." *Journal of Sociolinguistics* 6: 86–98.

Auer, Peter, Frans Hinskens, and Paul Kerswill, eds. 2004. *Dialect Change: Convergence and Divergence in European Languages.* Cambridge: Cambridge Univ. Press.

Bailey, Guy, and Marvin Bassett. 1986. "Invariant *Be* in the Lower South." In *Language Variety in the South: Perspectives in Black and White,* ed. Michael B. Montgomery and Guy Bailey, 158–79. University: Univ. of Alabama Press.

Bailey, Guy, and Natalie Maynor. 1987. "Decreolization?" *Language in Society* 16: 449–73.

———. 1989. "The Divergence Controversy." *American Speech* 64: 12–39.

Bernstein, Cynthia. 1993. "Measuring Social Causes of Phonological Variation in Texas." *American Speech* 68: 227–40.

Blake, Renée, Sonya Fix, and Cara Shousterman. 2009. "Vowel Centralization before /r/ in Two AAE Dialects: A Case of Regional Variation." Paper presented at the annual meeting of the Linguistics Society of America, San Francisco, Calif., Jan. 8–11.

Bloomquist, Jennifer. 2009. "Dialect Differences in Central Pennsylvania: Regional Dialect Use and Adaptation by African Americans in the Lower Susquehanna Valley." *American Speech* 84: 27–47.

Bucholtz, Mary, and Elena Skapoulli, eds. 2009. "Youth Language at the Intersection: From Migration to Globalization." Special issue of *Pragmatics* 19.1.

Butters, Ronald R. 1989. *The Death of Black English: Divergence and Convergence in Black and White Vernaculars.* Frankfurt am Main: Lang.

Chun, Elaine. 2009. "Speaking Like Asian Immigrants: Intersections of Accommodation and Mocking at a U.S. High School." In Bucholtz and Skapoulli 2009, 17–38.

Cobb, James C. 1984. *Industrialization and Southern Society, 1877–1984*. Lexington: Univ. Press of Kentucky.

Coupland, Nikolas. 2007. *Style: Language Variation and Identity*. Cambridge: Cambridge Univ. Press.

Deser, Toni. 1990. "Dialect Transmission and Variation: An Acoustic Analysis of Vowels in Six Urban Detroit Families." Ph.D. diss., Boston Univ.

Dillard, J. L. 1972. *Black English: Its History and Usage in the United States*. New York: Random House.

Dorrill, George Townsend. 1986. *Black and White Speech in the Southern United States: Evidence from the Linguistic Atlas of the Middle and South Atlantic States*. Frankfurt am Main: Lang.

Fasold, Ralph W. 1972. *Tense Marking in Black English: A Linguistic and Social Analysis*. Arlington, Va.: Center for Applied Linguistics.

Fasold, Ralph W., William Labov, Fay Boyd Vaughn-Cooke, Guy Bailey, Walt Wolfram, Arthur K. Spears, and John Rickford. 1987. "Are Black and White Vernaculars Diverging? Papers from the NWAVE XIV Panel Discussion." *American Speech* 62: 3–80.

Feagin, Crawford. 1997. "The African Contribution to Southern States English." In *Language Variety in the South Revisited*, ed. Cynthia Bernstein, Thomas Nunnally, and Robin Sabino, 123–39. Tuscaloosa: Univ. of Alabama Press.

———. 2004. "New South, New Town: Accounting for Contrasting Varieties of English in the White Community." Paper presented at the 33rd annual conference on New Ways of Analyzing Variation (NWAV 33), Ann Arbor, Mich., Sept. 30–Oct. 3.

Flood, Constance L. 2002. "Unconstricted /r/ in the SSE and AAVE of Lee County, Alabama." Paper presented at the 66th Southeastern Conference on Linguistics (SECOL LXVI), Memphis, Tenn., Apr. 18–20.

Fought, Carmen. 2003. *Chicano English in Context*. New York: Palgrave Macmillan.

Fridland, Valerie. 2003. "Network Strength and the Realization of the Southern Vowel Shift among African Americans in Memphis, Tennessee." *American Speech* 78: 3–30.

Fridland, Valerie, and Kathy Bartlett. 2006. "The Social and Linguistic Conditioning of Back Vowel Fronting across Ethnic Groups in Memphis, Tennessee." *English Language and Linguistics* 10: 1–22.

Giles, Howard. 1973. "Accent Mobility: A Model and Some Data." *Anthropological Linguistics* 15: 87–105.

———, ed. 1984. "The Dynamics of Speech Accommodation." Special issue of *International Journal of the Sociology of Language* 46.

Guy, Gregory R., and Cecelia Cutler. Forthcoming. "Speech Style and Authenticity: Quantitative Evidence for the Performance of Identity." *Language Variation and Change.*

Hall-Lew, Lauren. 2009. "Ethnicity and Sound Change in San Francisco English." Paper presented at the 35th Annual Meeting of the Berkeley Linguistics Society (BLS 35). Berkeley, Calif., Feb. 14–16.

Harwood, Jake, and Margaret J. Pitts, eds. 2009. "Current Research in Language and Social Psychology: Select Papers from ICLASP XI, Tucson, AZ." Special issue of *Journal of Language and Social Psychology* 28.4.

Henderson, Anita. 1996. "The Short 'a' Pattern of Philadelphia among African-American Speakers." In "(N)WAVES and MEANS: A Selection of Papers from NWAVE 24," ed. Miriam Meyerhoff, 127–40. *University of Pennsylvania Working Papers in Linguistics* 3.1.

Hinton, Linette N., and Karen E. Pollock. 2000. "Regional Variations in the Phonological Characteristics of African American Vernacular English." *World Englishes* 19: 59–71.

Jones, Jamilla. 2003. "African Americans in Lansing and the Northern Cities Vowel Shift: Language Contact and Accommodation." Ph.D. diss., Michigan State Univ.

Kerswill, Paul. 2002. "Koineization and Accommodation." In *The Handbook of Language Variation and Change,* ed. J. K. Chambers, Peter Trudgill, and Natalie Schilling-Estes, 669–702. Malden, Mass.: Blackwell.

Kerswill, Paul, and Ann Williams. 2000. "Mobility Versus Social Class in Dialect Levelling: Evidence from New and Old Towns in England." In *Dialect and Migration in a Changing Europe,* ed. Klaus Mattheier, 1–13. Frankfurt am Main: Lang.

Konopka, Kenneth, and Janet Pierrehumbert. 2008. "Vowels in Contact: Mexican Heritage English in Chicago." In "SALSA XVI: 2008," ed. Amy Brown and Josh Iorio, 94–103. Special issue of *Texas Linguistic Forum* 52.

Kurath, Hans. 1949. *A Word Geography of the Eastern United States.* Ann Arbor: Univ. of Michigan Press.

Labov, William. 1972. *Language in the Inner City: Studies in the Black English Vernacular.* Philadelphia: Univ. of Pennsylvania Press.

———. 1994. *Principles of Linguistic Change.* Vol. 1, *Internal Factors.* Oxford: Blackwell.

Labov William, Sharon Ash, and Charles Boberg. 2006. *The Atlas of North American English: Phonetics, Phonology, and Sound Change.* Berlin: Mouton de Gruyter.

Labov, William, Paul Cohen, Clarence Robins, and John Lewis. 1968. *A Study of the Non-standard English of Negro and Puerto Rican Speakers in New York City.* Cooperative research project no. 3288. 2 vols. New York: Columbia Univ.

Labov, William, and Wendell A. Harris. 1986. "De Facto Segregation of Black and White Vernaculars." In *Diversity and Diachrony*, ed. David Sankoff, 1–24. Amsterdam: Benjamins.

Ladefoged, Peter. 2005. *Vowels and Consonants: An Introduction to the Sounds of Languages.* 2nd ed. Malden, Mass.: Blackwell.

McDavid, Raven I., Jr., and Virginia Glenn McDavid. 1951. "The Relationship of the Speech of American Negroes to the Speech of Whites." *American Speech* 26: 3–17.

McNair, Elizabeth DuPree. 2005. *Mill Villagers and Farmers: Dialect and Economics in a Small Southern Town.* Publication of the American Dialect Society 90. Durham, N.C.: Duke Univ. Press.

Milroy, Lesley. 1980. *Language and Social Networks.* Oxford: Blackwell.

Nguyen, Jennifer G. 2006. "The Changing Social and Linguistic Orientation of the African American Middle Class." Ph.D. diss., Univ. of Michigan.

Payne, Arvilla Chapin. 1976. "The Acquisition of the Phonological System of a Second Dialect." Ph.D. diss., Univ. of Pennsylvania.

———. 1980. "Factors Controlling the Acquisition of the Philadelphia Dialect by Out-of-State Children." In *Locating Language in Time and Space*, ed. William Labov, 143–78. New York: Academic Press.

Pederson, Lee A., Susan Leas McDaniel, Guy Bailey, Marvin H. Basset, Carol M. Adams, Caisheng Liao, and Michael B. Montgomery, eds. 1986–92. *The Linguistic Atlas of the Gulf States.* 7 vols. Athens: Univ. of Georgia Press.

Pollock, Karen E., and Mary C. Berni. 1997. "Variation in Vocalic and Postvocalic /r/ in AAVE." Technical paper presented at the annual convention of the American Speech-Language-Hearing Association, Boston, Nov. 19–22.

Poplack, Shana, ed. 2000. *The English History of African American English.* Malden, Mass.: Blackwell.

Rickford, John R., and Faye McNair-Knox. 1994. "Addressee- and Topic-Influenced Style Shift: A Quantitative Sociolinguistic Study." In *Sociolinguistic Perspectives on Register*, ed. Douglas Biber and Edward Finegan, 235–76. New York: Oxford Univ. Press.

Roeder, Rebecca. Forthcoming. "Northern Cities Chicano English: Vowel Production and Perception." In "Accommodation to the Dominant

Norm in American Corpora," ed. Malcah Yaeger-Dror and Thomas C. Purnell. Special issue of *American Speech* 85.2.

Sankoff, David, and Suzanne Laberge. 1978. "The Linguistic Market and the Statistical Explanation of Variability." In *Linguistic Variation: Models and Methods*, ed. David Sankoff, 239–50. New York: Academic Press.

Smitherman, Geneva. 2000. *Black Talk: Words and Phrases from the Hood to the Amen Corner*. Rev. ed. Boston: Houghton Mifflin.

Thomas, Erik R. 1989a. "The Implications of /o/ Fronting in Wilmington, North Carolina." *American Speech* 64: 327–33.

———. 1989b. "Vowel Changes in Columbus, Ohio." *Journal of English Linguistics* 22: 205–15.

———. 1997. "A Rural/Metropolitan Split in the Speech of Texas Anglos." *Language Variation and Change* 9: 309–32.

———. 2001. *An Acoustic Analysis of Vowel Variation in New World English*. Publication of the American Dialect Society 85. Durham, N.C.: Duke Univ. Press.

———. 2007. "Phonological and Phonetic Characteristics of African American Vernacular English." *Language and Linguistics Compass* 1: 450–75.

Thomas, Erik R., and Guy Bailey. 1998. "Parallels between Vowel Subsystems of African American Vernacular English and Caribbean Anglophone Creoles." *Journal of Pidgin and Creole Languages* 13: 267–96.

Trudgill, Peter. 1986. *Dialects in Contact*. Oxford: Blackwell.

Wells, J. C. 1982. *Accents of English*. 3 vols. Cambridge: Cambridge Univ. Press.

Wolfram, Walter A. 1969. *A Sociolinguistic Description of Detroit Negro Speech*. Washington, DC: Center for Applied Linguistics.

Wolfram, Walt. 1974. "The Relationship of White Southern Speech to Vernacular Black English." *Language* 50: 498–527.

———. 2007. "Sociolinguistic Folklore in the Study of African American English." *Language and Linguistic Compass* 1: 292–313.

Wolfram, Walt, and Erik R. Thomas. 2002. *The Development of African American English*. Oxford: Blackwell.

Wolfram, Walt, Erik R. Thomas, and Elaine W. Green. 2000. "The Regional Context of Earlier African American Speech: Evidence for Reconstructing the Development of AAVE." *Language in Society* 29: 315–55.

Wong, Amy W. 2007. "Two Vernacular Features in the English of Four American-Born Chinese." In "Papers from NWAV 35," ed. Toni Cook and Keelan Evanini, 217–30. *University of Pennsylvania Working Papers in Linguistics* 13.2.

Woodward, C. Vann. 1951. *Origins of the New South, 1877–1913*. Baton Rouge: Louisiana State Univ. Press.

Yaeger-Dror, Malcah, and Crawford Feagin. 2005. "Elephants, Speech Styles, Accommodation, and Changes." Paper presented at the annual meeting of the Linguistic Society of America, Oakland, Calif., Jan. 6–9.

Yaeger-Dror, Malcah, and Thomas C. Purnell, eds. Forthcoming. "Accommodative Tendencies in Interdialect Communication." Special issue of *Journal of English Linguistics* 38.2.

Yaeger-Dror, Malcah, and Erik R. Thomas, organizers. 2007. "Vowel Phonology and Ethnicity." Symposium at the annual meeting of the Linguistic Society of America, Anaheim, Calif., Jan. 4–7.

———, organizers. 2008. "Urban Vowel Phonology and African American Identity." Symposium at the annual meeting of the Linguistic Society of America, Chicago, Jan. 3–6.

THE OLD RURAL SOUTH

2. VOWEL PHONOLOGY AND ETHNICITY IN NORTH CAROLINA

BECKY CHILDS

Coastal Carolina University

CHRISTINE MALLINSON

University of Maryland, Baltimore

JEANNINE CARPENTER

Duke University

IN THIS CHAPTER, we analyze a range of salient vowels for approximately 35 African American residents of four North Carolina communities, also comparing their vowel phonology to white speakers of the local predominant vernaculars. A state rich in geographic, ethnic, and linguistic diversity, North Carolina has been the site of extensive research by the North Carolina Language and Life Project, spearheaded by Walt Wolfram. Since 1992, the project has conducted fieldwork in over 15 different speech communities across North Carolina, from the coast to the mountains to the growing cities of the Piedmont in between. Of the four sites we examine, two are located on the coast: Roanoke Island (Carpenter 2004, 2005) and Hyde County (Wolfram and Thomas 2002). Two other sites are located in the mountains: Beech Bottom (Mallinson 2002; Mallinson and Wolfram 2002) and Texana (Childs and Mallinson 2004, 2006; Childs 2005; Mallinson 2006). Each of the four sites is indicated in the map in figure 2.1, with the location of Roanoke Island indicated by the marker for the town of Manteo.

One of the two main vowel patterns of American English is the so-called Southern Shift (Labov 1991; Thomas 2001). The Southern Shift—a series of sound changes that is generally considered to be completed among Southern white speakers—is characterized by the raising of short front vowels, the backing and lowering of front high vowels, the fronting of the back vowels BOOT, BOOK, and BOAT, and glide reduction in BITE and BIDE. The framework of the Southern Shift provides a template from which to describe particular varieties of Southern English, closely examine its characteristic

FIGURE 2.1

North Carolina Language and Life Project Field Sites

sounds, and detail how sound changes in its particular regions, lo-cales, and among specific ethnic groups operate in comparison to other areas in the South.

While this sound change pattern encompasses the South as traditionally defined, the spread and advancement of the change is not uniform throughout the region. The Southern Shift is more advanced and widespread in rural areas and less so in more urban areas. At the same time, considerable debate exists in the sociolin-guistic literature as to whether African American speakers (living in the South or in Southern transplant and/or diaspora communi-ties) participate in the Southern Shift and/or in local vowel pat-terns. As a result, research examining the vowel patterns of African Americans in and outside the South has been a highly active area of sociophonetic investigation in recent years. Multiple studies now indicate that many African American speakers do participate in re-gional vocalic patterns, but they may also show mixed vocalic align-ment—adapting pronunciations in ways that still align with local or regional patterns but that also reflect a speaker's ethnic status.

Fridland (1999, 2003) finds that African American speakers in Memphis show patterns of back vowel fronting as well as other indications of participation in the Southern Shift. Recent work in Atlanta (Kretzschmar et al. 2004) also reveals African American speakers using Southern vowel variants, even though white speak-ers in Atlanta did not use them. Similarly, Anderson (2003) finds that African Americans in Detroit are fronting high back vowels in ways similar to those of white speakers in the American South and English speakers all over the world. She argues that the use of Southern Shift characteristics among African Americans, even those not currently living in the South, can be a reflection of their identity and affiliation with the South. These and other similar studies thus underscore the need to take into account the confluence of regional, ethnic, and personal identity when examining the vocalic characteristics of African American residents of the South and elsewhere.

In our study, we find comparable trends. We analyze vowels that have been noted as crucial sites for variation: BITE and BIDE, BOAT, BOUT, BOOT, and BOOK. These vowels—in particular BITE, BIDE, BOAT, and BOOT—are noted for their unique productions in Southern English and are implicated in the Southern Shift (Thomas 2001). With respect to BITE and BIDE, the glide may be weakened or the segment monophthongized to [a] in many varieties of Southern English. In some regions of the South, including the Highland South (Hall 1942; Wolfram and Christian 1976), speakers show a weakened glide regardless of whether the following environment is voiceless (e.g., BITE) or voiced (e.g., BIDE). Other Southern varieties show glide weakening only before voiced segments, as in BIDE, and in open syllables, as in BUY (Bailey and Thomas 1998; Thomas 2001). Most descriptions of African American English (AAE) conclude that it aligns with those Southern varieties that reduce the glide only in pre-voiced positions (BIDE, BILE, PYRE, PINE); as such, the incidence of pre-voiceless-obstruent glide weakening (BITE) might suggest accommodation to local and/or regional dialect norms.

Among most speakers (particularly whites) throughout the South, the BOUT class is subject to fronting of the nucleus and lowering of the glide and may even show breaking, resulting in triphthongization to something like [æɛɒ]—a correlate of the "Southern drawl" (Thomas 2001, 2003, 2004). One variation occurs in the dialect of the Pamlico Sound region of North Carolina, whose speakers may front the glide of BOUT when the nucleus is low, producing variants such as [ay ~ ai] (Thomas 2001, 2003, 2004).

Finally, fronting of BOOT, BOOK, and BOAT is occurring throughout the English-speaking world; in addition, BOAT, when fronted,
is perceived by Americans as indicative of Southern affiliation, as
shown by Torbert (2004).

Based on data from a series of speakers in these sites across
North Carolina (see table 2.1), we find that African American speakers often do participate in local phonological patterns, although a
range of social and stylistic factors may subtly affect this regional
accommodation. Our data reveal that regionally situated ethnic enclave communities may align differently with regional norms and
the norms of a transregional AAE. Accordingly, we emphasize the
critical role of regionality that has recently reentered the discussion of AAE (Wolfram 2007) and suggest that further studies of
AAE spoken in regionally situated enclaves are necessary.

TABLE 2.1
Demographic Data for North Carolina Speakers by Field Site

Speaker	Gender	Date of Birth	Year of Interview	Interviewer's Race, Gender, & Age
Roanoke Island				
MS	F	1928	2003	WF22, BF22
DK	F	1962	2004	BF22, BF23
WC	M	1988	2003	WF22, BF22, BF21
Hyde County				
RS	M	1910	1997	WM31, WF36
OG	F	1909	1997	WF22, BF20
SS	F	1981	1997	BF18
Beech Bottom				
JCM	M	1929	2000	WF22, WF26
JM	M	1962	2001	WF22, WM30
Texana				
Gail Ann	F	1933	2003	WF25, WF27
Debbie	F	1964	2003	WF25, WF27
Zora	F	1957	2003	WF25, WF27
Michelle	F	1959	2003	WF25, WF27

ROANOKE ISLAND

Roanoke Island, a coastal community and the site of Carpenter's (2004, 2005) research, is a 13-mile island in the Croatan and Roanoke Sounds, located between the barrier islands of the Outer Banks and the mainland coast of North Carolina. Roanoke Island was the site of the first child born of English parents in the New World, Virginia Dare, and is the location of the mysterious Lost Colony.

Most of the slaves in the northern coastal region of North Carolina came through the coastal Virginia slave trade (Kay and Cary 1995). There was also an active slave trade in Wilmington, North Carolina, but transportation up and down the North Carolina coast was considerably more difficult. The majority of the African Americans on Roanoke Island during and following the Revolutionary War period were slaves of small farmers and fishermen. There also were some free African Americans who probably had migrated down from the Virginia settlements. However, as Wright and Zoby (2000, 24) explain, because these free blacks were of "little economic threat ... [they] shared the limited resources on more or less equal footing with their white counterparts." When the Civil War began, North Carolina's population was more than one-third black. At that time, the Roanoke Island slave population constituted almost 28% of the island's total population, which the 1850 U.S. Census lists as 610 residents (Stick 1970, 89).

Roanoke Island was a key battlefield in the Civil War. With the Union victory of the Battle of Roanoke Island (Feb. 7, 1862), the Confederates lost one of their most important maritime routes. As the Union army moved further into Confederate territory, runaway and freed slaves would go to the locations where Union armies established camps. One such camp was established on Roanoke Island (Stick 1958, 161) and resulted in the initiation of what would later become the Freedmen's Colony of Roanoke Island.

After the war ended in 1865, however, the vibrant community of over 3,000 freed slaves was lost. African Americans were displaced, and the land that the Freedmen's Colony occupied was returned to the former owners. Not all of the African American residents of Roanoke Island's Freedmen's Colony left, however (Bowser and Bowser 2002). By 1900, a group of around 300 African Americans continued to live on the island and formed their own neighborhood called California (Wright and Zoby 2000, 124). Although the national Civil Rights Act, passed in 1964, mandated large-scale desegregation, most African American residents still live in the same area of Roanoke Island with limited movement into the traditionally "white" parts of the island.

The contemporary African American community of Roanoke Island is the only long-established minority population of its kind on the Outer Banks. Its earlier isolation, historical continuity, community solidarity, and strong regional affiliation make this community a prime sociolinguistic situation for investigating patterns of language change in African American speech over time. Carpenter (2004, 2005) establishes a general sociolinguistic profile of Roanoke Island, analyzing data obtained from interviews with over 40 African American residents. European Americans on Roanoke Island are speakers of the well-documented variety of Pamlico Sound English (PSE), also known as Outer Banks English (Schilling-Estes 1996; Schilling-Estes and Wolfram 1997; Wolfram, Hazen, and Schilling-Estes 1999; Wolfram and Thomas 2002). African Americans, however, showed mixed dialect alignment. Some African Americans showed accommodation to PSE patterns, while others accommodated more to general norms of AAE. The analysis showed generational differences among the African American speakers, as well as considerable individual variation in each generation (see Carpenter 2004, 2005 for more detail).

Vowel trends for African American residents of Roanoke Island show similar mixed dialect alignment trends. Figures 2.2, 2.3, and 2.4 are vowel plots from three African American speakers. MS, an older African American female (b. 1928), is a lifelong resident of the community who worked in the crab houses with other women from the community and as a domestic for local white residents. DK, a middle-aged African American female (b. 1962), left the community for only two years while she was in school in a neighboring coastal community. WC, a young African American male (b. 1988) who at the time of the study was a prominent high school athlete, is the great nephew of MS, the oldest speaker in this study.

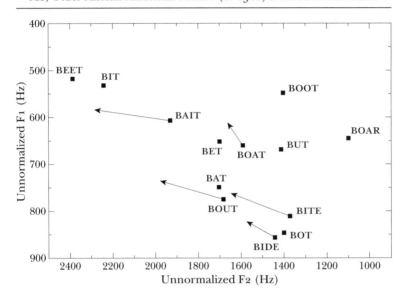

FIGURE 2.2

MS, Older African American Female (b. 1928) from Roanoke Island

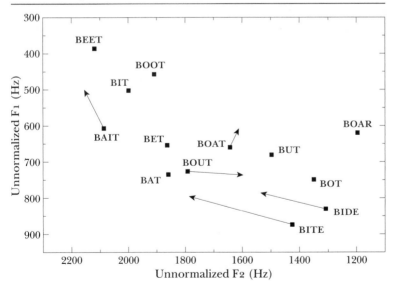

FIGURE 2.3

DK, Middle-Aged African American Female (b. 1960) from Roanoke Island

FIGURE 2.4

WC, Younger African American Male (b. 1988) from Roanoke Island

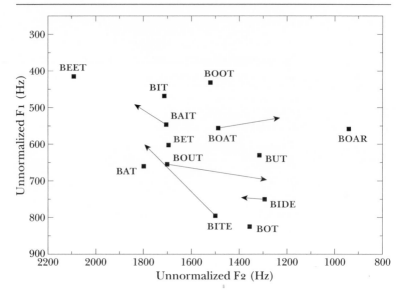

From these three vowel plots, we see that characteristics of PSE are evident among the speakers, who show lowered nuclei for both BAIT and BOAT. At the same time, these African American speakers front BOOT and BOAT, suggesting they are not accommodating to general vocalic norms of AAE. For both BITE and BIDE, as well as BOUT, the general pattern indicates alignment not with norms of AAE but with those of PSE (Schilling-Estes 1996; Schilling-Estes and Wolfram 1997; Wolfram, Hazen, and Schilling-Estes 1999; Thomas 2003, 2004). For the BITE and BIDE classes, differences in vowel productions are based on speaker age and identity. As the vowel plot in figure 2.2 exemplifies, middle-aged speakers produce a more backed nucleus. At the same time, speakers who identify more strongly with the regional area are more likely to use a regionally salient variant of /ai/ that sounds more like /oi/ (Carpenter 2004, 2005). For the BOUT class, middle-aged and older speakers exhibit the front-gliding variant that is characteristic of PSE in which *brown* comes to sound more like *brain* or *brine*, though younger speakers resist this pattern.

HYDE COUNTY

The second community, Hyde County, is the site of Wolfram and Thomas's (2002) extensive analysis. In contrast to Roanoke Island, which is an island located off of the coast, Hyde County consists of part of the mainland, as well as one of the barrier islands of North Carolina, Ocracoke Island. Hyde County, established by European Americans in the early 1700s, is one of the oldest and most physically isolated counties in North Carolina. Due to its rurality and the fact that the county is 85% wetlands, travel in the area prior to the draining of wetlands and the building of the first paved road in the 1920s mainly took place by boat. Fishing, logging, and grain farming have been the major occupations in the county; today, most people work in fishing and natural resources: for example, as local hunting and fishing guides. From 1790 to 1900, the population of Hyde County remained relatively stable, but from 1900 to 2000, the Hyde County population dropped by nearly half. Currently, around one-third of Hyde County residents are African American, and historically there has been high tension between black and white residents in this area.

Since the mid 1990s, 144 interviews have been conducted with residents of Hyde County: 92 with African American residents and 52 with European American residents (as documented in Wolfram and Thomas 2002). Most of the speakers were born and raised in Hyde County, as were their parents and grandparents, so they represent a sample of a long-standing population. Many residents never traveled outside the county or have only traveled to a limited extent, obtained only a few years of formal schooling, and worked in occupations such as tenant farming, fishery, and domestic labor.

In Wolfram and Thomas's (2002) analysis, generational differences were found, as well as individual differences within each generation (see also Wolfram and Beckett 2000). Among Hyde County's African American speakers, data revealed mixed dialect alignment. Just as in Roanoke Island, African American speakers in Hyde County were found to show some regional dialect features characteristic of the Outer Banks region, but at the same time they were also found to show some alignment with broader norms of AAE. In fact, the youngest generation of African American speakers in Hyde County have increased features of AAE in their speech, while distancing from local dialect traits found among cohort young European American speakers.

For Hyde County, we present vowel plots for RS, OG, and SS (figures 2.5, 2.6, and 2.7, resp.). None of these speakers has traveled extensively and all are second- or third-generation Hyde residents. Similar to what was found for Roanoke Island, in Hyde County both older African American and white speakers were found to share the distinctive vowel traits of the Ocracoke region: pronouncing BITE or BIDE as a diphthong approaching a BOY sound, pronouncing BOUT with a form close to a BAIT sound, and fronting BOAT. Despite the fact that older residents of Hyde County (both white and African American) showed these vowel patterns, however, the majority of traditional vowel variants have disappeared among younger speakers. Young African American and white speakers alike are losing the traditional variants for BITE, BIDE, and BOUT, although they are retaining fronted BOAT, which is characteristic of Southern speech more generally.

FIGURE 2.5
RS, Older African American Male (b. 1910) from Hyde County

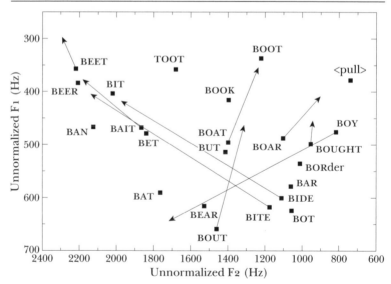

FIGURE 2.6

OG, Older African American Female (b.1909) from Hyde County

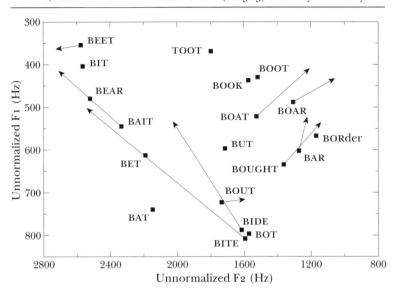

FIGURE 2.7

SS, Younger African American Female (b. 1981) from Hyde County

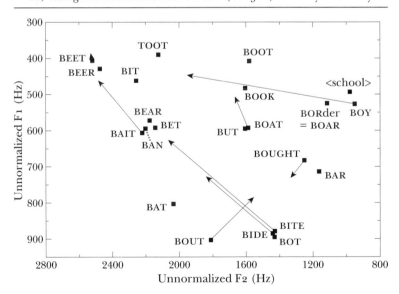

BEECH BOTTOM

Next, leaving the coastal region to examine the first of two sites located in the North Carolina mountains, we examine Beech Bottom, a tiny, highland community in the Appalachian region of western North Carolina, located along the Tennessee border. In some respects, the mountain community of Beech Bottom is quite different from that of Hyde County and Roanoke Island, but there are also some important parallels, notably their historical insularity and long-established continuity of the biethnic population. Of necessity, the investigation of Beech Bottom undertaken here uses a case study format for the few remaining African American residents; nonetheless, it offers an important complement to the analysis of Hyde County, Roanoke Island, and Texana.

The first African Americans to the Beech Bottom area were brought by Colonel Waightsill Avery (1741–1821), the namesake of Avery County, in which Beech Bottom is located. Small bands of Cherokees and other Native Americans also passed through the area as late as 1790, resulting in a population of mixed racial and ethnic heritage. Local history maintains that a man named Hampton Jackson formally settled Beech Bottom in the 1870s, after Appalachia had begun to develop as a diverse region, with establishments by English, Scotch-Irish, German, and Dutch inhabitants (Harris 1994). Although his own ethnicity is not recorded, Jackson was said to have raised two adopted sons, one of Native American and Polish descent and the other of Native American and German descent, and his family thus contributed to the settlement of Beech Bottom as a multiethnic community.

From 1900 to 1940 Beech Bottom's population ranged from 80 to 111 people (Turner 2000). During this period, 65 residents were classified as African American, which included those who were of mixed African American, European American, and Native American descent (Harris 1994). The primary community industry was feldspar mining, but as the mines began to close in the early 1940s, residents migrated north to seek work in the shipyards of Virginia or factories in Ohio. The mobilizing effect of World War II also took a toll on the community's population, as locals joined the service and resettled elsewhere upon their return.

Christmas tree farming is now Beech Bottom's primary industry, and two farms with about 100,000 trees employ several community residents full time; other residents tend trees on a part-time basis. Currently, only about ten longtime residents live in Beech Bottom, and several are related to each other. Three of the residents are European American while others have been categorized as African American although they currently claim mixed descent—African American, European American, and Native American (Harris 1994). The ethnic heritage of Beech Bottom residents is, of course, contrary to the stereotype that Southern Appalachia is a "reservoir of culturally-homogeneous, white Anglo-Saxon southerners," as discussed by Billings (1989).

Given Beech Bottom's historical diversity, it is an ideal community for the study of the relationship between European American Appalachian speech and the speech of Appalachian nonwhites. Mallinson (2002) and Mallinson and Wolfram (2002) provide an overview of data obtained from interviews with three African American residents from Beech Bottom and eight local whites. In general, Beech Bottom residents showed widespread accommodation to local norms of Appalachian English (AppE). The accommodation was so extensive that each generation of speakers showed little to no maintenance of selected features of AAE.

Vowel plots are provided for two African American male Beech Bottom speakers in figures 2.8 and 2.9. Both speakers were born and raised in Beech Bottom. The older speaker (b. 1929) traveled to some extent when he was in the army for five years, while the middle-aged speaker (b. 1962) has lived in the community all his life, working nearby at a medical supplies facility and farming Christmas trees on the side. From these vowel plots, we can see the speakers' accommodation to local Appalachian dialect norms. Both speakers have fairly fronted productions of back vowels BOOT and BOOK, which is documented for the South (Kurath and McDavid 1961; Labov 1991; Fridland 2003). However, this trend is suggested to be atypical of Southern African Americans, whose productions of these vowels, as Thomas (2001, 172) notes, "usually remain backed." The speakers show minimal fronting of BOAT but a more fronted nucleus in BOUT. Finally, the productions of BITE

FIGURE 2.8

JCM, Older African American Male (b. 1929) from Beech Bottom

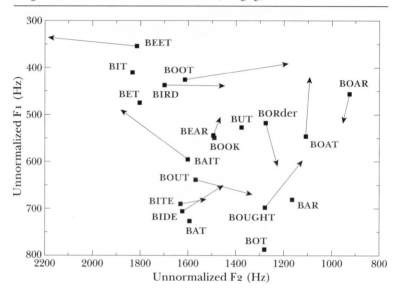

FIGURE 2.9

JM, Middle-Aged African American Male (b. 1962) from Beech Bottom

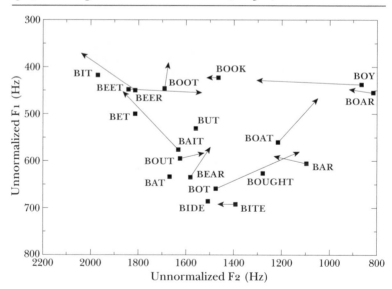

and BIDE are also essentially monophthongal, which shows the speaker's alignment with local vocalic patterns. Thus, the overall vowel systems of these two African American Beech Bottom speakers seem to be aligned toward a regional dialect norm.

TEXANA

Our last field site, Texana, is North Carolina's largest black Appalachian community and is located in the Great Smoky Mountain region of the Appalachian Mountains. The sociohistoric background of Texana dates to around 1880, when, according to local residents, an African American family named McClelland originally moved to Cherokee County from other western North Carolina counties and named the community after their daughter, Texana. The population of Texana, which now has approximately 150 residents, has remained relatively stable for over a century.

Despite the fact that Appalachia is largely considered to be an area with little ethnic diversity (Beaver and Lewis 1998; Hayden 2004), the area is more heterogeneous than is often thought, and nonwhite communities have persisted in Appalachia since its early settlement period. Many Texana residents have African, Cherokee, and Irish-European ancestors, which is the case for many black Appalachians, particularly those whose ancestors were former slaves (Dunaway 2003). Due to their mixed ancestry, many Texana residents have had to grapple with issues of ethnic identity and the fact that their heritage is often more diverse than the single term "African American" denotes. In fact, many of them feel that checkboxes for racial or ethnic categories, such as those found on the U.S. Census, are insufficient to categorize their heritage. Today, most Texanans self-identify as "black," which is the term they prefer since it is a designation based on the color of their skin rather than on any one racial or ethnic identity. At the same time, several Texanans have reported in their interviews with us that they also embrace their regional identity, considering themselves black Appalachians.

Texana residents do not exclude whites from their community; in fact, almost all the young people in the community date, live with, or are married to partners who are white or of mixed race or ethnicity (although, given the small size of Texana, the number of whites is very small, fewer than 10 individuals). Texana residents often cite the community's interconnected family ties and genealogical history as reasons for the frequent present-day interracial marriages. Still, interracial dating has been prevalent only among the youngest generations, largely because of past racial ideologies held by local whites and restrictions forced upon young Texanans by them.

In three years of fieldwork, Childs and Mallinson conducted interviews with 49 black residents of Texana. Previous work (Childs and Mallinson 2004) indicated that the Texana community in general is not following a widespread movement toward a more urban version of AAE that has been noted for other communities, both urban and rural and geographically disperse (Wolfram 1969, 1974, 2004; Labov 1972; Bailey and Thomas 1998; Rickford 1999; Cukor-Avila 2001; Poplack and Tagliamonte 2001; Wolfram and Thomas 2002). Over time, Texana speakers have shown increasing alignment to regional AppE phonology, while still maintaining a subtle effect of substrate AAE phonological norms and a weak alignment to AAE morphosyntax (which was once stronger in the speech of earlier generations of Texana residents).

This trajectory of language change finds young Texana residents not participating in the move toward urban norms of AAE that is often found taking place among young African Americans in nonurban areas—similar to what was found in Beech Bottom, but in contrast to what was found in Hyde County. We argue that unique social and cultural orientations are influencing Texanans' dialect development. Young Texana residents seem to feel little need to disassociate themselves from the regional variety of AppE by participating in a wide-scale adoption of the syntax and phonology of urban AAE. Instead, we see a more mixed and selective alignment—for example, through the use of lexical items associated with African American hip hop culture (Childs and Mallinson 2006). For young Texanans, such lexical items may serve as salient markers of in-group ethnic identity and thereby help establish ethnolinguistic boundaries, even (or especially) in the absence of typical morphosyntactic and phonological variation.

We now consider Texana residents' vocalic patterns. Two representative vowel plots from Texana speakers are given in figures 2.10 and 2.11. Both speakers are females and were born in Texana. The older speaker, Gail Anne, is a member of one of the long-established families in the community, while the middle-aged speaker, Debbie, is a first-generation Texana community member, her parents having moved to Texana from Georgia prior to her birth. As these plots show, Texana speakers show general Appalachian vocalic patterns, which are similar to those of Southern English. For example, Texana speakers show extensive fronting of BOOT, BOOK, and BOAT. They also show glide weakening in BITE and BIDE. In this regard, the Texana speakers' productions for these vowels follow the AppE pattern, the same trend found for Beech Bottom.

At the same time, the degree of regional vowel patterning still may be constrained by external and identity-based factors. In par-

FIGURE 2.10

Gail Anne, Older African American Female (b. 1933) from Texana

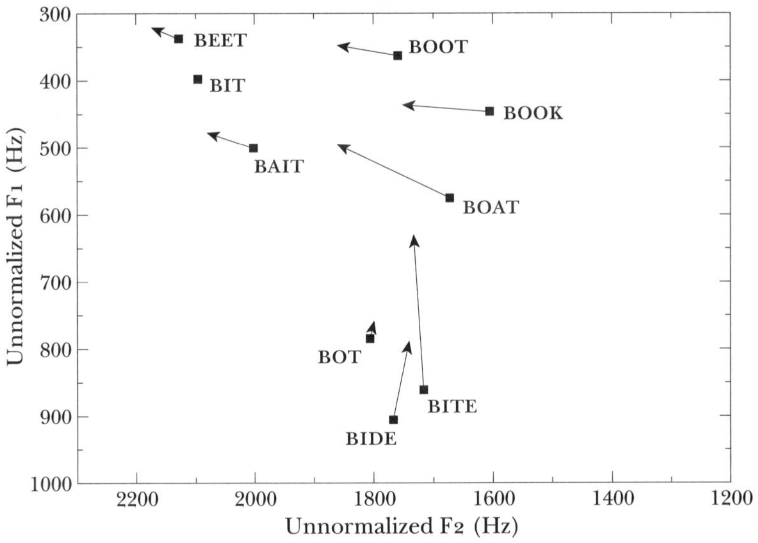

FIGURE 2.11

Debbie, Middle-Aged African American Female (b. 1964) from Texana

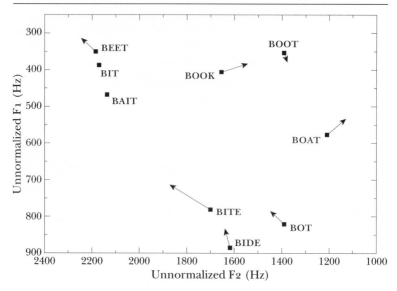

ticular, we found extensive variation in Texana across two communities of practice that consisted of middle-aged and older women—the "church ladies" and the "porch sitters" (Childs 2005; Mallinson and Childs 2005; Mallinson 2006). The women who showed more allegiance to the norms of the local church and community also used more regional vowel variants—namely, more fronted BOAT, BOOT, and BOOK. In contrast, in the community of practice that was less invested in local norms and more open toward outsiders, the women used vowel variants that were less local. Vowel plots for core members of each community of practice are given in figures 2.12 and 2.13, respectively.

FIGURE 2.12

Zora, Middle-Aged African American "Church Lady" (b. 1957)
from Texana

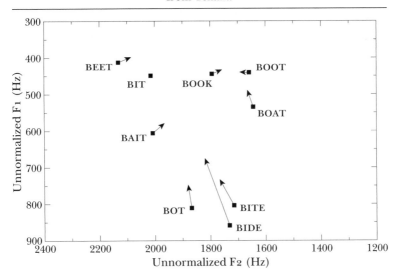

FIGURE 2.13

Michelle, Middle-Aged African American "Porch Sitter" (b. 1959)
from Texana

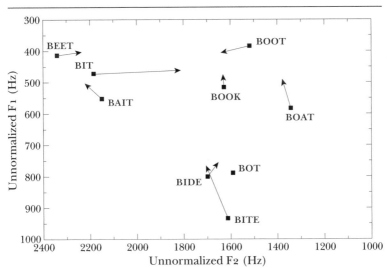

CONCLUSIONS

Our overview of vowel variation in these four coastal and mountain communities in North Carolina shows a few general trends. First, the two coastal North Carolina sites indicate that vowel patterns are affected by community dynamics. Both Hyde County and Roanoke Island showed that earlier generations of African American speakers showed more alignment to local PSE vocalic patterns. Both communities show a general decline of PSE vocalic features in younger generations, with some unique patterns for middle-aged speakers. For the younger African American speakers in particular, this movement away from local norms may also suggest a potential trajectory toward greater accommodation to general norms of AAE. These findings highlight the need to investigate different social, historical, and linguistic factors relevant to each community when examining linguistic patterns and the creation/maintenance of the sociophonetic system.

In the mountain sites located in western North Carolina, however, we find widespread accommodation to local Appalachian patterns, almost across the board. In general, only slight ethnolinguistic differences were found in the phonological systems of speakers from Beech Bottom and Texana, and when these differences were found, generally factors related to speaker identity were found to be important in explaining subgroup variation. The vowel patterns for the older African American speakers in both field sites—most notably, glide weakening in BITE as well as BIDE and the fronting of BOAT, BOOT, and BOOK—suggest the long-term presence and persistence of regional features. These trends are even more extensive among the younger African American speakers, among whom we see no indication that they are trending toward general norms of AAE and who instead exhibit nearly full accommodation to AppE norms.

In short, we have found that the vowel patterns of African American speakers in different rural communities throughout North Carolina may show sensitivity to both regional and ethnic norms. Thus, our study, like Thomas (2001), Anderson (2003), and Fridland (2003), suggests that African Americans do use regional vocalic patterns, which raises questions about assumptions that sociolinguists have often made regarding the presumed homogeneity of AAE (see Wolfram 2007). Yet, at the same time, across these speech communities and even within the same speech community, there may be considerable heterogeneity in speakers' vowel patterns. Often, it appears that these differences are due to the intersecting relationship of social, historical, linguistic, and identity-based factors.

We have presented data from four rural sites in North Carolina, and we acknowledge that different trends may be found in the quickly growing, and more ethnically diverse, cities in the state, as well as throughout the rest of the American South. The trends found within these communities are not necessarily representative of vocalic patterns found among African American communities in more urban areas or other rural areas of North Carolina. For this reason, it is hoped that further research will explore the ways that African American speakers in other rural, urban, suburban, and exurban communities throughout the American South employ regional and ethnic dialect features.

NOTES

We gratefully acknowledge the William C. Friday Endowment at North Carolina State University, National Science Foundation Grants BCS 0236838 and 9910224, and the University of Georgia Graduate School Dean's Award for funding this research. We would like to thank Erik Thomas and Bridget Anderson for assisting with data analysis. We also thank several colleagues who assisted with collecting interviews: Dani Schreier, Karen Lavarello Schreier, and Jaclyn Fried (Beech Bottom); Ceci Davis (Texana); Elaine Green, Erik Thomas, Tracey Weldon, Sherise Berry, and Tracie Fellers (Hyde County); and Sarah Hilliard and Janelle Vadnais (Roanoke Island). Last, but not least, we are indebted to Walt Wolfram for the mentorship and guidance he gave to each of us throughout the course of our work with the North Carolina Language and Life Project.

REFERENCES

Anderson, Bridget LeAnn. 2003. "An Acoustic Study of Southeastern Michigan Appalachian and African-American Southern Migrant Vowel Systems." Ph.D. diss., Univ. of Michigan.

Bailey, Guy, and Erik Thomas. 1998. "Some Aspects of African-American Vernacular English Phonology." In *African-American English: Structure, History and Use,* ed. Salikoko S. Mufwene, John R. Rickford, Guy Bailey, and John Baugh, 85–109. London: Routledge.

Beaver, Patricia D., and Helen M. Lewis. 1998. "Uncovering the Trail of Ethnic Denial: Ethnicity in Appalachia." In *Cultural Diversity in the U.S. South: Anthropological Contributions to a Region in Transition,* ed. Carole E. Hill and Patricia D. Beaver, 52–68. Athens: Univ. of Georgia Press.

Billings, Dwight B. 1989. "Appalachians." In *Encyclopedia of Southern Culture,* ed. Charles Reagan Wilson and William Ferris, 418. Chapel Hill: Univ. of North Carolina Press.

Bowser, Arvilla Tillett, and Lindsay Bowser. 2002. *Roanoke Island: The Forgotten Colony.* Chesapeake, Va.: Maximilian.

Carpenter, Jeannine. 2004. "The Lost Community of the Outer Banks: African American Speech on Roanoke Island." Master's thesis, North Carolina State Univ. Available at http://www.lib.ncsu.edu/theses/available/etd-03242004-100314/unrestricted/etd.pdf.

———. 2005. "The Invisible Community of the Lost Colony: African American English on Roanoke Island." *American Speech* 80: 227–55.

Childs, Becky. 2005. "Investigating the Local Construction of Identity: Sociophonetic Variation in Smoky Mountain African American Women's Speech." Ph.D. diss., Univ. of Georgia.

Childs, Becky, and Christine Mallinson. 2004. "African American English in Appalachia: Dialect Accommodation and Substrate Influence." *English World-Wide* 25: 27–50.

———. 2006. "The Significance of Lexical Items in the Construction of Ethnolinguistic Identity: A Case Study of Adolescent Spoken and On-line Language." *American Speech* 81: 3–30.

Cukor-Avila, Patricia. 2001. "Co-existing Grammars: The Relationship between the Evolution of African American and Southern White Vernacular English in the South." In *Sociocultural and Historical Contexts of African American English,* ed. Sonja L. Lanehart, 93–127. Amsterdam: Benjamins.

Dunaway, Wilma A. 2003. *Slavery in the American Mountain South.* Cambridge: Cambridge Univ. Press.

Fridland, Valerie. 1999. "The Southern Shift in Memphis, Tennessee." *Language Variation and Change* 11: 267–85.

———. 2003. "Network Strength and the Realization of the Southern Vowel Shift among African Americans in Memphis, Tennessee." *American Speech* 78: 3–30.

Hall, Joseph S. 1942. "The Phonetics of Great Smoky Mountain Speech." Ph.D. diss., Columbia Univ.

Harris, Jeffery. 1994. "Does Beech Bottoms Still Exist?" Senior thesis, Lees McCrae College.

Hayden, Wilburn, Jr. 2004. "Appalachian Diversity: African-American, Hispanic/Latino, and Other Populations." In "Appalachia Counts: The Region in the 2000 Census," ed. Phillip J. Obermiller, 293–306. Special issue of *Journal of Appalachian Studies* 10.3.

Kay, Marvin L., and Lorin Lee Cary. 1995. *Slavery in North Carolina, 1748–1775*. Chapel Hill: Univ. of North Carolina Press.

Kretzschmar, William, Sonja Lanehart, Betsy Barry, Iyabo Osiapem, and MiRan Kim. 2004. "Atlanta in Black and White: A New Random Sample of Urban Speech." Paper presented at the 33rd annual conference on New Ways of Analyzing Variation (NWAV 33), Ann Arbor, Mich., Sept. 30–Oct. 3.

Kurath, Hans, and Raven I. McDavid, Jr. 1961. *The Pronunciation of English in the Atlantic States: Based upon the Collections of the Linguistic Atlas of the Eastern United States*. Ann Arbor: Univ. of Michigan Press.

Labov, William. 1972. *Language in the Inner City: Studies in the Black English Vernacular*. Philadelphia: Univ. of Pennsylvania Press.

———. 1991. "The Three Dialects of English." In *New Ways of Analyzing Sound Change*, ed. Penelope Eckert, 1–44. New York: Academic Press.

Mallinson, Christine. 2002. "The Regional Accommodation of African American English: Evidence from a Bi-ethnic Mountain Enclave Community." M.A. thesis, North Carolina State Univ. Available from http://www.lib.ncsu.edu/theses/available/etd-20020404-142159/unrestricted/etd.pdf.

———. 2006. "The Dynamic Construction of Race, Class, and Gender through Linguistic Practice among Women in a Black Appalachian Community." Ph.D. diss., North Carolina State Univ.

Mallinson, Christine, and Becky Childs. 2005. "Communities of Practice in Sociolinguistic Description: African American Women's Language in Appalachia." In "Papers from NWAVE 32," ed. Maciej Baranowski, Uri Horesh, Keelan Evans, and Giang Nguyen, 1–14. *University of Pennsylvania Working Papers in Linguistics* 10.2.

Mallinson, Christine, and Walt Wolfram. 2002. "Dialect Accommodation in a Bi-ethnic Mountain Enclave Community: More Evidence on the Development of African American English." *Language in Society* 31: 743–75.

Poplack, Shana, and Sali Tagliamonte. 2001. *African American English in the Diaspora.* Malden, Mass.: Blackwell.

Rickford, John R. 1999. *African American Vernacular English: Features, Evolution, Educational Implications.* Malden, Mass.: Blackwell.

Schilling-Estes, Natalie. 1996. "The Linguistic and Sociolinguistic Status of /ay/ in Outer Banks English." Ph.D. diss., Univ. of North Carolina at Chapel Hill.

Schilling-Estes, Natalie, and Walt Wolfram. 1997. "Symbolic Identity and Language Change: A Comparative Analysis of Post-insular /ay/ and /aw/." In "A Selection of Papers from NWAVE 25," ed. Charles Boberg, Miriam Meyerhoff, Stephanie Strassel, and the PWPL editorial board, 83–109. *University of Pennsylvania Working Papers in Linguistics* 4.1.

Stick, David. 1958. *The Outer Banks of North Carolina, 1584–1958.* Chapel Hill: Univ. of North Carolina Press.

———. 1970. *Dare County: A History.* Raleigh, N.C.: State Dept. of Archives and History.

Thomas, Erik R. 2001. *An Acoustic Analysis of Vowel Variation in New World English.* Publication of the American Dialect Society 85. Durham, N.C.: Duke Univ. Press.

———. 2003. "Secrets Revealed by Southern Vowel Shifting." *American Speech* 78: 150–70.

———. 2004. "Rural Southern White Accents." In *A Handbook of Varieties of English,* vol. 1, *Phonology,* ed. Bernd Kortmann and Edgar W. Schneider, 300–324. Berlin: Mouton de Gruyter.

Torbert, Benjamin. 2004. "Southern Vowels and the Social Construction of Salience." Ph.D. diss., Duke Univ.

Turner, Morris, III. 2000. "Black Towns: North Carolina, Beech Bottoms." Soul of America.com http://www.soulofamerica.com/7773.0.0.1.0.0 .phtml.

Wolfram, Walter A. 1969. *A Sociolinguistic Description of Detroit Negro Speech.* Washington, D.C.: Center for Applied Linguistics.

Wolfram, Walt. 1974. "The Relationship of White Southern Speech to Vernacular Black English." *Language* 50: 498–527.

———. 2004. "Urban African American Vernacular English: Morphology and Syntax." In *A Handbook of Varieties of English,* vol. 2, *Morphology and Syntax,* ed. Bernd Kortmann and Edgar W. Schneider, 319–40. Berlin: Mouton de Gruyter.

————. 2007. "Sociolinguistic Folklore in the Study of African American English." *Linguistics and Language Compass* 1: 292–313.

Wolfram, Walt, and Dan Beckett. 2000. "The Role of the Individual and Group in Earlier African American English." *American Speech* 75: 3–33.

Wolfram, Walt, and Donna Christian. 1976. *Appalachian Speech.* Arlington, Va.: Center for Applied Linguistics.

Wolfram, Walt, Kirk Hazen, and Natalie Schilling-Estes. 1999. *Dialect Change and Maintenance on the Outer Banks.* Publication of the American Dialect Society 81. Tuscaloosa: Univ. of Alabama Press.

Wolfram, Walt, and Erik R. Thomas. 2002. *The Development of African American English.* Oxford: Blackwell.

Wright, David, and David Zoby. 2000. *Fire on the Beach: Recovering the Lost Story of Richard Etheridge and the Pea Island Lifesavers.* New York: Oxford Univ. Press.

3. MAPPING A DIALECT "MIXTURY": VOWEL PHONOLOGY OF AFRICAN AMERICAN AND WHITE MEN IN RURAL SOUTHERN LOUISIANA

MICHAEL WROBLEWSKI   THEA STRAND

University of Arizona   *University of Massachusetts, Amherst*

SYLVIE DUBOIS

Louisiana State University

THIS STUDY EXAMINES the vowel phonology of African American and white men in rural southern Louisiana, an area that has variously been described as a linguistic and cultural "gumbo" (White 1997; Melançon 2006), an "ethnic mosaic" (Henry and Bankston 1998), and "one of the most complex and fluid ethnolinguistic situations ever to develop in the United States" (Wolfram 2003). Given such complexity, we cannot expect to describe or explain the position of African American vowel phonology in southern Louisiana completely, but we do hope that this study will provide insight into the range of variation within African American English (AAE) throughout the United States, as well as help to establish a starting point for the acoustic analysis of vowel phonology in rural southern Louisiana, as very little acoustic work has been undertaken for this region previously.

As a site for sociolinguistic research, southern Louisiana does indeed present a tangled social and linguistic landscape. To begin with, this region has a long history of French-language use among both white and black residents. At the same time, the history of racial hierarchy and tension in Louisiana, further complicated by ethnicity and an institutionalized racial continuum, is even

48

more convoluted than in many other places in the South (e.g., see Dominguez 1986; Brasseaux 1992; Brasseaux, Fontenot, and Oubre 1994). Today, the local varieties of French spoken in ethnically Creole and Cajun communities are in decline, as younger generations have acquired English as their mother tongue. Still, the French language remains a salient component of local Cajun and Creole identities, and all of the speakers in this study claim at least some knowledge of one or more varieties of French. One older African American man's description of his linguistic repertoire as a "mixtury," including "a little of the French, a little of the Creole, and a little of the English" (speaker 2, b. 1918, interviewed 2002), conveys a sense of the region's sociolinguistic situation quite effectively.

In this chapter, we will be using the terms *Creole* and *Cajun* to describe local categories of group-affiliation that are emergent in sociolinguistic interviews focused on speakers' life histories, families, and local communities in three parishes in southern Louisiana: St. Landry, St. Martin, and Lafourche. *Cajun* and *Creole* thus represent self-designations for two historically distinct groups of southern Louisianans, as well as the linguistic varieties they use. Contemporary Cajuns claim ancestral ties to eighteenth-century French Canadian/Acadian (Dubois 1997) immigrants to Louisiana; they are almost exclusively white, while those who identify with Creole language and culture today are overwhelmingly African American.

At the time that the interviews used in this study were conducted (1995–2002), the populations of Saint Landry, Saint Martin, and Lafourche parishes were around 90,000, 88,000, and 49,000, respectively (U.S. Census Bureau 2000). Of these three parishes, Saint Landry has the highest percentage of African American residents at about 42% of the total population, followed by Saint Martin at about 32%. Lafourche, the parish of residence of all of the white speakers in this study, is a predominantly white parish, with African Americans making up only 13% of its total population. Regardless of race, many southern Louisianans also continue to report having French, French-Canadian, and/or Acadian/Cajun ancestry and speaking a language other than English, with percentages for these categories ranging from about 18% to 37% for the three parishes in this study. These demographic figures are displayed in table 3.1.

As noted above, AAE in rural southern Louisiana exists in a complex situation of long-term historical contact with other local language varieties, including Cajun French, Creole French, and Cajun Vernacular English (or CVE). Of these, only CVE is still widely used today, and, while it can be regarded as a "white" variety, it cannot be equated with Southern White Vernacular English (SWVE) in general.

CVE is spoken almost exclusively in southern Louisiana, but also in southern Texas and Mississippi by small groups of white Cajuns who have migrated from Louisiana. The contemporary CVE of southern Louisiana is a product of historical contact between Acadians from Nova Scotia, Canada, who fled to French Louisiana in 1765, and Louisiana inhabitants who spoke several varieties of French and non-French languages such as Canary Island Spanish, German, and English (Brasseux 1992; Melançon 2006). Historically Cajuns have been a stigmatized ethnic group in southern Louisiana, and they have generally resided in small, tightly knit, rural communities, with the majority living in relative poverty and receiving little education until fairly recently (Trépanier 1991; Dubois and Horvath 2004). Despite a 1929 state mandate instituting English as the sole language of education, Cajun French remained the primary language of Cajun communities outside the classroom, in familiar contexts, and among the majority of Cajuns who received little formal education until outside economic opportunities began

TABLE 3.1

Demographic Data for Louisiana Parishes Discussed in This Study
(based on 2000 U.S. Census)

	St. Landry	St. Martin	Lafourche
Total Population	89,974	87,700	48,583
Black	42%	32%	13%
White	56%	66%	83%
Claiming French ancestry	22%	32%	37%
Speaking non-English lang. at home	18%	31%	22%

to arise in the middle of the twentieth century. Since the 1950s, French has been in decline among Louisiana Cajuns, the majority of whom now use French only rarely, if at all.

CVE is currently spoken by both French-English bilinguals and English monolinguals in southern Louisiana. Although many of the defining sociolinguistic features associated with CVE are also common to SWVE and AAE varieties, Dubois and Horvath (2001, 2003c, 2004) have argued that the origins of CVE cannot be attributed to "interference" from French or surrounding English dialects and CVE, but instead that it represents an "innovation from within the Cajun community" (Dubois and Horvath 2003c, 35). Some of the phonological features of CVE previously identified include: final consonant and final consonant cluster reduction; nonaspiration of word initial /p/, /t/, and /k/; the substitution of stops for interdental fricatives; *r*-lessness in stressed syllables and in word-final and preconsonantal positions; and /l/ deletion in intervocalic and preconsonantal positions (Pedersen 1986–92; Dubois and Horvath 1998b, 2003c, 2004). Vocalic features include the monophthongization of the stressed vowels of BEET, BAIT, BOAT, and BOOT, which tend to be realized as monophthongs for CVE speakers. Previous impressionistic studies have also indicated that the diphthongs of BITE, BIDE, BOUT, and BOY are often realized as monophthongs—a feature that distinguishes CVE from other white Southern English varieties, where considerable lengthening and gliding are often produced (Dubois and Horvath 2004; Melançon 2006).

Paralleling the history and development of CVE is the story of Creole French speakers and their descendants. In the southern Louisianan context, the term *Creole* itself has a history that is indicative of the sweeping social, political, and economic upheavals that have shaped the region since colonial times (Dominguez 1986; Dormon 1996; Henry and Bankston 1998). During colonial settlement of Louisiana, *Creole* (or *créole* or *criollo*) originally referred to any person born in the new colonies, regardless of race. Throughout the eighteenth and nineteenth centuries, and especially after the Louisiana Purchase territory was incorporated into the United States in 1803, race became a more salient marker, and white, "colored," and black Creoles occupied different spaces in the social landscape, though the vast majority continued to speak French. While white Creoles tended to belong to the elite classes, colored Creoles, who were racially mixed but always free, could be found in all social classes, from the business-owning elite to poor share-croppers. Black Creoles, on the other hand, were enslaved prior to the Civil War, after which they were among the poorest and least-educated Louisianans until well into the twentieth century. Following the Civil War, white Creoles struggled to socially and legally exclude colored and black Creoles from Creole identification, but both groups continued to maintain their French language, culture, and Catholic religion. Its connection to the black population gradually transformed the Creole identity into a stigmatized one, and it was largely abandoned by whites in Louisiana during the first half of the twentieth century (Dubois and Melançon 2000).

Today, those identifying as Creole in Louisiana are overwhelmingly African American (Brasseaux, Fontenot, and Oubre 1994; Dubois and Melançon 2000). Within the contemporary Creole population are the descendants of French-speaking colored or black Creoles, as well as those whose ancestry includes both French-speaking Creoles and English-speaking former slaves brought to Louisiana in the mid-nineteenth century to work on cotton plantations (Brasseaux, Fontenot, and Oubre 1994). Like their Cajun counterparts, Creole African Americans lived in relative poverty and were among the least educated in the state until World War II, when they began to find employment in the new oil, gas, and chemical industries in Louisiana, which, in turn, brought them into closer contact with English-speaking Louisianans. Since then, English has rapidly replaced French as the dominant language among Creole African Americans (Dubois and Melançon 2000) and is the mother tongue of nearly all of today's younger generation.

Profound social and linguistic changes have thus affected both Cajun and Creole communities in similar ways, as both groups have benefited from economic and educational opportunities in the twentieth century, while at the same time experiencing a rapid shift from using primarily French to almost exclusively English in their everyday lives. Despite this sociolinguistic trend, a recent "Cajun Renaissance," boasting renewed interest in Cajun music, food, and literature, has garnered both popular and governmental support for the revitalization of Cajun French (Dubois and Melançon 1997), and, based on interviews with the youngest generation of African American speakers here, a revitalization of Creole language and culture, particularly zydeco music, may be on the horizon as well (Dubois and Horvath 2003b).

Until quite recently, research on the English spoken by African Americans in rural southern Louisiana was virtually nonexistent. However, recent work on Creole African American Vernacular English (CAAVE) by Dubois and Horvath (2003a, 2003b), Dubois and Melançon (2000), and Melançon (2000) has begun to fill this gap. To summarize their findings thus far, some of the most significant characteristics of CAAVE include the following: the substitution of interdental fricatives with stops; monophthongal BITE, BIDE, BOUT, and BOY; and glide weakening or absence for BEET, BOOT, BAIT, and BOAT in stressed position. All of these linguistic features are also characteristic of CVE, though Dubois and Horvath (2003a) have shown greater levels of persistence of these dialect features among CAAVE speakers across generations.

The present vowel analysis does not examine interdental fricatives, but it does support previous work by Dubois and Horvath

TABLE 3.2
Summary of Dialect Features

	Urban South (Labov et al. 2006)	AAE (Thomas 2007)	Rural La. AA (CAAVE)	Rural La. White (CVE)
BEET, BAIT, BOAT, BOOT monoph- thongization	−	−	+	+
BIDE monoph- thongization	+	+	+/−	−
BEET ↔ BIT	+	−	−	−
BAIT ↔ BET	+	+	−	−
BOOT, BOAT, BOOK fronting	+	+	+/−	+/−
BIN = BEN	+	+	+/−	+/−
BEN = BAN	−	−	+	−
BET ↔ BAT	−	−	+	+
r-lessness	−	+/−	+	+
BIRD → [ʌɪ]	−	+/−	+/−	−

(2003a, 2003b), which identified very high rates of monophthon-gization and glide weakening for the vowels listed above. In this study, we will be building on these previous findings by examin-ing the entire vowel system for Creole African Americans, while comparing it to that of Cajun English speakers from the same geo-graphic region (see table 3.2). We will also briefly address *r*-lessness and BIRD realization, which are treated in greater detail in Strand, Wroblewski, and Good (forthcoming).

DATA AND METHODOLOGY

For this study we carried out acoustic analysis of vowels in con-nected, socially occurring speech using audio recordings of 18 sociolinguistic interviews collected between 1995 and 2002. These interviews come from the Louisiana Creole African American Ver-nacular English Corpus and the Cajun French/English Sociolin-guistic Corpus, both of which are located at Louisiana State Uni-versity and were collected and transcribed by Sylvie Dubois and her colleagues. (See Dubois 1997 for a detailed description of the original fieldwork in white Cajun communities.) The interviews in this subsample are classic interview style and range in length from 20 to 60 minutes. All of the interviews analyzed here were conducted in English, although many interviewees also make some use of French or Creole lexical items and some speakers were also interviewed separately in French. The interviewers in the Louisiana CAAVE and Cajun corpora are matched to speakers according to race: interviews with Creole African American speakers were con-ducted by Creole African Americans or African Americans, while the Cajun men were interviewed by (white) native Cajun English speakers.

The sociolinguistic interviews were recorded in homes or more public gathering spaces; thus, the sound quality of these recordings varies. Background noise (e.g., other people talking, a child drib-bling a basketball) and apparent microphone misplacement make parts of some of the interviews unusable for acoustic analysis. We eventually excluded 1 of the 18 interviews from the vowel phonol-

ogy analysis due to poor sound quality, but the remaining recordings were generally clear enough that recording quality should not
have affected the study's outcome.

The 17 speakers whose vowels were analyzed in this study are
all fluent in English and have some knowledge of or exposure to at
least one local variety of French. Seven of the speakers have English
as their first language, with little or no conversational fluency in
Creole or Cajun French. Six of the interviews are native Creole or
Cajun French speakers who acquired English outside of the home,
generally in public elementary schools. Finally, three speakers
were considered fully bilingual English and Creole/Cajun French
speakers, having learned both languages at home as children. The
number of speakers we have analyzed here is obviously insufficient
to isolate all of the social variables that must be accounted for, but
it permits an overview of the range of variation possible within the
community.

Twelve of the speakers in this study are African American with
Creole ancestry from either St. Landry or St. Martin parish, in
rural southern Louisiana (see figure 3.1). Born between 1918 and
1981, these speakers ranged in age from 20 to 83 at the time of
the recordings and represent a diverse range of occupations, from
union and civil rights leader to sugar refinery worker to college student. For vowel phonology analysis, we have broken these speakers
into two age groups: an older group of six men born between 1918
and 1947 and a younger group of six men born between 1969
and 1981. While all of the African American speakers have lived in
either St. Landry or St. Martin parish for most of their lives, three
of the older speakers (b. 1918–47) also lived and worked in Texas
for short periods as young men, and two have traveled internation-
ally. Education varies according to age; none of the speakers born
before 1947 completed high school, but all completed between
4 and 8 years of primary education in local schools. Among the
younger African Americans, all speakers have completed at least
one year of post-secondary education.

The remaining six speakers in this study are white men from
rural, coastal Lafourche Parish in southern Louisiana (see figure
3.1), born between 1911 and 1968. At the time of the interviews,

FIGURE 3.1
Map of Louisiana Field Sites

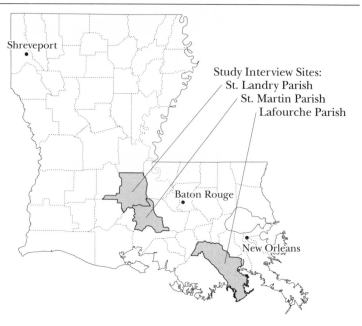

these speakers ranged in age from 27 to 85. Four of these six men are or have been employed in the major local industries of shipping, oil drilling, or oyster farming, and three of the six also have military experience. Like the African American speakers, the white speakers have been broken into an older group of four men born between 1911 and 1942, and a younger group of two men born in 1961 and 1968. Education varies somewhat less among the white men, as all of the older speakers for whom we have education data completed at least nine years of schooling. Additionally, both of the younger speakers and two of the four older speakers have completed at least some college.

Finally, for analysis of BIRD and r-lessness, both African American and white speakers were redivided into three age groups, born 1911–30, 1936–47, and 1961–81, as there appeared to be significant variation within the original older 1911–47 group for this locally distinctive phonological variable. (See Strand, Wroblewski, and Good forthcoming for a more complete discussion.)

Critical demographic data for each speaker in this study is summarized in table 3.3. For each speaker, we used Praat (v. 4.4.16) acoustic analysis software to measure F1 and F2 for tokens of the (locally) monophthongal vowels BEET, BIT, BET, BAIT, BAT, BOT, BOUGHT, BOAT, BOOT, BOOK, and BUT (also in prenasal and pre-liquid environments), as well as the key diphthongs BITE, BIDE, and BOUT. Measurements for monophthongal vowels were taken at the midpoint, and two sets of formants were taken at one-third and two-thirds into the vowel for diphthongs. We also recorded the surrounding phonetic environments for further analysis and separated tokens with following liquids and nasals. Based on previous studies of accuracy and problems with acoustic analysis software (Thomas 2002; Harrison 2004), we visually checked all automatic formant measurements against spectrograms in Praat, and we discarded and remeasured any automatic measurements that were either obviously inaccurate or suspicious.

We started with a target number of 10 tokens per vowel in our coding protocol, but, as a result of limited speech samples and low frequency for some vowels, we measured and recorded between 5 and 12 tokens of each vowel for each speaker. We also recorded data for tokens of vowels preceding nasals and liquids, though the number of tokens for these varied across speakers from 1 to 8, depending primarily on their frequency of occurrence. In total, we recorded formant measurements, including information on phonetic environment, for 90–130 vowel tokens per speaker. We then constructed vowel formant plots for each speaker for comparison across demographic categories and against findings from previous work on vowels in Louisiana and on AAE in other places.

In addition to vowel space analysis, we have also investigated the distinctive local production of "schwar" (Strand, Wroblewski, and Good forthcoming). For this portion of the study, we have identified, coded, and analyzed 50 tokens of BIRD, BURR, and botHER for each of the 18 speakers; the results are reported elsewhere (Strand, Wroblewski, and Good forthcoming), but will be briefly attended to here as well.

TABLE 3.3
Demographic Data for Louisiana Speakers

Spkr	Born	Sex	Race	Native Lang	Parish	Education	Occupation(s)
1	1925	M	AA	English	St. Landry	5th grade	local politics, NAACP
2	1918	M	AA	English	St. Martin	8th gr, extra in military	ex-military
3	1936	M	AA	Creole	St. Martin	some high school	agriculture, other manual labor
4	1945	M	AA	Creole	St. Martin	8th grade	road construction, suger refinery
5	1930	M	AA	Creole	St. Landry	4th grade	agriculture, comm., volunteer
6	1947	M	AA	Creole	St. Martin	8th grade, illiterate	agriculture, city employee
7	1981	M	AA	English, Creole	St. Landry	some college	industrial radiographer
8	1981	M	AA	English, Creole	St. Landry	some college	student
9	1970	M	AA	English	St. Landry	college	teacher (junior high)
10	1969	M	AA	English	St. Martin	1 year of college	agriculture, oil
11	1981	M	AA	English	St. Martin	some college	student
12	1980	M	AA	English	St. Martin	some college	student
13	1968	M	W	English	Lafourche	high school	telephone company, ex-marine
14	1961	M	W	English, Cajun	Lafourche	GED (some high school)	shipyard
15	1942	M	W	English	Lafourche	some college	shipyard owner, accountant
16	1949	M	W	English	Lafourche	college degree	B&B, gas station owner, ex-army
17	1926	M	W	English, Cajun	Lafourche	some high school	oil, oysters, ex-military
18	1911	M	W	Cajun	Lafourche	unknown	oil, oysters

RESULTS

MONOPHTHONGIZATION AND DIPHTHONGIZATION. As Dubois and Horvath have previously reported for CAAVE (2003b) and CVE (2004), both African American and white speakers in this study consistently displayed glide absence in the vowels in BEET, BAIT, BOAT, and BOOT. Previous perceptual studies by Dubois and Horvath (1998a) had shown that monophthongization or glide weakening of BITE and BIDE is also a prominent feature of CVE for male speakers. In a recent pilot study focused on diphthongs for four white Cajun women from the same corpus, Taha (n.d.) reports variable glide weakening, particularly among older women, but finds that complete monophthongization of the BITE-BIDE vowel is rare, typically occurring only in preliquid or prenasal positions. These are the environments that Labov, Ash, and Boberg (2006) found to favor monophthongization in the Midland region; consistent with their findings, Eberhardt (2010 [this volume]) also finds that her Pittsburgh speakers monophthongize mostly in these environments. Labov, Ash, and Boberg (2006) found that the rule generalizes at least to the environment before voiced obstruents throughout the South, including urban areas of Louisiana.

The monopthongization of the vowel in BIDE-BITE has long been listed as a common feature of SWVE, while use of the monophthong in BIDE, or prevoiced position, and in BUY, final position, along with diphthongal BITE, or prevoiceless position, has been reported for African Americans (e.g., Thomas 2001, 2007). The African American speakers in this study generally display this BIDE-BITE distinction, as we find a tendency toward use of the monophthong in BIDE, along with clearly diphthongal BITE, for both old and young African American and white speakers in this study, as shown in table 3.2. However, we note two exceptions to this pattern: first, the oldest African American speaker in this study (speaker 2, b. 1918; see figure 3.2) does NOT appear to have BIDE glide weakening. Second, speaker 4 (b. 1945) has only slight glide weakening in BIDE, despite clearly monophthongal productions of PINE.

High front vowels: BEET, BIT, and BAIT. The African American men in this study generally demonstrate considerable overlap in their

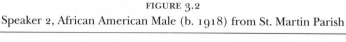

FIGURE 3.2

Speaker 2, African American Male (b. 1918) from St. Martin Parish

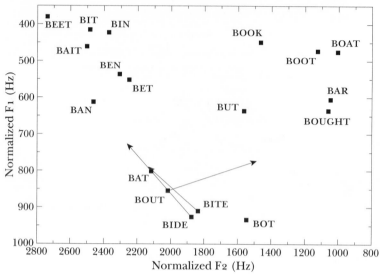

productions of the front vowels BEET, BIT, and BAIT. The raising of BAIT is particularly distinctive, and for many speakers, especially young African Americans, BAIT is consistently higher and fronter (lower F1, higher F2) than BIT, as shown in figures 3.3 and 3.4 (speaker 9, b. 1970, and speaker 7, b. 1981). This pattern is also present among white CVE speakers (e.g., see figure 3.5 for speaker 17, b. 1926), in addition to BIT fronting to [i], overlapping BEET, which has been noted previously (Dubois and Horvath 2004).

The fronting and raising of BIT and BAIT toward BEET, along with the lowering of BET into the BAT space (see below), appear to be features shared by both Creole and Cajun English speakers in rural southern Louisiana, as they contrast markedly with the general pattern for SWVE of BEET-BAIT and BIT-BET reversal or flip-flop (Labov, Ash, and Boberg 2006). Nor do these findings appear to align with the BIT, BET, BAT, BOT vowel shift proposed by Thomas (2007) for urban African Americans, indicating that this is most likely a local pattern presently restricted to southern Louisiana and other conservative Tidewater areas, as, for example, in

FIGURE 3.3
Speaker 9, African American Male (b. 1970) from St. Landry Parish

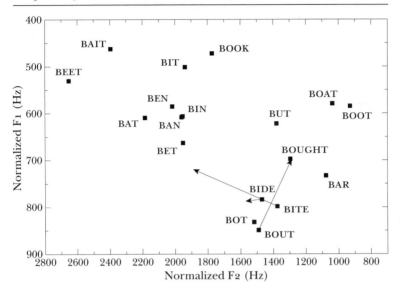

FIGURE 3.4
Speaker 7, African American Male (b. 1981) from St. Landry Parish

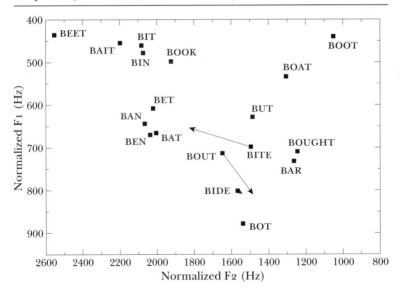

FIGURE 3.5

Speaker 17, White Male (b. 1926) from Lafourche Parish

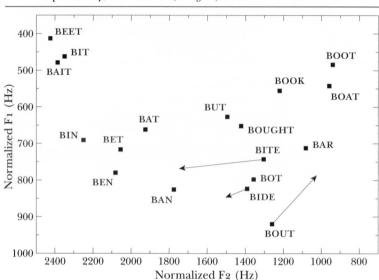

Charleston (see Baranowski 2007), which also shares the tendency to monophthongize BEET, BAIT, BOAT, and BOOT vowels.

BACK VOWELS: *BOAT, BOOT,* AND *BOOK.* Examination of the vowel formant plots in figures 3.2, 3.3, 3.4, and 3.6 clearly shows that the older African American speakers do not front BOOT, BOAT, and BOOK. While several speakers, including speaker 2 (b. 1918), also have a mean F2 for BOOT that is slightly higher than for BOAT, the majority of these speakers' F2 means for BOOT and BOAT fall around 1000 Hz, which is still unfronted according to Labov, Ash, and Boberg (2006). This also reflects the Tidewater pattern found by Baranowski (2007) but is contrary to recent findings reported for (urban) Louisianans in Labov, Ash, and Boberg (2006), where considerable BOOT and BOAT fronting were reported for whites, and BOOK fronting for African Americans, as in other urban areas in the South and elsewhere (Fridland and Bartlett 2006; Thomas 2007).

FIGURE 3.6

Speaker 6, African American Male (b. 1947) from St. Martin Parish

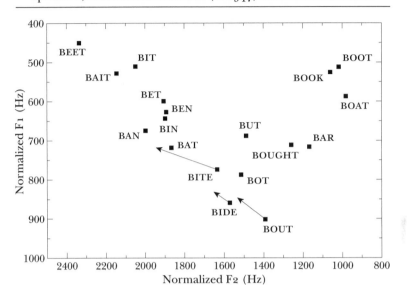

Furthermore, speakers 2 (b. 1918, figure 3.2), 4 (b. 1945), and 6 (b. 1947, figure 3.6) show considerable overlap, perhaps approaching a near-merger, in their productions of BOOT and BOAT, with several older African American speakers (including speaker 6, figure 3.6) also showing a fair amount of overlap of BOOK into the BOOT-BOAT space. In contrast to this pattern, the younger African American speakers in this study (speakers 7–12, b. 1969–81) display a trend toward BOOK fronting, as shown for speakers 7 (b. 1981) and 9 (b. 1970) in figures 3.4 and 3.3. These findings support Thomas's (2001, 2007) conclusions that Southern African American speakers are generally less likely to front BOOT and BOAT and more likely to front BOOK than their white counterparts. In our sample, none of the speakers fronts BOOT or BOAT, while both African American and white younger rural Louisianans front BOOK, as shown in figure 3.7 for speaker 13 (b. 1968); this is one important point of convergence for younger speakers across racial lines. This indicates that, as with the front vowels analyzed, both African

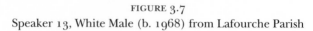

FIGURE 3.7

Speaker 13, White Male (b. 1968) from Lafourche Parish

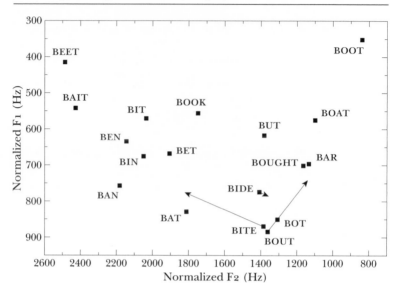

American and white speakers not only share the same vowel patterns, but the same shifts seem to have occurred nearly simultaneously in both communities.

MID-FRONT VOWELS AND FOLLOWING NASALS: *BIN, BEN, BAN, BET,* AND *BAT*. The apparent merger of BIN and BEN has long been recognized as a defining feature of AAE in general, as well as a defining feature of CVE by Dubois and Horvath (2004). In fact, Eberhardt (2010 [this volume]) and Purnell (2010 [this volume]) also attest that this feature is robust for AAE in Northern cities as well. On the other hand, we do not find the BIN-BEN merger across speakers for any age or racial group in this study, but a high degree of variability between speakers. Among older African Americans, BIN and BEN are unmerged in the vowel space of speaker 2 (b. 1918, figure 3.2) but are clearly merging in the vowel space of speaker 6 (b. 1947, figure 3.6). Similarly, for younger African Americans, speaker 9 (b. 1970, figure 3.3) displays the BIN-BEN merger, but speaker 7 (b. 1981, figure 3.4) clearly does not.

While there is very weak evidence for the BIN-BEN merger, there is a clear tendency toward a merger of BEN and BAN among both old and young African American speakers but no clear evidence indicating such a merger for the white speakers. Mean F1 values for BET and BAT for speaker 1 (b. 1925), for example, are around 420 Hz and 590 Hz, respectively, while mean F1 values for this speaker for BEN and BAN are both near 490 Hz. Speaker 2 (b. 1918, figure 3.2) displays significant raising and fronting of BAN toward BEN, and speakers 7 (born. 1981, figure 3.4) and 9 (b. 1970, figure 3.3) show movement of both BEN and BAN toward BIN. African Americans thus seem to have a BEN-BAN merger that may also involve BIN.

Although, as already mentioned, there is no evidence of the Southern flip-flop of BET and BAIT (Labov 1994; Thomas 2001; Labov, Ash, and Boberg 2006), our present results do indicate a somewhat inconsistent BET-BAT reversal among both African American and white speakers across age groups. Such reversals are clear in the vowel charts of African American speaker 9 (b. 1970, figure 3.3) and white speaker 17 (b. 1926, figure 3.5), where mean F1 values of BET are significantly higher than those of BAT. The patterned merger of BEN and BAN for African Americans, combined with the recurring reversal of BET and BAT for both African American and white speakers, thus does not appear to align with Thomas's (2007) suggestion of the movement of BET and BAT as part of a general urban AAE rotation involving BOT, BAT, BET, and BIT in a mirror image of the "Canadian Shift." Instead, such complex movements of BET, BAT, BEN, and BAN more directly support Dubois and Horvath's (2004) reports of widespread BET lowering and possible BET-BAT merging as features of local CVE.

LOW-CENTRAL/BACK VOWELS: *BOT, BOUGHT*, AND *BAR*. All of the speakers in this study, like other Southern speakers in this volume and elsewhere, show a clear differentiation between the low central/back vowels BOT and BOUGHT (Feagin 1979; Labov, Ash, and Boberg 2006; Baranowski 2007; Andres and Votta 2010 [this volume]; Childs, Mallinson, and Carpenter 2010 [this volume]), indicating that they do not have the well-known merger of these two sounds. This is not surprising given that previous surveys of both

African American and white Southern English, including those by Thomas (2001, 2007) and Labov, Ash, and Boberg (2006), generally find BOT and BOUGHT unmerged; however, this finding contrasts with previous reports that white Cajun speakers from this part of Louisiana often appear to have the BOT-BOUGHT merger (Dubois and Horvath 2004). Despite an unmerged BOT-BOUGHT pattern, however, most African American speakers in this study have BAR and BALL nuclei overlapping with BOUGHT (see figures 3.2, 3.3, 3.4, and 3.6), a pattern that has also been described for white CVE speakers (Dubois and Horvath 2004).

R-LESSNESS AND *BIRD*. While this study was primarily concerned with vowel phonology and did not examine overall *r*-lessness in great detail, it is interesting to note that the speakers analyzed here show widely varying degrees of *r*-lessness. Although Thomas (2001, 2007) and Labov, Ash, and Boberg (2006) find that Southern African American phonology tends to be moving in the same direction as general (white) Southern trends, but somewhat more slowly, we found the African American speakers in our study to be more *r*-less than their white counterparts, which has been a pattern in the South for some time (e.g., Pedersen 1986–92; Thomas 2001; Labov, Ash, and Boberg 2006). For older black speakers (b. 1918–36), in particular, postvocalic *r*-lessness is dominant, while older whites (b. 1911–26) are somewhat more *r*-ful. The youngest African American speakers (b. 1969–81), who are considerably more educated than the old and middle-aged speakers, are more *r*-ful than previous generations. At the same time, the youngest white speakers (b. 1961–68) are less *r*-ful than middle-aged white Cajuns (1939–42). While this may represent a case of the "recycling" of a traditionally Cajun linguistic feature (Dubois and Horvath 2003a), it is also important to consider that the youngest white speakers in this study are less educated than both their African American counterparts and the middle-aged white speakers.

One particularly distinctive feature related to *r*-lessness that we have investigated more closely elsewhere (Strand, Wroblewski, and Good forthcoming) is the highly variable realization of BIRD. For the African American men in this study, particularly the older and

middle-aged speakers, among whom *r*-lessness is also most prominent, the BIRD sound is frequently realized as [ʌɪ], particularly in
stressed, monosyllabic environments. That is, for words like *work*,
learn, and *heard*, where the "schwar" vowel is followed by a consonant, a nonrhotic vowel is diphthongized. Based on GoldVarb
analysis, we have found patterned variation of the *r*-ful, *r*-less, and
diphthongal ([ʌɪ]) realizations of BIRD, in which African American
men born prior to World War II with less than high school education are most likely to produce the diphthongal ([ʌɪ]) variant,
while middle-aged African Americans use it less, and the youngest (and most educated) generation uses it only very infrequently.
Among white men, the older speakers use the diphthongal variant
only rarely, while middle-aged and younger speakers almost never
realize BIRD as [ʌɪ]. Our study thus suggests further consideration
of this varying realization of BIRD as a feature that continues to
distinguish the AAE of southern Louisiana from other Southern
varieties, and also as a variable that indexes both race and age in
the region.

DISCUSSION AND CONCLUSIONS

No single speaker in our sample exhibits all of the dialect characteristics described above in a neat package; however, there do
appear to be certain trends across speakers that can be described as
distinctive dialect markers. Generally speaking, we found that African American speakers in rural southern Louisiana tend to have
vowel spaces similar to those of local whites of the same age. The
differences appear to be more prominent for older speakers than
younger ones. In fact, the younger African American and white
speakers have nearly identical vowel patterns. This apparent convergence may be related to recent shifts in local race relations, in
which old antagonisms between Creole and Cajun languages and
cultures are becoming less salient in daily interaction, and the years
of segregation, when education and life expectations isolated these
two groups, fall further into the past.

It is important to note that taken as a demographic whole, both groups of speakers differ considerably from SWVE and AAE vowel norms discussed in either Thomas (2007) or Labov, Ash, and Boberg (2006) and share a distinctive local Cajun/Creole phonology. Moreover, rural southern Louisiana African Americans do not seem to be participating in extralocal AAE patterns, despite the evidence of trends among African Americans in urban New Orleans and Baton Rouge that indicate some degree of convergence toward extra-local AAE norms (Labov, Ash, and Boberg 2006). Instead, these rural Creole African American men have maintained a surprisingly distinctive English phonology, which appears to be resultant from internal innovations arising during the dramatic social, economic, and linguistic transitions they experienced during the twentieth century. As other studies in this volume show, it is not unusual for rural dialect speakers to share more features with their local age-mates (across racial groups) than with an abstract "pan-AAE" dialect, both in the North and elsewhere in the South.

Our findings suggest a number of important considerations for future studies of AAE and, perhaps, for regionally focused phonetic studies more broadly. Whereas the phonetic characteristics of the Northern cities African American diaspora have been comprehensively described, supplementary work remains to be conducted on AAE in the Southern and Western United States in order to make adequate regional comparisons. As Wolfram (2007) has recently argued, the idea of a supraregional AAE that is spoken (or exists as a linguistic target) throughout the United States must be viewed as a myth in light of recent studies demonstrating significant regional and local variation across AAE speakers. Furthermore, the findings of this study also point to the importance of looking at urban and rural differences in phonological patterns for AAE, as well as other varieties of English, to develop a more complete understanding of both urban and rural patterns. Here, rural-urban distinctions should be analyzed at a fine-grained phonetic level AND in terms of the relationship between phonology and the social-interactional sphere. Clearly, locally salient issues surrounding social identity, particularly ethnic differentiation, as the case of southern Louisiana demonstrates, can have profound effects at all levels of linguistic expression, from phonology to discourse.

In other words, there is a definite need for a renewed focus on the sociohistorical context of phonetic (and other linguistic) variation, especially in situations of interethnic contact. The above findings clearly demonstrate the potential phonological imprints of ethnic and socioeconomic division in community language practices, while also indicating that generational differences may reveal ongoing social changes in apparent time. Studies of regional phonological characteristics must thus take into account local socioeconomic categories and histories of migration, contact, and social stratification, as well as contemporary ethnic and cultural community practices that continue to influence local patterns of sociolinguistic variation.

NOTES

The interviews used in this research were gathered with the support of National Science Foundation grants SBS9808994, SBR9514831, and BCS#091823, as well as a grant from the Louisiana Board of Regents ATLAS Program, all to Sylvie Dubois at Louisiana State University. We gratefully acknowledge the participation of all of the southern Louisianans whose interviews were used in this study, as well as the work of student interviewers at Louisiana State University. The analysis and writing of this chapter were also supported by grants from the University of Arizona's Department of Anthropology and the University of Arizona's Graduate and Professional Student Council. Special thanks to Mary K. Good for her part in coding and analyzing the BIRD data, to Malcah Yaeger-Dror and Norma Mendoza-Denton for their assistance with data analysis, and to Erik Thomas for help with vowel formant plots.

REFERENCES

Andres, Claire, and Rachel Votta. 2010. "African American Vernacular English: Vowel Phonology in a Georgia Community." In Yaeger-Dror and Thomas, 75–98.
Baranowski, Maciej. 2007. *Phonological Variation and Change in the Dialect of Charleston, South Carolina*. Publication of the American Dialect Society 92. Durham, N.C.: Duke Univ. Press.

Brasseaux, Carl A. 1992. *Acadian to Cajun: Transformation of a People, 1803–1877.* Jackson: Univ. Press of Mississippi.

Brasseaux, Carl A., Keith P. Fontenot, and Claude F. Oubre. 1994. *Creoles of Color in the Bayou Country.* Jackson: Univ. Press of Mississippi.

Childs, Becky, Christine Mallinson, and Jeannine Carpenter. 2010. "Vowel Phonology and Ethnicity in North Carolina." In Yaeger-Dror and Thomas, 23–47.

Dominguez, Virginia R. 1986. *White by Definition: Social Classification in Creole Louisiana.* New Brunswick, N.J.: Rutgers Univ. Press.

Dormon, James H. 1996. "Ethnicity and Identity: Creoles of Color in Twentieth-Century South Louisiana." In *Creoles of Color of the Gulf South,* ed. James H. Dormon, 67–86. Knoxville: Univ. of Tennessee Press.

Dubois, Sylvie. 1997. "Field Method in Four Cajun Communities in Louisiana." In *French and Creole in Louisiana,* ed. Albert Valdman, 47–70. New York: Plenum.

Dubois, Sylvie, and Barbara M. Horvath. 1998a. "From Accent to Marker in Cajun English: A Study of Dialect Formation in Progress." *English World-Wide* 19: 161–88.

———. 1998b. "Let's Tink about Dat: Interdental fricatives in Cajun English." *Language Variation and Change* 10: 245–61.

———. 2001. "Do Cajuns Speak Southern English: Morphosyntactic Evidence." In "Papers from NWAV 29," ed. Tara Sanchez and Daniel Ezra Johnson, 27–41. *University of Pennsylvania Working Papers in Linguistics* 7.3.

———. 2003a. "Creoles and Cajuns: A Portrait in Black and White." *American Speech* 78: 192–207.

———. 2003b. "The English Vernacular of the Creoles of Louisiana." *Language Variation and Change* 15: 255–88.

———. 2003c. "Verbal Morphology in Cajun Vernacular English: A Comparison with Other Varieties of Southern English." *Journal of English Linguistics* 31: 34–59.

———. 2004. "Cajun Vernacular English: Phonology." In *A Handbook of Varieties of English,* vol. 1, *Phonology,* ed. Bernd Kortmann and Edgar W. Schneider, 407–16. Berlin: Mouton de Gruyter.

Dubois, Sylvie, and Megan Melançon. 1997. "Cajun Is Dead—Long Live Cajun: Shifting from a Linguistic to a Cultural Community." *Journal of Sociolinguistics* 1: 63–93.

———. 2000. "Creole Is, Creole Ain't: Diachronic and Synchronic Attitudes toward Creole Identity in Southern Louisiana." *Language in Society* 29: 237–58.

Eberhardt, Maeve. 2010. "African American and White Vowel Systems in Pittsburgh." In Yaeger-Dror and Thomas, 129–57.

Feagin, Crawford. 1979. *Variation and Change in Alabama English: A Sociolinguistic Study of the White Community.* Washington, D.C.: Georgetown Univ. Press.

Fridland, Valerie, and Kathy Bartlett. 2006. "The Social and Linguistic Conditioning of Back Vowel Fronting across Ethnic Groups in Memphis, Tennessee." *English Language and Linguistics* 10: 1–22.

Harrison, Philip. 2004. "Variability of Formant Measurements." M.A. thesis, Univ. of York. Available at http://www.jpfrench.com/docs/harrison -formant-dissertation.pdf.

Henry, Jacques M., and Carl L. Bankston, III. 1998. "Propositions for a Structuralist Analysis of Creolism." *Current Anthropology* 39: 558–66.

Labov, William. 1994. *Principles of Linguistic Change.* Vol. 1, *Internal Factors.* Oxford: Blackwell.

Labov, William, Sharon Ash, and Charles Boberg. 2006. *The Atlas of North American English: Phonetics, Phonology and Sound Change.* Berlin: Mouton de Gruyter.

Melançon, Megan Elizabeth. 2000. "The Sociolinguistic Situation of Creoles in South Louisiana: Identity, Characteristics, Attitudes." Ph.D. diss., Louisiana State Univ.

———. 2006. "Stirring the Linguistic Gumbo (Cajun English)." In *American Voices: How Dialects Differ from Coast to Coast,* ed. Walt Wolfram and Ben Ward, 238–43. Malden, Mass.: Blackwell.

Pederson, Lee A., ed. 1986–92. *The Linguistic Atlas of the Gulf States.* 7 vols. Athens: Univ. of Georgia Press.

Purnell, Thomas C. 2010. "The Vowel Phonology of Urban Southeastern Wisconsin." In Yaeger-Dror and Thomas, 191–217.

Strand, Thea, Michael Wroblewski, and Mary K. Good. Forthcoming. "Variation and Accommodation in Schwar Realization among African American, White, and Houma Men in Southern Louisiana." In "Accommodative Tendencies in Interdialect Communication," ed. Malcah Yaeger-Dror and Thomas C. Purnell. Special issue of *Journal of English Linguistics* 38.2.

Taha, Maisa C. N.d. Unpublished MS, Univ. of Arizona.

Thomas, Erik R. 2001. *An Acoustic Analysis of Vowel Variation in New World English.* Publication of the American Dialect Society 85. Durham, N.C.: Duke Univ. Press.

———. 2002. "Instrumental Phonetics." In *The Handbook of Language Variation and Change,* ed. J. K. Chambers, Peter Trudgill, and Natalie Schilling-Estes, 168–200. Malden, Mass.: Blackwell.

————. 2007. "Phonological and Phonetic Characteristics of African American Vernacular English." *Language and Linguistics Compass* 1: 450–75.

Trépanier, Cécyle. 1991. "The Cajunization of French Louisiana: Forging a Regional Identity." *Geographical Journal* 157: 161–71.

U.S. Census Bureau. 2000. "2000 U.S. Census: Louisiana." http://factfinder.census.gov.

White, David R. M. 1997. "Cultural Gumbo: An Ethnographic Overview of Louisiana's Mississippi River Delta and Selected Adjacent Areas." New Orleans, La.: Report Prepared for Jean Lafitte National Historical Park and Preserve.

Wolfram, Walt. 2003. "Language Variation in the American South: An Introduction." *American Speech* 78(2):123-129.

————. 2007. "Sociolinguistic Folklore in the Study of African American English." *Language and Linguistics Compass* 1: 292–313.

Yaeger-Dror, Malcah, and Erik R. Thomas, eds. 2010. *African American English Speakers and Their Participation in Local Sound Changes: A Comparative Study.* Publication of the American Dialect Society 94. Durham, N.C.: Duke Univ. Press.

THE URBAN SOUTH

4. AFRICAN AMERICAN VERNACULAR ENGLISH: VOWEL PHONOLOGY IN A GEORGIA COMMUNITY

CLAIRE ANDRES

*University of Georgia at Athens/
University of Texas at San Antonio*

RACHEL VOTTA

University of Georgia at Athens

ALTHOUGH A LARGE BODY of linguistic research has explored the syntactic and morphological features of African American English (AAE), little focus has been placed on the vowel phonology of the dialect. In addition, research into AAE is often carried out under the assumption that AAE can be "seen as a system in itself, [and] analyzed without reference to other dialects" (Labov 1998, 110). As Labov points out, this "monolithic" approach has been a source of insight but has often resulted in descriptions that are "far removed from linguistic and social reality." We attempt to address these problems using speech data drawn from an ongoing project in Roswell, Georgia.

The Roswell Voices Project began when a local community member, Jim Mcyntire, saw a presentation of Walt Wolfram's work on Ocracoke, North Carolina. Enamored with the idea of having the speech of Roswell, Georgia, captured in such a way, he contacted Wolfram, who suggested that Mcyntire get in touch with William Kretzschmar at the University of Georgia. Shortly thereafter, the Roswell Voices Project, a combination oral history and dialect study, was begun as a cooperative effort of the Roswell Folk and Heritage Bureau and the Linguistics Program at the University of Georgia. We are exceptionally grateful to the Roswell Folk and Heritage Bureau for its continued sponsorship of this project.

THE COMMUNITY

Roswell, Georgia, is often referred to as a fringe city of Atlanta, an "exurb"—one step beyond a suburb, but not a full-fledged metropolis. With a population that now tops 80,000, Roswell certainly could be described as a city in its own right, but it lacks any central area of large buildings that reach for the sky. Roswell's "downtown" is instead a collection of small old buildings, two to three stories at most, that wrap around a town square complete with a gazebo and large oak and magnolia trees. This town center hearkens back to the earliest days of Roswell's history.

The town was founded in the 1830s by Roswell King, who was responsible for building a textile mill that provided much of the employment for the town, with about 400 employees by the time of the Civil War. Most of the other 600 or so residents were subsistence farmers, though there were some large plantations along with their attendant populations of wealthy whites and nonwealthy slaves. While it is apparent from interviews with older speakers that almost everybody in town—from the very wealthy to the very poor—knew each other in one way or another, it is also the case that three major groups, African Americans, non-mill-village whites, and those who lived in the mill village were clearly distinguishable. Many threads of language history converged in these groups. While the original language spoken in the vicinity was Cherokee, governmental policy resulting in the Trail of Tears in 1838 effectively ended any Cherokee influence. With the founding of the textile mill in 1849, many new residents were drawn to the town. Roswell King brought both family and friends with him from the Georgia coast, where "plantation speech" was the norm. African Americans, transported to Roswell to work the fields, also shared some features of plantation speech. Workers for the mill came from a number of regions, bringing with them the mountain speech of Appalachia as well as Southern upland varieties.

The town's population remained between 1,000 and 2,000 between the years of 1860 and 1950, with most of the townspeople living "within shouting distance" of the town square. However, by the time the last mill in town closed in 1975, the population had jumped to around 15,000, and by 1990 the population topped 48,000. As of 2000, the population in Roswell was 79,334—75.3% non-Hispanic white, 8.3% non-Hispanic black, and 10.6% Hispanic—and by all estimates is still growing (U.S. Census Bureau 2000). The population growth, then, has been rather astounding, increasing from around 2,000 to nearly 80,000 in less than 60 years.

The vast amount of change in the community is alluded to in all of the interviews conducted thus far, but our favorite story demonstrating this is one from Hank, now 42 years old, who recalled walking down Main Street with his boyhood friends, each with a shotgun over his shoulder and a passel of recently acquired squirrels over the other. As Hank tells us, "You can tell that things have really changed; people have gotten to be awfully narrow-minded these days about you walking down Main Street with a shotgun." The changes in the Roswell community are certainly related to the growth of the population, but also involve changes in attitudes, economic prosperity, and interaction patterns of the population.

Many of the small houses of the mill village which used to hold economically impoverished white members of the community now house offices and shops rather than families. The economic landscape of the community has also changed drastically. Roswell is now considered to be an affluent community. Census figures report the per capita income in 1999 at $36,012, well above the overall Georgia per capita income of $21,154 (U.S. Census Bureau 2000). In and of themselves, these figures do not tell us much about how the wealth is divided among members of the community. A more complete picture can be drawn from our own forays into the city as well as from the interviews conducted with residents.

Unlike many cities of equivalent size, Roswell does not seem to have any clearly definable "black areas," and it might also be said that there are no areas that would be considered "poor" by the standards of similarly sized cities. While it does seem to be the case that the majority of the African American population of Roswell tends to cluster on the lower rungs of the economic scale, there also seems to be a greater degree of economic parity between the African American and white populations of Roswell than exists in many communities across the United States. Moreover, while the older participants in our interviews attended segregated schools, the younger residents, of course, have not experienced this division. More importantly—compared with many other communities—the public schools in Roswell are considered "good" schools, with well-maintained facilities and comparatively large proportions of college-bound students. Because of these factors, Roswell appears to have a highly integrated community. The interviews with both African Americans and whites provide statements that appear to substantiate this conclusion and support the notion that this is not merely a surface phenomenon. One college-aged African American, for instance, told us about his experience during what was called a Minority to Majority program that occurred during his high school years. In this program African American students from nearby Atlanta were bussed into the schools in Roswell. This young man indicated that it seemed to him that the students did not think that Roswell's African American students were "black enough." This is not to say that no boundaries exist between the ethnic populations of Roswell—rather that the boundaries seem less harshly drawn. One instance of a division of the population that can be seen is in the churches established in Roswell early in the twentieth century, which remain as predominantly "white churches" and "black churches." These churches now, however, are sprinkled across the broader landscape, which includes "megachurches," synagogues, and smaller racially mixed churches of various denominations.

Roswell provides an interesting community for linguistic research. Although this type of community is becoming increasingly frequent, it is underrepresented in linguistic regional studies, which focus on the extremes of rural versus metropolitan communities.

THE PROJECT

Phase 1 of the project began in 2003, with interviews conducted by Sonja Lanehart, Becky Childs, Bridget Anderson, William Kretzschmar, and Rachel Votta; 8 African Americans and 13 whites

were interviewed. Phase 2 began in 2005 with interviews conducted by Claire Andres, Sasha Johnson, Votta, and Kretzschmar.
Eight African Americans and 22 whites were interviewed—for a
total thus far of 16 African Americans and 35 whites. The interviews with African Americans were conducted by African American
interviewers, and those with white interviewees with white interviewers. Interviews were recorded on a Marantz CDR 300 with a
Shure SM58 microphone. Most were conducted in Best Western
hotel rooms in the Roswell area, although some interviews were
conducted in participants' homes. The hour-long interviews were
semistructured, with most questions designed to simply engage the
participants in conversations about their own lives in Roswell. The
results of both phases of the project were presented to Roswell community members, and two booklets were produced with short tran-
scriptions from each participant along with a CD of corresponding
audio clips (Kretzschmar et al. 2004, 2006). In the Roswell Voices
Project, we are interested in what people have to say as well as how
they say it. In this way we can give back to the community—ful-
filling Wolfram's (1993) Principle of Linguistic Gratuity—both
by preserving an oral history of community life in Roswell and by
documenting the linguistic features of the area. In this chapter,
however, we are primarily concerned with the speakers' vowel phonology.

BACKGROUND

Researchers of Southern dialects have noted that throughout the
South, a series of vowel shifts appear to be occurring in Southern
White Vernacular English (SWVE) (Labov 1994; Thomas 2003,
2007; Bailey and Tillery 2006; Labov, Ash, and Boberg 2006).
Taken in combination, these changes are referred to as the Southern (Vowel) Shift. The shift primarily involves a fronting of back
vowels and a reversal of the positions of tense and lax nuclei of the
high and mid front vowels. The Southern Shift is generally seen as
applying to white speakers, but not to African American speakers.
Labov (1991), for instance, has argued that AAE does not fit the
pattern of the shift and constitutes a "fourth" dialect, the other

three being the Southern Shift, the Northern Cities Shift, and the dialect complex that merges the BOT and BOUGHT vowels. Descriptions of Southern vowel phonology often include the following six features as characteristically Southern, most of which are involved in the shift:

1. Reversal of the positions of the vowels in BEET and BIT.
2. Reversal of the positions of the vowels of BAIT and BET.
3. Glide weakening of BIDE (before voiced obstruents) and less often of BITE (before voiceless obstruents).
4. Merger of BOUGHT and BOT (among younger speakers).
5. Fronting of the nuclei of BOOT and BOUT, with BOAT slightly behind.
6. Glide weakening in BOY.

While these features are generally considered to be Southern, research on their ethnic patterning remains quite limited. Work by Bailey and Thomas utilizing mechanical recordings of African Americans born between 1844 and 1984 and a comparable set of recordings of white speakers suggests that the African American community in the South may not be participating fully in the changes in vowel phonology affecting whites (Thomas 1997; Bailey and Thomas 1998; Thomas and Bailey 1998). In a comparison of the present-day vowel systems of AAE and SWVE features, Bailey and Thomas (1998) reported that African Americans lack the BOUGHT-BOT merger and have glide weakening of the diphthong in BIDE (before voiced obstruents) but not in BITE (before voiceless obstruents). In addition, they indicate that African Americans have "back back vowels," which is to say that the fronting of the vowels in BOOT and BOAT, according to Bailey and Thomas, is widespread in SWVE but not common in AAE. Other features of the shift are not addressed by Bailey and Thomas, though they note that African Americans and whites in the South share other features, such as the BIN-BEN merger.

In a contradictory finding, Fridland's (2003) research on Memphis speech indicates that both African American and white speakers adopt particular features of the Southern Shift with both African Americans and whites reversing the positions of BAIT and BET, but neither group reverses the positions of BEET and BIT.

Unpublished data supplied by Kretzschmar from 10 African American and 8 white speakers in the Atlanta area, like the Memphis data, show no reversal of the positions of BEET and BIT by either white or African American speakers. Conversely, Kretzschmar's data show that Atlanta differs from Memphis in that African American speakers reverse BAIT and BET while white speakers do not. Table 4.1 summarizes the information from these three studies, with features reported for the Southern Shift for comparison.

In this chapter, we examine the features in table 4.1 and ask the following questions:

1. Do any of the 12 speakers in this study have the first three features in table 4.1, which Labov (1994) suggests constitute the Southern Shift, and, if so, are the speakers African American or white?
2. Which group has which Southern features, and how do these features compare to the findings of the previously discussed research?
3. Does the vowel phonology of African American speakers and white speakers in Roswell differ and, if so, how?

TABLE 4.1
Summary of Observations Regarding African American
Vowel Phonologies in Southern Area

Feature	Southern Shift	South	Memphis	Atlanta
BEET-BIT reversal				
African American	no		no	no
White	yes		no	no
BAIT-BET reversal				
African American	no		yes	yes
White	yes		yes	no
Glide shortened in BITE or BIDE				
African American	no[a]	yes[a]		
White	yes[b]	yes[b]		
BOUGHT-BOT merger				
African American		no		
White		yes		

a. Before voiced obstruents.
b. Before voiced and voiceless obstruents.

METHODOLOGY

In order to address these questions, we examine the vowel phonology of 12 speakers from Roswell, 6 African Americans and 6
whites. These speakers were born between 1915 and 1983, and
the two groups are roughly comparable in terms of date of birth,
sex, and education level. All of the speakers were born in Roswell,
or in counties that are now part of Roswell, and spent the majority
of their youth living in Roswell. Table 4.2 shows the demographic
information for these speakers. The speakers are also divided into
age groups, the older of which is composed of three African American speakers born in the years 1915 through 1936 (Mark, Emma,
and Hazel) and three white speakers born in the same time span
(Alfred, Betty, and Jane). The younger speakers were born in the
years 1964 through 1984. The young African American group consists of Doug, Shakra, and George, and the white group consists of
Bill, Mary, and John.

Although we attempted to attain comparable education levels
between African Americans and whites as well as for the older and
younger groups, a one-to-one correspondence was not achieved.
It is simply the case that African Americans in our group of older
speakers, born in 1936 or before, did not generally have access to
the same level of education as the white population did. This edu-

TABLE 4.2

Demographic Information for 12 Speakers Born in Roswell, Georgia

African Americans			Whites		
Name	Birth Year	Education	Name	Birth Year	Education
Females					
Emma	1920	read & writing	Betty	1915	B.A. part of M.A.
Hazel	1936	2½ years college	Jane	1935	high school
Shakra	1980	high school	Mary	1983	college
Males					
Mark	1915	7th grade	Alfred	1923	10th grade
Doug	1972	in college in 2006	Bill	1964	high school
George	1984	in college in 2006	John	1983	college

NOTE: Speakers in the older age group, born 1915–36, are highlighted.

cation gap seems to have narrowed substantially in the interven-
ing years, allowing us to more closely equate the education level of
our younger speakers; although, here as well, the overall education
level of the African American group is slightly lower than that of
the white speakers. There is a trade-off here. On the one hand, we
do not have a one-to-one correspondence in education level, which
would be beneficial for purposes of correlation; on the other hand,
the education levels of those interviewed probably more accurately
reflect the comparative education levels of these groups in the
broader population of Roswell.

Following the suggestions of the volume editors, Malcah Yaeger-Dror and Erik R. Thomas, tokens of vowels with preceding or
following laterals or nasals and tokens with a preceding /w/ were
excluded. Also, given their limitations, there were not enough
tokens of preceding and following environments for BOOT and BOY
to provide reliable measurements. Hence, we look only at the four
features listed in table 4.1. Vowels were cut at the top of the first
peak of the quasi-periodic wave and in the trough of the last cycle.
F_1 and F_2 values were measured at the peak of the wave using the
PRAAT program. Measurements of monophthongs were taken
halfway through the duration of the vowel, and measurements of
diphthongs at 35 milliseconds from onset and 35 milliseconds from
offset, as suggested by Yaeger and Thomas. A minimum of seven
tokens of each vowel were averaged for individual speakers. No
normalization techniques were applied. Vowels were plotted with
Ladefoged's (1993) measurements of American English vowels as
reference points using the Excel Charts and Graphing Program.

The protocol outlined by Yaeger and Thomas was followed in
order to maintain consistency with the other studies in this volume;
however, this protocol did present some difficulties. The most significant difficulty in terms of the vowels measured for this study
arose in the measurement of diphthongs. Although it was quite
apparent from viewing the spectrograms that many vowel tokens
were diphthongal, a significant number of these vowels were short
in duration, many being around the 70 millisecond range. This, of
course, means that measurements of 35 milliseconds from onset

and offset place the measurements right at the center of the vowel and, hence, do not capture the diphthongal nature of the token. For this reason, tokens with durations under 120 milliseconds were discarded.

RESULTS

The reversal of the positions of the BEET and BIT vowels is characteristic of the Southern Shift, although, as discussed above, Fridland and Kretzschmar found that neither African Americans nor whites in Memphis or Atlanta, respectively, exhibited this feature. Figure 4.1 shows the mean positions of the six African American and six white speakers for the BEET vowel and the BIT vowel.

As can be seen in figure 4.1, locations for BIT, represented by circles, are clustered together in a lower and more backed space from the BEET tokens. We have drawn a black line on the plot to

FIGURE 4.1

Unnormalized Mean Positions of the BEET and BIT Vowels
for African American and White Speakers

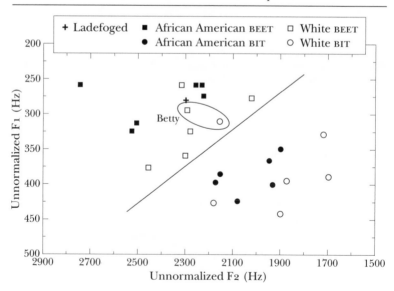

underscore this relationship. None of the positional relations for any individual speaker's plot point for BEET and BIT are reversed. Only one speaker, Betty, a white female born in 1915, has a vowel position for BIT that could be said to be moving toward a reversal—at least more so than the rest of the speakers. This speaker's vowels are circled on the plot. It should be noted that, for her time, Betty's social circumstances were anomalous. She received not only a B.A. but also part of an M.A. from nearby University of Georgia. This suggests that although Betty did not live far from Roswell during her college years, she may well have had greater exposure to a wider range of regional varieties of language than most Roswell residents of the time. We could tentatively suggest that Betty adjusted her speech patterns to "fit in" with the college students of her day. Overall, however, our data correspond with both Fridland's and Kretzschmar's in that neither group exhibits reversal of the positions of the BEET and BIT vowels. Comparison of the African American and white realizations shows that the African American tokens for both BEET and BIT appear to be slightly higher and more fronted on average than those of the white speakers.

In explaining the reversal of positions in the BAIT and BET vowels, Labov and Ash (1997) describe the primary motion of the shifting of BAIT in the South as being created by the monophthongization and fronting of the BITE vowel, which removes BITE from the path of BAIT, allowing the nucleus of BAIT to fall to the "same degree of opening" as the nucleus of BITE. To put this more simply, the nucleus of BAIT becomes centralized and more lowered than that of BET. Fridland (2003) found that both African Americans and whites in Memphis reversed the positions of BAIT and BET, but Kretzschmar's data indicate that only African Americans in Atlanta reverse these vowels, the opposite of what would be expected if the Southern Shift were operating. Figure 4.2 illustrates the relationship between the mean position of the nucleus of BAIT and the position of BET for the white speakers in our study. As can be seen be seen in this plot, the white speakers, with the exception of Mary, Jane, and John, have some degree of reversal in the position of these two vowels, although the nucleus of BAIT for these speakers is somewhat scattered in relation to BET. Bill and Betty have a BAIT

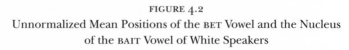

FIGURE 4.2

Unnormalized Mean Positions of the BET Vowel and the Nucleus
of the BAIT Vowel of White Speakers

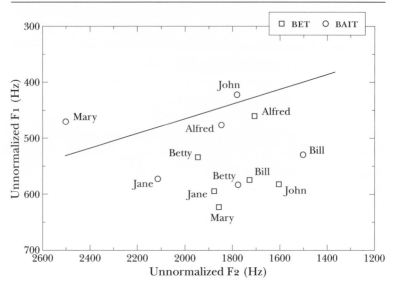

nucleus that is more centralized than BET, but Bill's BAIT nucleus is higher than BET, while Betty's is lower. In Alfred's case, the BAIT nucleus is more fronted than BET, but is also higher than BET. Mary and John, the youngest white speakers—both born in 1983—not only do not show a reversal, but also have positions which show the most differentiation between the nuclei of the BAIT and BET vowels. This difference is indicated by the black line drawn on the vowel plot, which separates the points for these two speakers' BAIT vowels and the rest of the points on the chart.

Figure 4.3 illustrates the relationship between the mean position of the nucleus of BAIT and the mean position of BET for our African American speakers. In this vowel plot, it can be seen clearly that none of the older group of African American speakers—Mark, Emma, and Hazel—reverse the positions of the nucleus of BAIT and the vowel in BET. This is indicated by the black line drawn on the plot, which separates these speakers' BAIT vowel positions from all other points. In the younger group, George and Doug reverse the

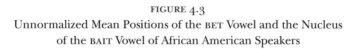

FIGURE 4.3
Unnormalized Mean Positions of the BET Vowel and the Nucleus
of the BAIT Vowel of African American Speakers

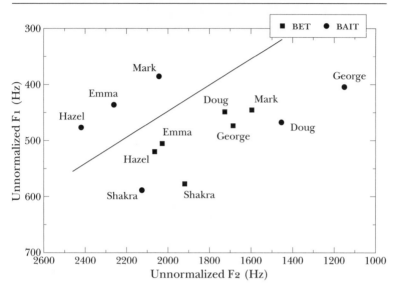

positions, with George's BAIT nucleus backed and higher than that of his BET vowel and Doug's BAIT nucleus backed and slightly lower that his BET vowel. Shakra shows a somewhat different pattern, with her BAIT nucleus fronted in comparison to her BET vowel, but also lowered.

When we compare the African American and white speakers' reversal of the nucleus of BAIT and BET, it seems that we must first specify what counts as a reversal. None of the speakers of either group appears to have as extreme a differentiation of the positions of these sounds as is suggested by Labov and Ash's (1997) description. That is to say, in no case do we see the nucleus of BAIT falling to the "same degree of opening" as the nucleus of BITE. However, we do see clear cases where the positions of these vowels are reversed along both the dimensions of front/back and high/low: the nucleus of BAIT is both lower and more backed than the BET vowel. If we require that the vowels must take on this position—that is, that they must reverse on both dimensions—then one white speaker and one African American speaker can be said to show the reversal. If a less stringent requirement is applied—that the positions must reverse on only one dimension, with the nucleus of BAIT being EITHER lower or backed from BET for the vowel to be considered reversed—then the situation changes strikingly. Using this criterion, we can say that two of the older white speakers and one of the younger white speakers show a reversal; in the African American group, none of the older speakers show the reversal, but all of the younger speakers do. Using either requirement, our data correspond with Fridland's (2003) Memphis study, which found that both African Americans and whites reversed the positions of the vowels, although with the more restricted requirements, it is only one speaker from each group who does so. Kretzschmar's Atlanta data show that African Americans reverse BAIT and BET; again, our data show that both groups reverse the positions of these vowels and do so in equal proportions using either criterion for "reversal."

The third feature investigated is glide weakening of BITE and BIDE. Bailey and Thomas (1998) were careful to differentiate offglides according to the following environment, reporting that whites may show weakened offglides of the BITE and BIDE vowels, while African Americans show glide weakening of the BIDE vowel only. Figure 4.4 shows the BITE and BIDE vowels for white females, and figure 4.5 does so for African American females. Figures 4.6 and 4.7 show the same features for white males and African American males, respectively.

There is one consistent factor represented in all the BITE and BIDE vowel plots: for all speakers, African American and white, the glide of the BIDE vowel is either similar in spectral movement or shorter than that of the glide of the BITE vowel. For both African American and white speakers, the males' offglides of BITE and BIDE are on average considerably shorter than the females'. Also, the white females have a greater internal consistency to their glide lengths than do African American females and represent the group with the longest glides (overall).

Alfred, a white speaker, produces completely monophthongal forms for BITE and BIDE. John, also white, as well as Mark and Doug, African American speakers, have full monophthongs for BIDE and noticeably short glides for BITE. The only female speaker

FIGURE 4.4

Unnormalized Mean Onset and Offglide Positions of the BITE
and BIDE Vowels for White Females

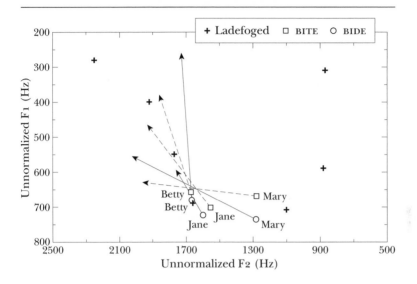

FIGURE 4.5

Unnormalized Mean Onset and Offglide Positions of the BITE
and BIDE Vowels for African American Females

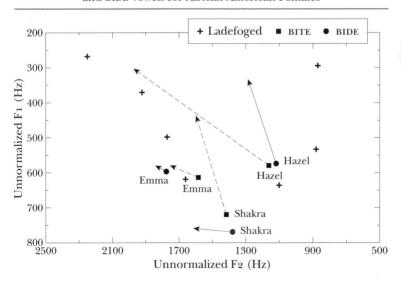

FIGURE 4.6

Unnormalized Mean Onset and Offglide Positions of the BITE
and BIDE Vowels for White Males

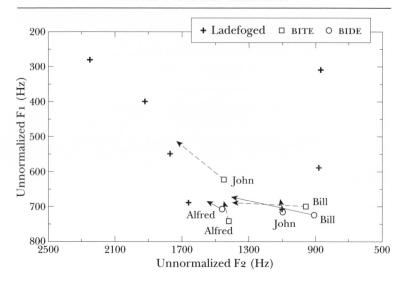

FIGURE 4.7

Unnormalized Mean Onset and Offglide Positions of the BITE
and BIDE Vowels for African American Males

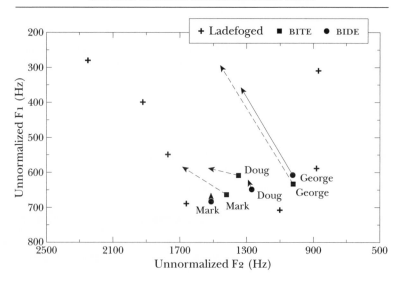

with a full monophthong is Emma, an African American, who, like John, Mark and Doug, has monophthongal BIDE and a quite short glide for BITE. Shakra and Hazel, African American speakers, and Jane, a white speaker, exhibit glide weakening of BIDE, with lesser degree or possibly no glide shortening of BITE. Mary, the youngest white female speaker, born in 1983, and Bill, a white speaker born in 1964, have "flat" offglides, as does Shakra, the youngest African American female speaker, born in 1980. By "flat," we mean that the F2 value increases considerably through the course of the diphthong but the F1 value hardly changes at all. A notable difference between Mary's and Bill's glides as opposed to Shakra's is that Mary's and Bill's are flat for both BITE and BIDE, while Shakra's is flat for BIDE only. George, the youngest African American, born in 1984, is the only male speaker with offglides that approach full diphthongal status.

In contrast to Bailey and Thomas's (1998) finding—that whites may show weakened offglides for BITE while African Americans do not—we find that the African American speakers of Roswell do produce weakened offglides for BITE and that for all speakers glides for BIDE are either very similar in length or shorter than their voiceless counterparts for each speaker.

The last vowel plot, figure 4.8, shows the mean positions for the BOUGHT and BOT vowels. As noted previously, Bailey and Thomas (1998) identified the merger of the BOUGHT and BOT vowels as a feature of SWVE, but not of AAVE. Mark, an African American, is the only speaker in our investigation who can be said to have a complete merger. Four of our white speakers, John (b. 1983), Bill (b. 1964), Alfred (b. 1923), and Betty (b. 1915), as well as one African American, Shakra (b. 1980), have these vowels in comparatively close proximity. These speakers' tokens are circled on the plot. It is difficult to discern which of the tokens close in proximity should be considered merged without a specific standard of measurement, but it would seem likely that at a minimum, Alfred is extremely close to showing this merger. It appears, then, that both African Americans and whites exhibit some degree of formant approximation.

FIGURE 4.8

Unnormalized Mean Onset and Offglide Positions of the BOT
and BOUGHT Vowels for African American and White Speakers

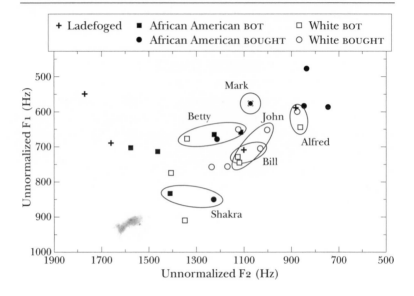

DISCUSSION

Regarding the questions we originally asked, we consider first the
question of whether any of the Roswell speakers in this study exhibit
the three features identified by Labov (1994) as indicative of the
Southern Shift—BEET-BIT reversal, BAIT-BET reversal, and glide
weakening of the BITE vowel. Data from this study are summarized
in table 4.3, along with reports on Southern features found in the
other studies mentioned previously. None of the 12 speakers featured in this study have all three diagnostic Southern Shift features
because nobody reverses the positions of the BEET and BIT vowels.
This, of course, does not mean that no speakers in Roswell reverse
the BEET and BIT vowel positions, but in this particular group of
speakers it is not found. This finding corroborates both Fridland's
(2003) Memphis findings and Kretzschmar's data from Atlanta.

As far as the reversal of the vowels in BAIT and BET is concerned,
both African American and white speakers exhibit the feature. Our

TABLE 4.3

Summary of African American and White Vowel Phonologies
in Southern Areas

Feature	Southern Shift	South	Memphis	Atlanta	Roswell
BEET-BIT reversal					
African American	no		no	no	no
White	yes		no	no	no
BAIT-BET reversal					
African American	no		yes	yes	yes
White	yes		yes	no	yes
Glide shortened in BITE or BIDE					
African American	no[a]	yes[a]			yes[b]
White	yes[b]	yes[b]			yes[b]
BOUGHT/BOT merger					
African American		no			yes
White		yes			yes

a. Before voiced obstruents.
b. Before voiced and voiceless obstruents.

findings regarding this feature correspond with Fridland's Memphis finding in that both African Americans and whites reverse the positions of these vowels (although not all do). In Atlanta, however, Kretzschmar found that African Americans reverse, while white speakers do not. This would appear at first to be a sharp contrast between Atlanta and Roswell speakers; it should be remembered, however, that we found only one white speaker and one African American who exhibited complete reversal—that is, along both the front/back and high/low dimensions.

There are some differences that stand out between the groups. The youngest white speakers, Mary and John, both college graduates born in 1983, are most definitely not reversing BAIT and BET, and they are the only white speakers, regardless of education level, with the exception of Jane, who do not reverse on at least one dimension (front/back or high/low). Among African Americans, the opposite pattern holds: the oldest speakers, Hazel, Emma, and Mark, who have vast differences in education level—ranging from knowledge of reading and writing to two and a half years of college—do not reverse in either dimension, while all of the younger speakers, two of whom were in college at the time of the interviews and one who had completed high school, reverse on at least one dimension. In very general terms, then, we can posit that in this small group of speakers, the younger African Americans are advancing in their reversal, while young whites are receding in their use of the feature; this difference does not appear to have any clear correspondence to education level, but rather suggests a generational change in the three young African Americans and the two youngest whites in divergent directions.

It should be mentioned here that during the course of writing this chapter we realized that our initial divisions of age groupings should be revised in our future investigations of Roswell. We divided speakers into two groups, those born between 1915 and 1936 and those born between 1964 and 1984. The gap between 1936 and 1964 seemed to present a reasonable dividing line. However, considering the population growth of Roswell, this dividing gap was, perhaps, not the best place to make the division. The population of Roswell was less than 2,000 prior to 1950, grew from around 2,000 to 15,000 between 1950 and 1975, and grew from around 15,000 to 48,000 between 1975 and 1990. This means that Bill, a white speaker born in 1964, was born into a very different community (one of only about 15,000 to maybe 25,000 residents) than those speakers born shortly after this period, who were born into a community that had nearly doubled in population. We tentatively suggest that the impact of this population boom may also have differed somewhat for young African American speakers and young white speakers.

There are at least two dominant organizations that tend to bind both older and younger African Americans in Roswell. These are the older "black churches," which provide a number of differing services as well as activities—many of which are geared toward the younger population—and a very active local community center, which primarily serves the African American community. These organizations provide centers around which local ties can be maintained and seem to provide a continuity for the younger African American community between what might be best termed the old "small town" Roswell and the new "exurban" Roswell. In addition, the African American population is smaller than the white population, and, as mentioned earlier, African Americans in Roswell tend to be on the lower economic rungs of the community. These factors, taken together, suggest that maintenance of strong local network ties is more important for African Americans, both old and young, than for white speakers.

White residents also, of course, participate in a number of institutionalized activities. However, given the size of the white population, the diversity in the economic scale of the population, and the vast number of differing organizations to which whites belong, in conjunction with the fact that these organizations are not as likely to have overlapping participation as do, for instance, the "black churches" and the community center mentioned above, the emphasis on multiplex local network ties that are tightly entwined seems to be smaller for whites than for African Americans.

One group of whites stands out in contrast to this situation. There is a group of white long-term residents of Roswell who meet every morning at a local restaurant, the Southern Skillet. The core group—those who show up nearly every day—consists of about 15 older white men. In addition there are probably another 30 or so who join the group less regularly, a few times a week or less, and there are a few wives who sometimes join their husbands. This group, however, rarely includes individuals born after 1960. It is mostly, then, older male whites who lived there when Roswell was still a small town and who maintain the local network ties developed in that community.

Taking these factors into account, we offer a tentative explanation for the divergence of the young African American and young white speakers in their reversal of BAIT and BET. We propose that the younger African Americans are raised in a community that has a greater density of local network ties that provide continuity back to the old linguistic norms of "small town" Roswell, whereas younger whites diverge from the norms of old Roswell as a result of the relative looseness of their network ties. These network ties also seem to have some implications in glide shortening of the BITE and BIDE vowels, although there may be a general attitude that this feature indicates "roughness," "coarseness," or lack of education by those who use it, especially among white speakers.

We found that both African Americans and whites, contrary to Bailey and Thomas's (1998) findings in the South, weaken the glides of the BITE and BIDE vowels, although for both groups glides are noticeably shorter for BIDE than for BITE. The group that demonstrates the most internal consistency in their glide lengths is the white females, who on average have longer glides than any of the other groups. Among the other groups, white males and African Americans of both sexes, the most salient social characteristic that appears to correlate with glide length or glide flatness is the level of education of the speaker. In these groups, Shakra, Hazel, John, George, and Doug have the longest offglides, and the latter four are the only speakers of these groups who attended college. Another speaker, Bill, shows a glide comparable in length to those of these individuals, but Bill's glide is exceptionally flat.

With regard to the last feature investigated here, the convergence of the vowels in BOUGHT and BOT, our findings are also inconsistent with Bailey and Thomas's (1998). Only one speaker in our group appears to merge these vowels, and he is African American. At least one white speaker appears "close enough" that we feel justified in deeming his BOT and BOUGHT nuclei convergent. There do not seem to be any social factors that can be correlated with the merger of the BOUGHT and BOT vowels among the Roswell speakers represented here.

Overall, the findings presented here suggest that a monolithic approach to correlations of linguistic features and regional or social features, whether it qualitatively divides the North and the South, African Americans and whites, more educated and less educated, or men and women, tends to overgeneralize the data. This overgeneralization can be useful in creating a broad picture of the distribution of certain features, but it seems worthwhile to keep in mind that this broad picture is a result of a generalization and one often made from a very small set of speakers. In generalizing from a very small sample of speakers, we must rely on the assumption that the sample is representative of the wider population, who are using features in the same way as the sample set. This may not be the case from community to community, or even within a community. Of course, a very large sample, certainly one that would achieve the numbers necessary to reach statistical significance, is often unattainable on a pragmatic level. We suggest that to consider a sample a reliable estimate of what a broader population does, it is necessary to continue to add speakers until the sample correlations become stable—that is, until the addition of new sets of speakers does not alter the overall picture. We have not yet done this with the Roswell speakers, so we are very hesitant to suggest that the data presented here can be said to reflect the broader population of Roswell. We have, rather, presented data that seem to indicate some correlated features that may hold true in the wider community. If they actually do hold true, we can say that what occurs in the vowel phonology of the African American speakers raised in Roswell differs in some ways and is similar in others to that of the white speakers raised in Roswell. At the same time, we can add that the ways that African Americans and whites in Roswell employ these features differ both quantitatively and qualitatively from the findings regarding the Southern Shift, the South, Memphis, and Atlanta.

REFERENCES

Bailey, Guy, and Erik Thomas. 1998. "Some Aspects of African-American Vernacular English Phonology." In *African-American English: Structure, History and Use*, ed. Salikoko S. Mufwene, John R. Rickford, Guy Bailey, and John Baugh, 85–109. London: Routledge.

Bailey, Guy, and Jan Tillery. 2006. "Sounds of the South." In *American Voices: How Dialects Differ from Coast to Coast*, ed. Walt Wolfram and Ben Ward, 11–16. Malden, Mass.: Blackwell.

Fridland, Valerie. 2003. "Network Strength and the Realization of the Southern Vowel Shift among African Americans in Memphis, Tennessee." *American Speech* 78: 3–30.

Kretzschmar, William A., Jr., Claire Andres, Rachel Votta, and Sasha Johnson. 2006. *Roswell Voices: A Community Oral History and Dialect Study, Phase II*. Roswell, Ga.: Roswell Folk and Heritage Bureau.

Kretzschmar, William A., Jr., Sonja Lanehart, Bridget L. Anderson, and Becky Childs. 2004. *Roswell Voices: A Community Oral History and Dialect Study*. Roswell, Ga.: Roswell Folk and Heritage Bureau.

Labov, William. 1991. "The Three Dialects of English." In *New Ways of Analyzing Sound Change*, ed. Penelope Eckert, 1–44. New York: Academic Press.

———. 1994. *Principles of Linguistic Change*. Vol. 1, *Internal Factors*. Oxford: Blackwell.

———. 1998. "Co-existent Systems in African-American Vernacular English." In *African-American English: Structure, History and Use*, ed. Salikoko S. Mufwene, John R. Rickford, Guy Bailey, and John Baugh, 110–52. London: Routledge.

Labov, William, and Sharon Ash. 1997. "Understanding Birmingham." In *Language Variety in the South Revisited*, ed. Cynthia Bernstein, Thomas Nunnally, and Robin Sabino, 508–73. Tuscaloosa: Univ. of Alabama Press.

Labov, William, Sharon Ash, and Charles Boberg. 2006. *The Atlas of North American English: Phonetics, Phonology, and Sound Change*. Berlin: Mouton de Gruyter.

Ladefoged, Peter. 1993. *A Course in Phonetics*. 3rd ed. Fort Worth, Texas: Harcourt Brace.

Thomas, Erik R. 1997. "A Rural/Metropolitan Split in the Speech of Texas Anglos." *Language Variation and Change* 9: 309–32.

———. 2003. "Secrets Revealed by Southern Vowel Shifting." *American Speech* 78: 150–70.

———. 2007. "Phonological and Phonetic Characteristics of African American Vernacular English." *Language and Linguistics Compass* 1: 450–75.

Thomas, Erik R., and Guy Bailey. 1998. "Parallels between Vowel Subsystems of African American Vernacular English and Caribbean Anglophone Creoles." *Journal of Pidgin and Creole Languages* 13: 267–96.

U.S. Census Bureau. 2000. United States Census 2000. http://www.census .gov.

Wolfram, Walt. 1993. "Ethical Considerations in Language Awareness Programs." *Issues in Applied Linguistics* 4: 225–55.

THE URBAN NORTHEAST

5. THE VOWEL PHONOLOGIES OF AFRICAN AMERICAN AND WHITE NEW YORK CITY RESIDENTS

ELIZABETH L. COGGSHALL
KARA BECKER
New York University

This study presents a new perspective on the regional variety of New York City English (NYCE) by considering the speech of two local ethnic groups, white and African American New Yorkers.[1] Regional dialectology traditionally considers only the speech of white Americans, and as a result we know little about local varieties of American English used by other ethnic groups, only noting that in general they do not participate in regional phonology (Labov, Ash, and Boberg 2006). This asymmetry has been the case in New York City, where the regional variety was described in depth by Labov (1966), based primarily on a sample of speakers of European descent. Since then, little research has looked at nonwhite New Yorkers and the extent to which they participate in local regional vowel phonology (see Wong 2007; Becker and Wong 2009). Our study provides insight into the extent of ethnic integration in the New York City speech community by comparing African American and white speakers of similar demographic backgrounds.

African American English (AAE) is well documented in the sociolinguistic literature; in fact, another seminal work by Labov, *Language in the Inner City* (1972), described African American speech using data from Harlem speakers. Labov's work, however, was part of the trend in AAE scholarship seeking commonalities among African American speakers across the United States rather than identifying regional differences within AAE. This focus has led to the assumption that there is a homogeneous, supraregional

AAE, particularly in northern urban centers (Labov 1968, 1972; Wolfram 1969; Fasold 1972; Thomas 2001). More recent scholarship, such as Wolfram (2007), Childs, Mallinson, and Carpenter (2010 [this volume]), Eberhardt (2010 [this volume]), Durian, Dodsworth, and Schumacher (2010 [this volume]), Purnell (2010 [this volume]), and Wroblewski, Strand, and Dubois (2010 [this volume]), has questioned this supraregional assumption. New York City, a Northern city with a large African American population in contact with a highly stigmatized regional variety, is an ideal site for exploring questions about regionality in AAE. Our results find that African Americans in New York City do in fact produce some local regional phonology, which may help to dispel the supraregional myth (Wolfram 2007). However, African American New Yorkers also produce some features considered central to AAE, linking these speakers to a larger African American identity. The relationship that emerges between AAE and local regional phonology is complex, and we contribute thoughts on the divergence controversy (Fasold et al. 1987; Bailey and Maynor 1989) as manifested in the local context of New York City.

If African American New Yorkers interact with local phonology in unique ways, so too do the white speakers of NYCE presented here. Despite the importance of *The Social Stratification of English in New York City* (Labov 1966) as foundational in the field of sociolinguistics, little work has followed up on the state of NYCE in the 40 years since (see Fowler 1986; Labov, Ash, and Boberg 2006; Becker 2009; Becker and Wong 2009). Our results show that younger white New Yorkers are not producing characteristic NYCE features, suggesting change in progress. The behavior of white New Yorkers only further complicates our understanding of convergence/divergence between white and African American speakers. Our data do not support a characterization of African American and white phonology in New York City as either converging or diverging, since individual features show unique trajectories of convergence, divergence, and maintenance over time. Like Wolfram (2007), we question the notion of identifying a unilateral path of change for AAE or any variety.

This study examines several vowels from the full vowel spaces of 36 New Yorkers, selected to provide insight into African American

and white speech in New York City. Four are locally salient phonological features of NYCE: the raising and ingliding of BOUGHT, the
split short-*a* system, and the BEAR-BEER and BOOR-BOAR mergers.
Other features (the fronting of BOAT, BOOT, BOOK, BUT, and the
nucleus of BOUT) are part of larger white sound changes in North
America. We contrast these with phonological features considered
characteristic of AAE and Southern English: glide-weakening of
BIDE and BOY and the apparent mergers of BIN-BEN, PEEL-BILL, and
BAIL-BELL. Finally, we examine features of what Thomas (2007)
calls the African American shift: the fronting of BOT and the raising
of BIT, BET, and BAT.

METHODOLOGY

THE SAMPLE. Our goal in compiling a sample of New York City
speakers was to control as much as possible for such social characteristics as age, sex, and social class, so that any differences between
African American and white speakers would be reliably based on
ethnicity. We had access to interview data of white New Yorkers
collected by various sociolinguists at New York University; these
data provided a sample of 18 white speakers stratified by age and
gender. We then compiled the African American sample to match
the social characteristics of the white New Yorkers as much as possible. The result is a matrix of 36 New Yorkers divided equally by
ethnicity, age (young, 18–35; middle, 36–55; old, 55 and older),
and gender (see table 5.1 for a full list of speakers).

The speakers represent a range of neighborhoods and boroughs across New York City, raising the possibility of cross-neighborhood or cross-borough differences. We accept Labov's (1966,
1972) reasoning that, at least for English speakers, New York City
is one unified speech community and that perceived differences
in New York City accent by area of residence, like the stigmatized
"Brooklynese," are actually class differences, with working-class
speakers using more salient NYCE features. We proceed from this
assumption that speakers with similar socioeconomic backgrounds
will not show cross-borough or cross-neighborhood differences and
compile a sample of speakers whose combined characteristics of

TABLE 5.1

Social Demographics of the New York City Sample

	Born	Sex	Ethnicity	Location	Occupation	Education
Joan	1915	F	AA	Lwr East Side	hospital worker	high school
Frank	1927	M	W	Lwr East Side	garment worker	some college
Mae	1928	F	W	Lwr East Side	lab supervisor	college
Lucille	1930	F	W	Lwr East Side	secretary	high school
Anne	1932	F	W	Lwr East Side	homemaker	elementary
Lewis	1932	M	AA	Lwr East Side	car detailer	high school
Michael	1933	M	W	Lwr East Side	pastor	graduate
Lillian	1935	F	AA	Bronx	court reporter	some college
Joe	1935	M	W	Brooklyn	nurse	graduate
Donnie	1940	M	AA	Bronx	coach	college
Roger	1941	M	AA	Bronx	salesperson	high school
Norma	1946	F	AA	Bronx	nurse	high school
Duke	1950	M	AA	Bronx	youth worker/coach	graduate
Tobias	1951	M	W	Lwr East Side	unemployed	elementary
Sandra	1954	F	AA	Bronx	postal worker	college
Ella	1956	F	AA	Bronx	homemaker	some college
Edith	1958	F	AA	Bronx	teacher	college
Martin	1959	M	W	Bronx	craftsman	high school
Lindsey	1960	F	W	Lwr East Side	bank supervisor	college
Kathy	1960	F	W	Brooklyn	waitress	college
Janet	1965	F	W	Brooklyn	law clerk	high school
Clay	1966	M	AA	Harlem/Bronx	hip hop archivist	high school
Jerry	1968	M	W	Brooklyn	police officer	college
John	1969	M	AA	Bronx	salesperson	high school
Jane	1977	F	W	Brooklyn	office administration	college
Sara	1977	F	W	Lwr East Side	homemaker	college
Mary	1977	F	AA	Bronx	unemployed	high school
Evan	1978	M	W	Queens	comedian	high school
Leon	1978	M	AA	Bronx	businessperson	college
Elaine	1980	F	W	Brooklyn	salesperson	college
Gary	1980	M	W	Brooklyn	teacher	graduate
Justice	1984	F	AA	Bronx	student	some college
Seamus	1984	M	W	Brooklyn	substitute teacher	some college
Alisa	1985	F	AA	Brooklyn	student	some college
Marcus	1985	M	AA	Bronx	student	some college
Matthew	1986	M	AA	Bronx	student	some college

occupation and education would locate them in either the upper-working class or lower-middle class, with few exceptions. Other studies of large urban centers (Sankoff and Cedergren 1971; Lennig 1978; Milroy 1980) have also drawn speakers from various neighborhoods in order to get an adequate demographic sample.

Nearly half of the white speakers live on the Lower East Side of Manhattan, the setting for Labov's (1966) foundational work. The Lower East Side today continues to diversify from the white immigrant port of entry that it was one hundred years ago, with growing Latino, Asian, and African American populations as well as a gentrifying middle class. The additional white speakers in the sample are not from the Lower East Side, but come from multiple neighborhoods and boroughs across New York City. This diversity of residence is further complicated by the African American speakers, who participated in oral history interviews conducted by the Bronx African American History Project (BAAHP) at Fordham University (Naisan, Purnell, and LaBennet 2007). As a result, 16 of the 18 African American speakers are from the Bronx (the other two are from the Lower East Side and Brooklyn). In the present instance, we argue that whites from the Lower East Side and African Americans from the South Bronx live in areas with similar sociodemographic characteristics. In the Bronx, upwardly mobile African Americans migrated from Harlem in the 1940s and 1950s, settling in what were then primarily white neighborhoods (Naison 2005). But the borough soon diversified, so that today it is an urban mix of many ethnicities, similar to the current Lower East Side. Both the Lower East Side and the Bronx experienced a period of disinvestment, unemployment, and crime in the 1970s and 1980s and are now dealing with conflict over urban renewal and gentrification. To the extent that the two areas show similar social characteristics, we argue that a comparison of these speakers according to ethnicity does not reflect neighborhood or borough distinctions. Another benefit of the choice of these particular neighborhoods is that they are far more ethnically mixed than other parts of the city, increasing chances of contact. (New York City overall has a very high index of dissimilarity for African Americans and whites, at 83 [Lewis Mumford Center 2004], meaning that 83% of one group would have to move in order to achieve an equal distribution across the city.) Another factor increasing the likelihood of contact is that most speakers in our sample are second- or third-generation New Yorkers. This reflects the fact that both ethnic groups have a long history in the city: waves of European immigrants began settling in large numbers in New York City in the mid-nineteenth century, while African Americans came north in large numbers following World War I during the Great Migration (although there were certainly African Americans in the city before then).

A potential limitation of the sample is the varied backgrounds of the interviewers in terms of ethnicity, gender, and regional variety. We have drawn from multiple sources for our interview data and were therefore unable to control for the social characteristics of the interviewers themselves. Another potential limitation is the use of varied methods for data collection. All of the white interviews were conducted by sociolinguists, following the traditional methods for sociolinguistic interviews, whereas 13 of the 18 African American interviews were conducted by oral historians at the BAAHP. We argue that all the interviews are comparable, following similar topic paths and eliciting both casual and careful speech. The oral histories do not contain language-oriented tasks, like reading passages or word lists, but the body of these interviews resembles a sociolinguistic interview. Other sociolinguistic studies have utilized oral histories as sources for sociolinguistic data, and we would argue these are an underutilized resource for sociolinguistic research (Bailey, Maynor, and Cukor-Avila 1991; Myhill 1995; Thomas 2001).

METHODS. The acoustic analysis that we present here consists of the full vowel spaces of 36 New Yorkers. Tokens were drawn from interview speech, excluding data from word lists or reading passages. Each interview was a minimum of one hour, and some were as long as two and a half hours. A total of 7,560 tokens (an average of 210 words per speaker) were analyzed in Praat, using a script that allowed the researcher to designate points of extraction. Pitch, F_1, F_2, F_3, and duration were measured for each token. With the exception of vowels that were shorter than 90 milliseconds in duration (often BIT, BET, BUT, and BOOK), two measurements were taken for each vowel, at 25 to 35 milliseconds from the onset and offset of the vowel, unless the point of inflection occurred later. Five to ten tokens were taken of each vowel; occasionally, a scarcity of tokens necessitated the use of as few as one, and occasionally a speaker had no tokens of a vowel, particularly those in specific environments, such as before /l/ or /r/. Vowels following glides, /l/, and /r/ were excluded; vowels before /r/, /l/, and nasals were excluded unless specified. Neither duration nor pitch are considered in the analysis being presented here.

The NORM program was used to normalize the formant data across speakers (Thomas and Kendall 2007). We selected the normalization procedure developed by Labov, Ash, and Boberg (2006) for *The Atlas of North American English,* allowing us to make direct comparisons with their findings, which include some of the most recent acoustic data on NYCE and related varieties. Other papers in this volume have used the same methods. Labov, Ash, and Boberg's method is both vowel and speaker extrinsic, so that a vowel is normalized by being compared both to other vowel tokens and to the vowels of other speakers (Thomas and Kendall 2007).

ANALYSIS

NYCE FEATURES. We first consider the data from the perspective of New York City English to see if African American New Yorkers use local NYCE phonology. Labov, Ash, and Boberg (2006) cite two features of NYCE that distinguish it from surrounding regional varieties: the vocalization of postvocalic /r/ and its unique short-*a* system. We do not consider /r/-vocalization here except to note that both white and African American New Yorkers are variably /r/-less (Becker 2009). Instead we focus on the parallel raising of the low vowels, BAD and BAN in the front and BOUGHT in the back, as distinctive NYCE features.

In 1966, Labov noted that the raising of BOUGHT was a stigmatized feature of NYCE, characteristic of stereotypical pronunciations of words like *coffee* and *dog.* Today, BOUGHT is still raised in NYCE above the midline, with an F_1' (i.e., normalized F_1) less than 700 Hz (Labov, Ash, and Boberg 2006). In addition, the glide of BOUGHT is both in- and downgliding in NYCE (Thomas 2001; Labov, Ash, and Boberg 2006). In contrast, we expect African Americans either to glide in the opposite direction (up and back), a characteristic of Southern speech, or to produce a monophthong (Thomas 2001).

In table 5.2 we see evidence that African American New Yorkers are producing this local phonological feature, so much so that there are no obvious differences by ethnicity in the means of the F1' of BOUGHT nuclei. Both groups show what Labov, Ash, and Boberg (2006) consider raised BOUGHT, with mean F1' values far less than 700 Hz. In addition, the means for both groups show in- and downgliding forms, although whites have a slightly longer downglide.

These findings for BOUGHT are surprising in two ways. First, African American New Yorkers have adopted a regional raised and in- and downgliding pronunciation of BOUGHT (see appendix for speakers' vowel plots). Similar results for BOUGHT have been found for Chinese Americans (Wong 2007) and Latinos (Slomanson and Newman 2004) in New York City. In fact, one African American informant in this study, Marcus (b. 1985), points to this variable (particularly his pronunciation of *talk*) as something that separates him from Southern African Americans. (Note that none of the other studies in this volume finds a raised BOUGHT nucleus that is ingliding for African Americans in other locales.) Second, white speakers show significant differences by age, with the youngest white speakers showing the least-raised BOUGHT for any group of

TABLE 5.2
Mean Normalized Formant Values for BOUGHT by Ethnicity and Age

	F1	F2	F1 Glide	F2 Glide
White	565	1036	621	1199
Young	623	1085	644	1178
Middle	583	1017	667	1169
Old	488	1007	569	1239
African American	563	1045	596	1190
Young	582	1039	610	1170
Middle	544	1051	579	1242
Old	561	1043	598	1157

either ethnicity. This suggests that white NYCE speakers are moving away from raised BOUGHT over time, while African American New Yorkers retain the local variable.

Young white speakers are also moving away from the short-*a* system of NYCE, in which a long /æː/ is expected to raise in parallel with BOUGHT. The NYCE short-*a* split is described as early as Babbitt (1896) and by Labov (1966, 2007). In Labov's system, shown in figure 5.1, the commonly referred to "tense/lax" character of the low front vowel is conditioned by the following environment, with long, or "tense," before the front nasals /n/ and /m/, voiceless fricatives, and voiced stops, and with short, or "lax," before the velar nasal, voiceless stops, voiced fricatives, and laterals (Labov 2007). There are a number of exceptions as well, such as laxing in open syllables, in function words, and in initial position. Following Labov, we refer to this as the complex short-*a* system.

The complexity of the system is ideal because it allows us to investigate partial diffusion to other groups, as Labov has argued for northern New Jersey, New Orleans, Cincinnati, and Albany (Labov 2007). The short-*a* tokens here are categorized using Labov's classifications, so BAN represents a following front nasal, BAD represents the other environments where Labov predicts a "tense" phoneme will occur, and BAT represents environments he predicts will be

FIGURE 5.1

Codas That Condition Raising of Short-*a* in New York City
(from Labov 2007)

p	t	ʧ	k
b	d	ʤ	g
m	n		ŋ
f	θ	s	ʃ
v	ð	z	ʒ
l		r	

"lax." All the New York speakers "tense" the BAN class; this in itself
is not surprising, as a nasal raising system is common in American
English (Thomas 2001). But the white speakers show significant
age stratification for the NYCE short-*a* split, as seen in figure 5.2.
Each age group shows the short-*a* system to varying extents, but
as speakers get younger, the distinction gets smaller. Older white
speakers have BAN and BAD about equally raised and fronted and
very far from BAT; the middle-aged group shows a lowered BAD
relative to BAN, and less of a distinction overall; and the younger
speakers show an even smaller distinction between BAD and BAT
and a general lowering and backing in all environments—Thomas
(2001) notes this is a widespread phenomenon in American English. Remember that the young white speakers also had the lowest
BOUGHT of any group; combined with the parallel backing and lowering of the low front class, this suggests a change in progress away
from these two characteristic NYCE features.

In contrast, African Americans show variable systems, the
means of which are plotted in figure 5.3. Some older and mid-

FIGURE 5.2
Short-*a* Split of White New Yorkers by Age

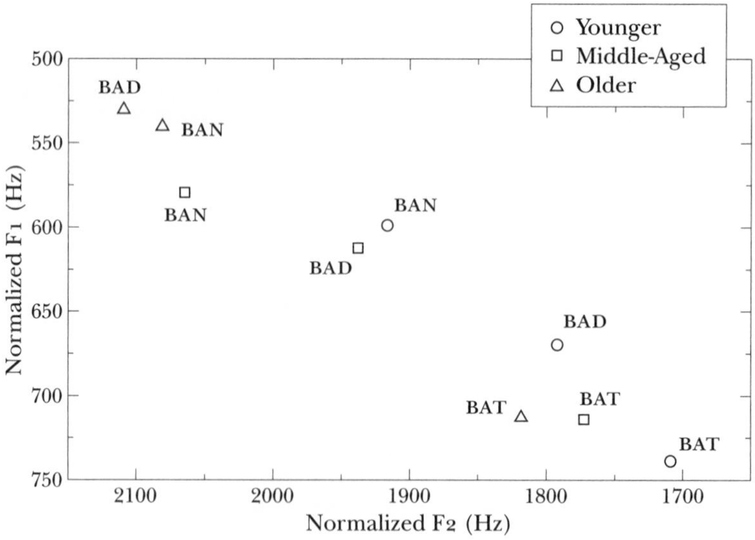

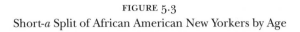

FIGURE 5.3
Short-*a* Split of African American New Yorkers by Age

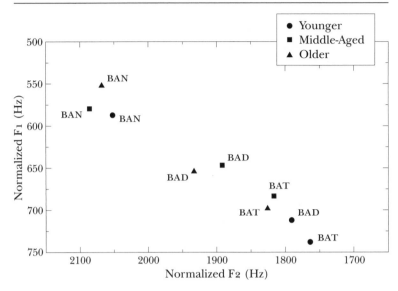

dle-aged speakers appear to make a distinction between BAD and BAT, although this is not the clear NYCE split we expect to see. The younger speakers, and some older speakers, do have a "nasal raising" system—with raising in the BAN class only. Gordon (2000) also found that African Americans in northwest Indiana raise BAN, which he argued was a nasal raising system and not the beginning stages of a split in progress, as suggested by Labov, Yaeger, and Steiner (1972). It appears that African Americans are not acquiring the split short-*a* system of NYCE, while at the same time white speakers are moving away from the complex system. These findings have been corroborated by Becker and Wong (2009), who found that Puerto Rican and Chinese New Yorkers, like African Americans, were also producing nasal systems, while young white New Yorkers also appeared to be moving toward a nasal system.

Labov (1966) also argues that NYCE shows apparent merger of the mid and high vowels before /r/ when /r/ is variable, so that both pairs BEER and BEAR and BOOR and BOAR have overlapping nuclei.[2] BEER and BEAR should also merge with the vowel of "tense" BAD, which has raised to meet them (Labov 1966). One older white male does appear to merge BAD, BEAR, and BEER, but none of the other white speakers shows apparent merger of BEER and BEAR, although a few show overlapping nuclei for BEAR and BAD. Interestingly, few scholars note that African Americans may overlap the nuclei of BEER and BEAR; yet our data show African Americans of all ages appear to merge or nearly merge these vowels. Not all speakers produced BOOR in interview speech, but for those who did, we see differences by ethnicity. Whites show apparent merger or near merger of BOOR and BOAR, particularly along the height dimension. African Americans show variable overlap of BOOR and BOAR, with many speakers clearly unmerged. Like white speakers, evidence of overlapping nuclei is stronger along the height dimension. On average, both African American and white speakers have ingliding BOOR and BOAR, as opposed to the up-glide found in the South for both whites and African Americans.

"WHITE" SOUND CHANGES. The fact that African American New Yorkers produce a "white" NYCE feature like raised and ingliding BOUGHT introduces the possibility that these speakers may also participate in larger sound changes thought to be restricted to white speakers of American English. The fronting of the back vowels BOAT and BOOT, recent changes in progress, and the fronting of BOOK, BUT, and the nucleus of BOUT, which are earlier changes, have all been investigated for evidence of divergence or convergence between whites and African Americans. The majority view is that African Americans resist these sound changes, keeping their back vowels backed (Bailey and Maynor 1989; Thomas 1989, 2001; Labov, Ash, and Boberg 2006). Recently, however, studies like Childs, Mallinson, and Carpenter in North Carolina (2010 [this volume]), Eberhardt in Pittsburgh (2010 [this volume]), and Durian, Dodsworth, and Schumacher in Columbus, Ohio (2010 [this volume]), have found that many African Americans participate in the fronting of back vowels. Like the raising of BOUGHT, we are starting to find evidence that these "white" sound changes are not restricted to white speakers.

Further, not all white speakers in the United States participate in "white" sound changes, as is the case for our white NYCE speakers. As shown in table 5.3, some white New Yorkers show mild fronting of BOAT, with an overall mean of 1296 Hz, just barely front of Labov, Ash, and Boberg's (2006) criterion for fronted BOAT of F2' > 1200 Hz. This slight fronting does not appear to be a change advancing by age in NYCE, as the oldest speakers have the most fronted BOAT. No whites front BOOT; even TOOT, which is considered to be fronted for all American English speakers, is just front of center (F2' > 1550 Hz) for white New Yorkers. This is in line with Labov, Ash, and Boberg's (2006) findings that NYCE is conservative in BOAT and BOOT fronting, though there is a slight preference to front BOAT.

African American speakers also show some fronting of BOAT, although they remain less advanced than the white speakers by 100 Hz. African Americans are similar to whites in keeping BOOT back, with the exception of one outlier, a middle-aged African American man who fronts BOOT significantly. Neither group meets the criteria for fronted BOOT, described by Labov, Ash, and Boberg (2006) as an F2' > 1200 Hz.

Because white New Yorkers do not front BOAT or BOOT, we lose the potential for investigating contact and diffusion of these features to African American New Yorkers. This is also the case for another phonological process many think African Americans do not produce—the merger of BOT and BOUGHT. Since white NYCE distinguishes these vowel classes, we cannot use this as a point of comparison for the two ethnic groups. However, white New Yorkers do moderately front the nucleus of BOUT, an older change that Thomas (2007) notes is common in American English. African

TABLE 5.3
Mean Normalized F2 Values for NY Speakers' Back Vowels by Ethnicity

	BOAT F2	*BOOT* F2	*TOOT* F2	*BOOK* F2	*BUT* F2
White	1296	1023	1615	1399	1407
African American	1174	1047	1554	1382	1351

TABLE 5.4
Mean Normalized Values for NYC BOUT by Ethnicity

	F1	F2	F1 Glide	F2 Glide
White	735	1617	664	1314
African American	745	1532	692	1257

Americans as a group show a BOUT nucleus very close to that of white speakers, though slightly less fronted (table 5.4).

We must note that neither group produces the very fronted BOUT characteristic of Southern speech, with F2' > 1800 Hz; instead, F2's for both groups hover around the midline (F2' = 1500 Hz), with whites slightly front and African Americans slightly back. There is some age stratification, with young African Americans showing the most backed nuclei of BOUT, slightly back of the midline and more backed than their nuclei for BITE. What is interesting is that African American and white speakers seem to be matching each other, fronting BOUT to about the same degree. In addition to the location of the nucleus, Thomas (2001, 2007) suggests that African Americans may weaken the glide of BOUT. There is some evidence for that here, particularly with some of the young African American speakers, but overall this difference is not great. There is also no difference by ethnicity for the location of BOOK or BUT, suggesting that African Americans approximate the local target. Overall, African American New Yorkers produce few fronted back vowels, yet they are fronted by the local white community. Neither group fronts BOAT or BOOT, but both groups slightly front BOOK, BUT, and the nucleus of BOUT.

SOUTHERN ENGLISH FEATURES. Most literature on African American vowel systems has looked at those features that are often considered "core" to AAE. These are features shared with white Southern speech, which is unsurprising given the contact between these two groups before the Great Migration (Bailey and Thomas 1998). The most studied is the monophthongization or weakening of the glide of /ai/ before voiced obstruents (BIDE). African American speakers have long been thought to monophthongize BIDE but not BITE, with the latter characteristic of the Inner South region (Labov, Ash, and Boberg 2006). However, recent evidence demonstrates that

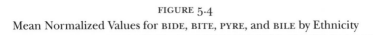

FIGURE 5.4

Mean Normalized Values for BIDE, BITE, PYRE, and BILE by Ethnicity

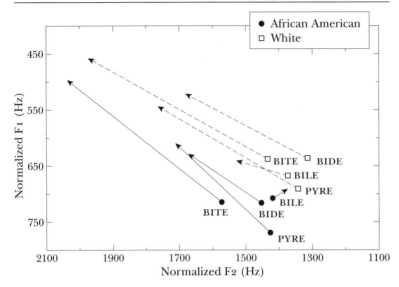

African American speakers in urban centers weaken the glide of BITE as well (Fridland 2003).

Figure 5.4 shows the means of BIDE, BITE, BILE, and PYRE for speakers of both ethnicities. All speakers show some glide reduction in BIDE compared to BITE, common in American English. The African American New Yorkers, however, show significantly weaker glides relative to white New Yorkers for BIDE. African American New Yorkers do not appear to weaken the glide in BITE at all, having lengths comparable to those of the white New Yorkers. African American New Yorkers show even stronger glide weakening before /l/, with monophthongal pronunciations of BILE, although they only moderately weaken the glide in PYRE, as predicted by Thomas (2001). There are no significant differences among African American New Yorkers by age; all groups weaken the glides of BIDE, BILE, and PYRE. The African American speakers also have a nucleus for both BIDE and BITE that is lower and more fronted than those of the white speakers. NYCE has a characteristically backed nucleus for [aɪ] (Labov 1966; Thomas 2001), whereas Southern and AAE forms often have a fronted nucleus. In sum, African American New Yorkers produce a characteristic feature of AAE—glide weakening in BIDE, BILE, and PYRE (a finding corroborated for the other locales in this volume)—but without the accompanying weakening for BITE.

Another diphthong, BOY, also shows glide weakening in the South and AAE. African American New Yorkers do weaken the glide of BOY relative to their white counterparts, although this difference is significant only along the frontness/backness dimension and not for height. African American New Yorkers do not monophthongize or weaken the glide of BOIL relative to white New Yorkers, as Southern whites and African Americans speakers do (Thomas 2001).

There are a number of mergers found in Southern English believed to be supraregional features of AAE, including the mergers of BIN and BEN, PEEL and BILL, and BAIL and BELL (Bailey and Thomas 1998; Rickford 1999; Gordon 2000). Thomas (2001, 461) notes that the merger of BIN and BEN "appears to occur virtually everywhere in African American speech"; yet only three of the older African American New Yorkers show an apparent merger of BIN and BEN, while the young speakers show no overlap of the nuclei of these vowels, as shown in table 5.5. No African American New Yorkers of any age appear to merge PEEL and BILL or BAIL and BELL, with one exception, a young woman.

As we can see, the supposed AAE "core" features discussed above may not be a part of the speech of New York African Americans, with the exception of BIDE and BOY glide weakening. Perhaps the mergers of BIN and BEN, PEEL and BILL, and BAIL and BELL have a stronger link to Southern identity than they do to ethnicity for New York African Americans, because these features are shared with Southern whites. This theory would not explain why African American New Yorkers weaken the glide of BIDE and BOY, however.

UNIQUE AFRICAN AMERICAN ENGLISH PHONOLOGY. African American English does not follow a one-to-one relationship with Southern English, and much work, particularly in morphosyntax, has

TABLE 5.5
BIN/BEN Merger by Age and Ethnicity

	F1 Difference	F2 Difference
African Americans	83	146
Old	84	30
Middle	66	142
Young	101	267
White	130	163

explored the unique features of AAE (Rickford 1999). More recently, Thomas (2007) discusses what he calls the "African American shift," defined as the raising of BAT, BET, and BIT, and the fronting of the nucleus of BOT. Compared to white New Yorkers, African American New Yorkers do not raise BET and BIT, with no significant differences by ethnicity or age. There is some variation in the raising of BAT (see, for example, Matthew, born 1986, in the appendix). Overall, African American New Yorkers have BAT raised higher than white New Yorkers; this raising would only increase if, on the assumption that African American New Yorkers do not have a split short-*a* system, we collapsed the BAT and BAD classes. However, African Americans do not front BOT, showing no differences in mean F2' from white speakers. Thus, we can conclude that African American New Yorkers are not participating in the "African American shift."

CONCLUSION

The results from our New York City corpus present a complicated picture for the divergence/convergence controversy over the trajectories of AAE and white dialects (Fasold et al. 1987; Bailey and Maynor 1989). If we assume that African Americans who migrated to New York City during the Great Migration and after brought with them some of the "core" AAE phonology, then we might view the lack of mergers for BIN and BEN and for PEEL and BILL as evidence of convergence, as African American New Yorkers adopt the local phonology. However, other features with a similar history, like BIDE and BOY monophthongization, have not converged with local norms but instead are maintained in African American New York speech. There is also divergence in the New York City sample, although it is not the African Americans who are doing the diverging, but young white speakers who are moving away from the raising of BOUGHT and the split short-*a* system. For BOUGHT, African Americans of all ages are equally raised, suggesting that there was convergence to this local pronunciation early on and continued maintenance. There is also some evidence of early convergence by African American New Yorkers to the short-*a* split, although the amount of variability in speakers' systems makes a generalization difficult. If some older African Americans did converge in part with the split short-*a* system, then younger African Americans are certainly diverging, using a nasal system. Henderson (1996) argued for her short-*a* data in Philadelphia that a lack of African Americans under age 40 who showed a split was an indication of divergence, citing the famous quote from Labov and Harris (1986, 139): "The Philadelphia speech community is separating into two distinct speech communities: White and Black." The African American New York speech community, however, if diverging from local white speech, is not converging with a supraregional AAE, whether in older core features (like BIN-BEN) or newer changes like Thomas's (2007) African American shift. Our data therefore adhere, nominally, to Bailey and Maynor's (1989, 31) loosest definition of divergence as "simply ... that the black and white vernaculars are developing in different ways." This finding is neither surprising nor particularly telling. Young white speakers are moving away from some of the more marked NYCE variables, which in the case of BOUGHT takes them farther away from African American New York speech but in the case of short-*a* brings them closer together. African American speakers are in a sense picking and choosing among variables available to them via ethnicity and region to create an identity based on both. Although we may identify a particular feature as convergent or divergent from local white phonology, the overall picture of African American New York phonology resists a unilateral characterization of "convergent" or "divergent." This mirrors the resistance by Wolfram (2007) and others to characterize the larger variety of AAE as "convergent" or "divergent." At present, the data do not allow such a simplified characterization of African American New York phonology.

Like the other papers in this volume, our study joins a growing body of literature that shows the unique ways in which ethnic groups acquire and use local regional phonology (Fought 1999; Anderson 2002; Fridland 2003; Coggshall 2006; Wolfram 2007; Wong 2007). African Americans in New York City neither completely adhere to supraregional AAE nor completely produce local New York City English. Further, we argue (with Fought 1999 and Eckert 2008) that we cannot interpret the utilization of white NYCE resources as the assimilation of minority groups to the dominant white group, but rather, that we need new ways of understanding how groups in contact cross ethnic and other identity boundaries in utilizing each other's resources. The results of this study suggest that we are only just beginning to understand how ethnicity and geography interact linguistically. In rejecting a characterization of AAE as homogeneous, we also reject a conception of African American identity, or any identity, as monolithic. This perspective helps explain the complex set of features used by the African American speakers in our study. The speakers raise BOUGHT but do not use the NYCE short-*a* system, and they weaken the glide of BIDE but do not appear to merge BIN and BEN or PEEL and BILL. Perhaps, as the time since the Great Migration of rural, Southern African Americans to the urban North lengthens, the strong tie between Southern and African American identity has weakened. We cannot yet explain the choices of our African American New Yorkers to preserve some Southern features while not utilizing others, but argue that the expectation of complete clarity may be one of the major drawbacks of previous work on this subject. We are left with a view of African American speech in New York that is not static. In the same way, white NYCE appears to be evolving. Both varieties reveal the complexity that results from the interaction between ethnicity and regional variety in New York City.

APPENDIX
Representative Vowel Plots

1. Michael, White Male (b. 1933) from Lower East Side, New York City

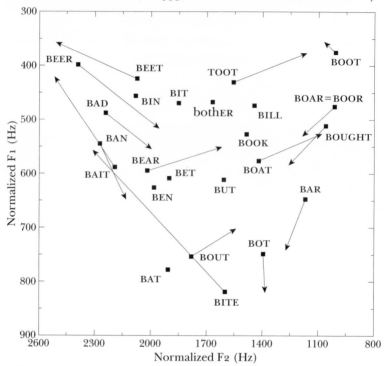

Michael's BAN and BAD are raised and fronted, higher than BAIT. BOUGHT is raised, higher than BOAT. BOAT is slightly fronted but BOOT remains backed. The nucleus of BOUT is fronted. BOAR and BOOR overlap, but BEER and BEAR are quite distinct.

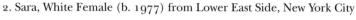

2. Sara, White Female (b. 1977) from Lower East Side, New York City

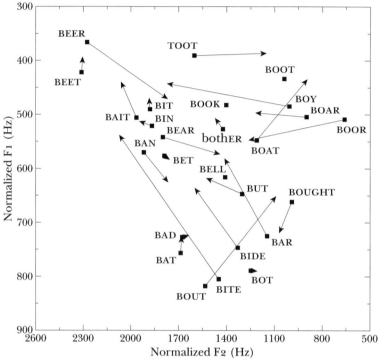

Sara's BOUGHT is raised only slightly above the midline, and her BAT and BAD are lax and back, while BAN is raised and fronted. She does not appear to merge BEER and BEAR, but BOOR and BOAR are close. BOAT and BOOT are both backed, although BOAT is more fronted than BOOT. The nucleus of BOUT is fronted.

3. Lillian, African American Female (b. 1935) from Bronx, New York City

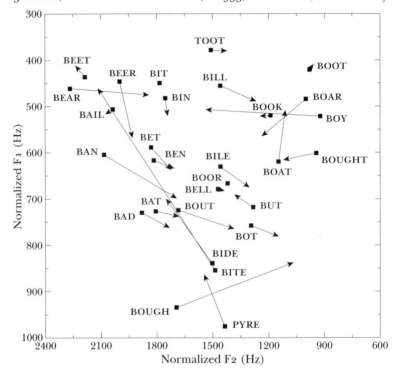

Lillian has a raised and ingliding BOUGHT. She shows a nasal system for short-*a*. The back vowels BOAT, BOOT, BOOK, and BUT are backed, but the nucleus for BOW is fronted. She has reduced glides for BIDE, PYRE, BILE, and BOY. She does not appear to merge BIN and BEN, BAIL and BELL, or BEER and BEAR, though the last two are close. Her BIT is raised, but not above BEET.

4. Clay, African American Male (b. 1966) from Harlem and the Bronx

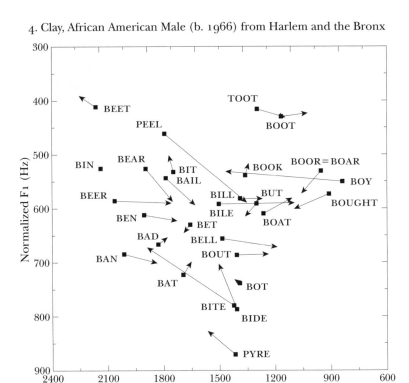

Clay's BOUGHT is raised above 700 Hz and is in- and downgliding. BAT is raised some, but BAN and BAD even more so, approximating the NYCE short-*a* split. His BOOR overlaps with BOAR, but his BEAR and BEER show no overlap. He shows reduced glides for BIDE, PYRE, and BOY, but he does not appear to merge BIN and BEN or BAIL and BELL. TOOT, BOOT, BOAT, and the nucleus of BOUT are back.

5. Matthew, African American Male (b. 1986) from Bronx, New York City

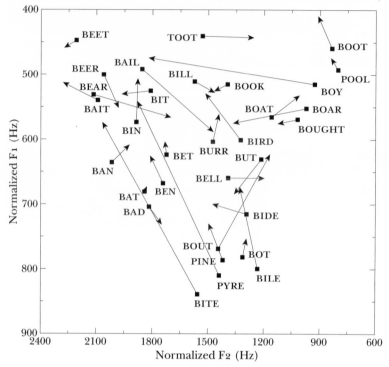

Matthew has a raised and ingliding BOUGHT. His short-*a* shows a nasal system, and a raised BAT and BAD. Neither BET nor BIT is raised. BILE and BIDE show glide-weakening, but PYRE and BOY do not. BEAR and BEER appear to show a near-merger. Matthew shows distinction between BIN and BEN, and BAIL and BELL. BOOT and BOAT are back, while the nucleus of BOUT is slightly fronted.

NOTES

This study would never have been possible without the hard work of Cara Shousterman, Elaine Devora, and Corey Silverstein, or without the Praat script created by Paul DeDecker. We thank Malcah Yaeger-Dror and Erik Thomas for all their help and support in making this volume happen. We also thank John Singler, Gregory Guy, and Donna Coggshall for their technical and moral support. Finally, we owe a great debt to the Bronx African American History Project at Fordham University, including Mark Naisan, Brian Purnell, and Oneka LaBennet: http://www.fordham.edu/academics/programs_at _fordham_/bronx_african_americ/index.asp. All mistakes are our own. In this and other writings together, we are coauthors, regardless of the ordering of the names.

1. We use the term *white* to refer to speakers of various European descents. *African American* is used in a narrow sense to refer to American slave descendants, in keeping with Baugh (1999); we specifically excluded speakers of Caribbean descent, some of whom may also claim the term African American. Parents of African American speakers were either native to New York City or migrated from the South. All speakers in the sample are native, monolingual speakers of English.

2. Note that the historical classes of BOAR (/or/) and BORDER (/ɔr/) have been merged in both NYCE and AAE (Kurath and McDavid 1961; Labov 1966; Bailey and Thomas 1998). A preliminary look at this New York corpus suggests that both ethnicities merge BOAR and BORDER. So for speakers who merge BOOR and BOAR, really there is a merger of all back rounded vowels before /r/: BORDER, BOAR, and BOOR.

REFERENCES

Anderson, Bridget L. 2002. "Dialect Leveling and /ai/ Monophthongization among African American Detroiters." *Journal of Sociolinguistics* 6: 86–98.

Babbitt, E. H. 1896. "The English of the Lower Classes in New York City and Vicinity." *Dialect Notes* 1: 457–64.

Bailey, Guy, and Natalie Maynor. 1989. "The Divergence Controversy." *American Speech* 64: 12–39.

Bailey, Guy, Natalie Maynor, and Patricia Cukor-Avila, eds. 1991. *The Emergence of Black English: Text and Commentary*. Amsterdam: Benjamins.

Bailey, Guy, and Erik Thomas. 1998. "Some Aspects of African-American Vernacular English Phonology." In *African-American English: Structure, History, and Use*, ed. Salikoko S. Mufwene, John R. Rickford, Guy Bailey, and John Baugh, 85–109. London: Routledge.

Baugh, John. 1999. *Out of the Mouths of Slaves: African American Language and Educational Malpractice*. Austin: Univ. of Texas Press.

Becker, Kara. 2009. "/r/ and the Construction of Place Identity on New York City's Lower East Side." *Journal of Sociolinguistics* 13: 634–58.

Becker, Kara, and Amy Wong. 2009. "The Short-*a* System of New York City English: An Update." *University of Pennsylvania Working Papers in Linguistics* 15.2.

Childs, Becky, Christine Mallinson, and Jeannine Carpenter. 2010. "Vowel Phonology and Ethnicity in North Carolina." In Yaeger-Dror and Thomas, 23–47.

Coggshall, Elizabeth L. 2006. "Differential Vowel Accommodation among Two Native American Groups." M.A. thesis, North Carolina State Univ. Available at http://www.lib.ncsu.edu/pubweb/www/ETD-db/web_root/collection/available/etd-04272006-113514/unrestricted/etd.pdf

Durian, David, Robin Dodsworth, and Jennifer Schumacher. 2010. "Convergence in Urban Blue-Collar Columbus, Ohio." In Yaeger-Dror and Thomas, 161–90.

Eberhardt, Maeve. 2010. "African American and White Vowel Systems in Pittsburgh." In Yaeger-Dror and Thomas, 129–57.

Eckert, Penelope. 2008. "Where Do Ethnolects Stop?" *International Journal of Bilingualism* 12: 25–42.

Fasold, Ralph W. 1972. *Tense Marking in Black English: A Linguistic and Social Analysis*. Arlington, Va.: Center for Applied Linguistics.

Fasold, Ralph W., William Labov, Fay Boyd Vaughn-Cooke, Guy Bailey, Walt Wolfram, Arthur K. Spears, and John Rickford. 1987. "Are Black and White Vernacular Varieties Diverging? Papers from the NWAVE XIV Panel Discussion." *American Speech* 56: 3–80.

Fought, Carmen. 1999. "A Majority Sound Change in a Minority Community: /u/-Fronting in Chicano English." *Journal of Sociolinguistics* 3: 5–23.

Fowler, Joy. 1986. "The Social Stratification of (r) in New York City Department Stores, 24 Years after Labov." Unpublished MS.

Fridland, Valerie. 2003. "'Tie, Tied and Tight:' The Expansion of /ai/ Monophthongization in African-American and European-American Speech in Memphis, Tennessee." *Journal of Sociolinguistics* 7: 279–98.

Gordon, Matthew J. 2000. "Phonological Correlates of Ethnic Identity: Evidence of Divergence?" *American Speech* 75: 115–36.

Henderson, Anita. 1996. "The Short 'a' Pattern of Philadelphia among African-American Speakers." In "(N)WAVES and MEANS: A Selection of Papers from NWAVE 24," ed. Miriam Meyerhoff, 127–40. *University of Pennsylvania Working Papers in Linguistics* 3.1.

Kurath, Hans, and Raven I. McDavid, Jr. 1961. *The Pronunciation of English in the Atlantic States: Based upon the Collections of the Linguistic Atlas of the Eastern United States*. Ann Arbor: Univ. of Michigan Press.

Labov, William. 1966. *The Social Stratification of English in New York City*. Washington, D.C.: Center for Applied Linguistics.

———. 1968. *A Study of the Non-standard English of Negro and Puerto Rican Speakers in New York City*. New York: Columbia Univ.

———. 1972. *Language in the Inner City: Studies in the Black English Vernacular*. Philadelphia: Univ. of Pennsylvania Press.

———. 2007. "Transmission and Diffusion." *Language* 83: 344–87.

Labov, William, Sharon Ash, and Charles Boberg. 2006. *The Atlas of North American English: Phonetics, Phonology, and Sound Change*. Berlin: Mouton de Gruyter.

Labov, William, and Wendall A. Harris. 1986. "De Facto Segregation of Black and White Vernaculars." In *Diversity and Diachrony*, ed. David Sankoff, 1–24. Philadelphia: Benjamins.

Labov, William, Malcah Yeager, and Richard Steiner. 1972. *A Quantitative Study of Sound Change in Progress*. Philadelphia: U.S. Regional Survey.

Lennig, Matthew. 1978. "Acoustic Measurement of Linguistic Change: The Modern Paris Vowel System." Ph.D. diss., Univ. of Pennsylvania.

Lewis Mumford Center. 2004. "Metropolitan Racial and Ethnic Change." http://mumford.albany.edu/census/WholePop/CitySegdata/361000City.htm.

Milroy, Lesley. 1980. *Language and Social Networks*. Oxford: Blackwell.

Myhill, John. 1995. "The Use of Features of Present-Day AAVE in the Ex-Slave Recordings." *American Speech* 70: 115–47.

Naison, Mark. 2005. "Memories of Morrisania: Introduction." *Bronx County Historical Society Journal* 42: 5–22.

Naisan, Mark, Brian Purnell and Oneka LaBennet. 2007. http://www.fordham.edu/academics/programs_at_fordham_/bronx_african_americ/index.asp.

Purnell, Thomas C. 2010. "The Vowel Phonology of Urban Southeastern Wisconsin." In Yaeger-Dror and Thomas, 191–217.

Rickford, John R. 1999. *African American Vernacular English: Features, Evolution, Educational Implications.* Malden, Mass.: Blackwell.

Sankoff, Gillian, and Henrietta J. Cedergren. 1971. "Some Results of a Sociolinguistic Study of Montreal French." In *Linguistic Diversity in Canadian Society,* ed. Regna Darnell, 61–87. Edmonton, Alta.: Linguistic Research.

Slomanson, Peter, and Michael Newman. 2004. "Peer Group Identification and Variation in New York Latino English Laterals." *English World-Wide* 25: 199–216.

Thomas, Erik R. 1989. "The Implication of /o/ Fronting in Wilmington, North Carolina." *American Speech* 64: 327–33.

———. 2001. *An Acoustic Analysis of Vowel Variation in New World English.* Publication of the American Dialect Society 85. Durham, N.C.: Duke Univ. Press.

———. 2007. "Phonological and Phonetic Characteristics of African American Vernacular English." *Language and Linguistics Compass* 1: 450–75.

Thomas, Erik R., and Tyler Kendall. 2007. NORM: The Vowel Normalization and Plotting Suite. Version 1.0. http://ncslaap.lib.ncsu.edu/tools/norm/.

Wolfram, Walt. 1969. *A Sociolinguistic Description of Detroit Negro Speech.* Washington, D.C.: Center for Applied Linguistics.

———. 2007. "Sociolinguistic Folklore in the Study of African American English." *Language and Linguistics Compass* 1: 292–313.

Wong, Amy. 2007. "Two Vernacular Features in the English of Four American-Born Chinese." In "Papers from NWAV 35," ed. Toni Cook and Keelan Evanini, 217–30. *University of Pennsylvania Working Papers in Linguistics* 13.2.

Wroblewski, Michael, Thea Strand, and Sylvie Dubois. 2010. "Mapping a Dialect 'Mixtury': Vowel Phonology of African American and White Men in Rural Southern Louisiana." In Yaeger-Dror and Thomas, 48–72.

Yaeger-Dror, Malcah, and Erik R. Thomas, eds. 2010. *African American English Speakers and Their Participation in Local Sound Changes: A Comparative Study.* Publication of the American Dialect Society 94. Durham, N.C.: Duke Univ. Press.

6. AFRICAN AMERICAN AND WHITE VOWEL SYSTEMS IN PITTSBURGH

MAEVE EBERHARDT

University of Vermont

Aлтноugн тнеre наs alwaуs been a great deal of interest in the study of African American English (AAE), the bulk of this work has focused on the morphosyntactic properties of the variety, leaving its phonological system largely unexplored (Bailey and Thomas 1998). As a result, sociolinguists have gained little formal knowledge of cross-regional phonetic and phonological variation in AAE or of how regional AAE varieties compare to white local vernaculars (see Fought 2002; Wolfram 2007). In recent years, however, scholars have turned their attention to investigations of the phonological systems of regional varieties of AAE, focusing on the extent to which African Americans and whites in a given area share features of the local dialect and to what extent their speech remains distinct (e.g., Anderson 2002; Mallinson and Wolfram 2002; Fridland 2003b; Childs and Mallinson 2004; Nguyen 2005; see also other chapters in this volume). Such investigations have revealed that African American English is much less uniform than was once believed (see Wolfram 2007). The current paper joins the growing body of literature that examines the linguistic character of AAE in regional context.

Pittsburgh, Pennsylvania, is an appealing site for the study of ethnicity and sociolinguistic variation for several sociohistorical reasons. Pittsburgh is a mid-sized city in southwestern Pennsylvania, home to about 315,000 residents in the metropolitan area, roughly 27% of whom are African American (U.S. Census Bureau 2009). Beginning in the late nineteenth century, large numbers of both European immigrants and African Americans were drawn to Pittsburgh for work in the steel industry (Baldwin 1937; Epstein 1969;

Dickerson 1986). Large-scale migration of African Americans to Pittsburgh occurred slightly earlier (1875) than the Great Migration to other areas (1910–30) (Glasco 2006). As groups settled in the city, the hilly terrain of Pittsburgh helped create isolated, self-contained ethnic enclaves (Baldwin 1937; Johnstone, Bhasin, and Wittkofski 2002), which forced fragmentation of the African American community into several neighborhoods across the city (Glasco 1989). In the late nineteenth and early twentieth centuries, there was a great deal of contact between African American and white immigrant groups, as they worked side by side in the steel industry (Dickerson 1986; Hinshaw 2002) and lived in close proximity in the neighborhood of the Hill District through the middle of the twentieth century (Lubove 1969; Bodnar, Simon, and Weber 1982; Dickerson 1986; Glasco 1996). Today, however, the situation is quite different, with much less contact between the races than there once was, and an index of dissimilarity of 67 (Lewis Mumford Center 2004),[1] putting segregation in Pittsburgh higher than the national average (Logan 2001).

Linguistically, Pittsburgh is part of the Midland (Labov 1991; Labov, Ash, and Boberg 2006), and as such, exhibits a split short-*a* system, in which the vowel is raised before front nasals and before /d/, but remains low elsewhere. Pittsburgh is also participating in the fronting of the BOAT and BOOT nuclei, a widespread change occurring in the Midland, the South, and the West (Labov, Ash, and Boberg 2006). Fronting and unrounding of the BOAT nuclei may have been present in western Pennsylvania as early as the Civil War (Thomas 2001), although fronting of the BOAT vowel is a newer development in other areas (Labov, Ash, and Boberg 2006). Consistent with Labov, Ash, and Boberg's (2006) results for this area, the diphthongs in BILE, PINE, and PYRE are often monophthongal in Pittsburgh (McElhinny 1999; Johnstone, Bhasin, and Wittkofski 2002), as they also found them to be throughout the Midland. Hankey (1972) found that white speakers in western Pennsylvania show weak BIDE-gliding as well, but that is supported neither by my results nor by those of Labov, Ash, and Boberg (2006), who reported that only one speaker in the Midland (in Kansas) showed glide-deletion before obstruents (e.g., BIDE).

Western Pennsylvania has been called "a hotbed of vowel mergers" (Thomas 2001). Tense vowels tend to lax before /l/, creating several conditioned mergers: PEEL-BILL, BAIL-BELL, and POOL-PULL. McElhinny (1993) found PEEL-laxing prevalent in the speech of both whites and African Americans, with higher rates among African Americans (51%, compared to 37% for white speakers). Conversely, McElhinny found no POOL-laxing in Pittsburgh AAE, although whites exhibited laxing in 27% of POOL tokens.

Other conditioned mergers present in the area include the three-way collapse of BORDER, BOAR, and BOOR, as in many other regions (Thomas 2001). Additionally, the unconditioned merging of the low back vowels BOT and BOUGHT is a completed change (Wetmore 1959; Kurath and McDavid 1961; Herold 1990; Labov, Ash, and Boberg 2006) in the white community of western Pennsylvania. In Eberhardt (2008), I report that African Americans in Pittsburgh also exhibit the low-back merger, although other studies have reported that this merger is limited among African Americans in other regions (e.g., Bernstein 1993), where BOT fronting precludes the need for a merger with BOUGHT (Thomas 2007). In Pittsburgh, sociohistorical conditions seem to have fostered the spread of this merger from white to African American speech. In particular, the fact that the merger is a longstanding feature of Pittsburgh speech (Wetmore 1959; Kurath and McDavid 1961) as opposed to its status as a change in progress in other regions, and the extensive contact between ethnic groups around the turn of the twentieth century, created conditions for the merger to spread to African American speech. In addition, as Labov (1994) has discussed, mergers have a tendency to expand at the expense of distinctions, which would have facilitated the spread of this merger. The low-back merger has additionally triggered the Pittsburgh Chain Shift (Labov, Ash, and Boberg 2006; Kiesling and Johnstone 2007), in which BUT lowers into the space provided by the merger of BOT and BOUGHT. Labov, Ash, and Boberg (2006) report a substantially lower BUT for western Pennsylvania than the rest of the Midland, with an average F_1 of 787 Hz. Kiesling and Johnstone (2007) recently confirmed this as a change in progress among white speakers in the city.

A final local feature is the monophthongization of BOUT. Monophthongal BOUT is unique to Pittsburgh as a regional characteristic in North America (Labov, Ash, and Boberg 2006), though it does surface in other areas (almost categorically in the possessive pronominal *our*). Thomas (2001, 2003, 2007) has noted that BOUT glide loss may be more common in African American speech than in white speech, particularly in the South. In Pittsburgh, BOUT-monophthongization has been widely identified for, and is seen as characteristic of, white regional speech (Gagnon 1999; McElhinny 1999; Thomas 2001; Johnstone, Bhasin, and Wittkofski 2002; Labov, Ash, and Boberg 2006). There is some indication that BOUT-monophthongization is receding in Pittsburgh, though more slowly among men (Kiesling and Wisnosky 2003) and the working class (Johnstone, Bhasin, and Wittkofski 2002).

Whether monophthongal BOUT is present in Pittsburgh AAE remains to be determined. Based on impressions and experience from having lived in the city, Johnstone, Bhasin, and Wittkofski (2002) write, "Monophthongal /aw/ ... is rare in local African Americans' speech," a claim also made by McElhinny (1999), similarly based on unmeasured observation. In an exploratory analysis of BOUT-gliding, Gooden and Eberhardt (2007) found that the feature is limited in Pittsburgh AAE; however, this study was based solely on an auditory analysis. Therefore, while previous research suggests that Pittsburgh African Americans do not share this regional feature, in order to firmly establish that claim, an acoustic comparison of BOUT in African American and white Pittsburgh speech is needed. The current study provides such an analysis, in addition to a description of the vowel systems of several Pittsburgh speakers, both white and African American.

The overall goal of this chapter is to provide a more complete picture of Pittsburgh AAE, in comparison to the region's white speakers. The analysis begins with the full vowel system of 8 speakers (4 African American and 4 white), describing features of both regional speech and those identified as belonging to a supraregional variety of AAE (see, e.g., Bailey and Thomas 1998; Rickford 1999). I then turn to an investigation of BOUT-gliding, expanding the sample to 32 speakers (17 African Americans, 15 whites) and comparing the two ethnic groups with respect to this local Pittsburgh feature.

DATA AND METHODS

Sociolinguistic interviews (Labov 1984) were conducted between 2004 and 2007 with both African American and white Pittsburghers as part of the Pittsburgh Speech and Society Project (Johnstone and Kiesling 2008). These interviews generally lasted 1–2 hours, covered a variety of topics, and elicited a range of speech styles. Interviews were conducted by one of three female field-workers: African Americans were interviewed either by Trista Pennington (African American) or Maeve Eberhardt (white); white speakers were interviewed by Barbara Johnstone (white) or Maeve Eberhardt. Biographical information of the participants is provided in table 6.1. The African American speakers come from the Hill District, a predominantly African American neighborhood adjacent to Pittsburgh's central business district. The Hill District was at one time a vibrant area, and regarded as the center of cultural life for African Americans (Glasco 1989, 1996). The neighborhood today is severely depressed, having suffered more than one phase of urban renewal, all of which have yet to benefit the community (see Fullilove 2004). The white speakers are from Lawrenceville, a historically white working-class neighborhood. Lawrenceville sits on the banks of the Allegheny River and for many years housed workers in the mills that lined the same river. It has remained predominantly white (City of Pittsburgh 2000), although the overall demographics are changing as the neighborhood is undergoing gentrification.

In the following section, I discuss the vowel systems for the 8 speakers described above. Five to ten tokens of each vowel were selected from conversational portions of the interviews, with no more than 2 tokens of the same lexical item included. In the analysis of BOUT, 10–30 tokens of the vowel were selected, with no more than 3 of the same word represented. Measurements of the first three formants were taken using Praat (Boersma and Weenink 2007), at

TABLE 6.1

Speaker Characteristics

Speaker	Birth Year	Interview Year	Gender	Social Class	Interviewer
African Americans					
Albert	1926	2007	M	working	ME
Marilyn	1929	2004	F	working	TP
Booker	1933	2005	M	lower middle	TP
Esther	1935	2005	F	working	TP
Victor	1936	2005	M	working	TP
Rodney	1940	2005	M	lower middle	TP
Gladys	1946	2004	F	upper middle	TP
Barbara	1951	2004	F	working	TP
Tammy	1960	2005	F	lower middle	TP
Keith	1967	2004	M	working	TP
Sabrina	1974	2004	F	working	TP
Tanesha	1978	2007	F	working	ME
Antoine	1982	2007	M	working	ME
Janice	1984	2007	F	working	TP
Daryl	1986	2006	M	working	TP
Terrance	1992	2006	M	lower working	TP
Maurice	1993	2007	M	lower middle	ME
Whites					
Rita	1917	2004	F	working	BJ
Bill	1922	2004	M	upper middle	BJ
Rich	1932	2004	M	working	BJ
Marie	1932	2004	F	working	BJ
Diane	1941	2005	F	lower middle	ME
Wanda	1941	2004	F	working	BJ
Tina	1948	2004	F	lower middle	BJ
Anne	1953	2005	F	lower middle	ME
Glen	1955	2004	M	lower middle	BJ
Tom	1956	2005	M	working	ME
Debbie	1961	2005	F	lower middle	ME
Joanne	1967	2005	F	lower middle	ME
Mike	1978	2004	M	upper middle	BJ
Jessica	1991	2004	F	working	BJ
Matt	1992	2004	M	working	BJ

the midpoint for monophthongs and at 35 ms from the onset and offset for diphthongs. Data were normalized using Labov, Ash, and Boberg's (2006) method, to allow for cross-speaker comparison, using NORM, the online vowel normalization suite (Thomas and Kendall 2007).

RESULTS

Figures 6.1–6.8 provide the individual vowel plots for 8 speakers, beginning with women in the older age group, followed by their male cohorts, and then moving on to women and men in the younger generation. Black squares represent vowel nuclei, and arrows indicate offglides. Vowels paired with an equal sign have an apparent merger of F1 and F2, as determined by substantial overlap of individual tokens and nonsignificant results obtained in *t*-tests of independent samples.

The vowel systems of the women in the older generation, Esther and Diane, shown in figures 6.1 and 6.2, display several areas of overlap. Both women exhibit mergers characteristic of Pittsburgh (Thomas 2001; Labov, Ash, and Boberg 2006). Both women have the BOT-BOUGHT merger, a defining feature of speech in western Pennsylvania. Furthermore, the merger in each case converges closer to where BOUGHT would be in other dialect regions, as is characteristic of the realization of the merged vowel in Pittsburgh (Wetmore 1959; Kurath and McDavid 1961; Labov, Ash, and Boberg 2006). Both also have a merger of PEEL and BILL, common to Pittsburgh speech (Thomas 2001; Johnstone, Bhasin, and Wittkofski 2002), as well as AAE cross-regionally (Labov, Ash, and Boberg 2006; Thomas 2007). In contrast, while Diane (white, b. 1941) exhibits merged POOL and PULL, Esther (African American, b. 1935) keeps the vowels distinct, consistent with McElhinny's (1993) findings for African Americans in Pittsburgh. Both women merge the back vowels before /r/ (BORDer = BOAR = BOOR), a contrast that has been lost in many areas in North America (Thomas 2001). Also characteristic of the Midland, both women show mild fronting of BOAT nuclei, though this fronting is not substantial in

FIGURE 6.1

Esther, Older African American Female (b. 1935) from Pittsburgh

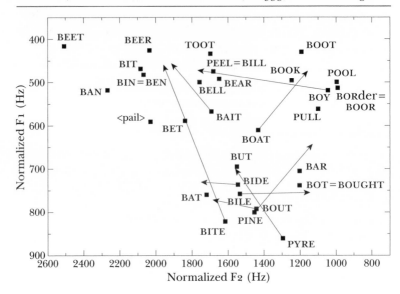

FIGURE 6.2

Diane, Older White Female (b. 1941) from Pittsburgh

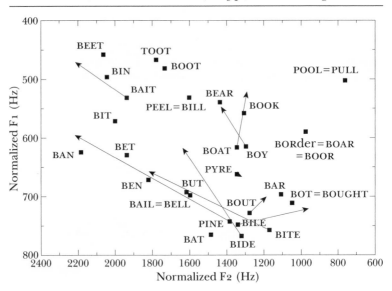

either case. The women also show some fronting of BOOT, though Esther exhibits fronting only when the vowel is preceded by an alveolar (TOOT), a context conducive to fronting (Labov, Ash, and Boberg 2006). Finally, the women both show a raised BAN, while keeping BAT low. Esther additionally shows some features that have been associated with a supraregional variety of AAE (Bailey and Thomas 1998; Rickford 1999). Esther exhibits the BIN-BEN merger, while Diane maintains a contrast, as we would expect for a white Northern speaker. A pronounced distinction between the women exists in terms of the monophthongization of BIDE. Esther exhibits a heavily weakened glide, with just slight movement away from the nucleus. Diane, on the other hand, produces a glide, reaching the height of BET. A similar pattern is present for gliding on PINE. Both women exhibit very little gliding on BILE and PYRE, both of which are characteristic to Pittsburgh speech (McElhinny 1993, 1999; Johnstone, Bhasin, and Wittkofski 2002). Both women show full gliding on BITE.

The men in this generation, shown in figures 6.3 and 6.4, exhibit many of these same tendencies, though some differences are evident as well. Both men show mergers of BOT-BOUGHT and PEEL-BILL, and both have a raised BAN relative to BAT. With respect to the fronting of BOAT and BOOT, there is a considerable difference. While Booker (African American, b. 1933) does not show any fronting of BOAT nuclei, Rich's (white, b. 1932) vowel is strongly fronted. Rich also shows fronting of BOOT and TOOT, while for Booker, both vowels are at the back edge of the vowel space. With regard to the supraregional AAE features, we find similar patterns to the women in this age group. Booker has the BIN-BEN merger, while Rich maintains distance between the vowels. Booker is monophthongal in his pronunciation of BIDE, and Rich shows some weakening of the glide, though it certainly is not monophthongal. Both speakers exhibit full gliding on BITE. Additionally, both men show a merging of the back vowels before /r/.

The younger women and men are presented in figures 6.5–6.8. We see many of the same patterns present among the older speakers with respect to features of Pittsburgh speech: speakers show a raised BAN, BOT-BOUGHT merger, a merger of back vowels before

FIGURE 6.3

Booker, Older African American Male (b. 1933) from Pittsburgh

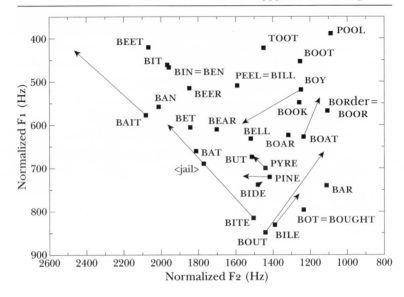

FIGURE 6.4

Rich, Older White Male (b. 1932) from Pittsburgh

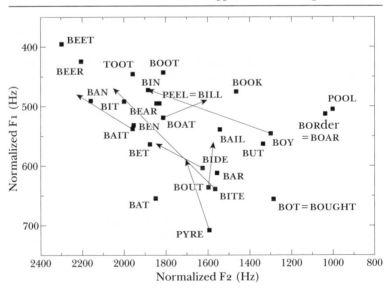

FIGURE 6.5

Tanesha, Younger African American Female (b. 1978) from Pittsburgh

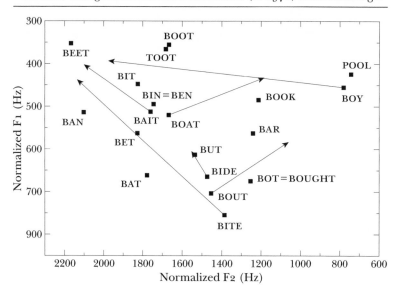

FIGURE 6.6

Jessica, Younger White Female (b. 1991) from Pittsburgh

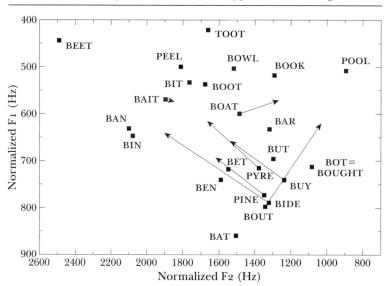

FIGURE 6.7

Maurice, Younger African American Male (b. 1993) from Pittsburgh

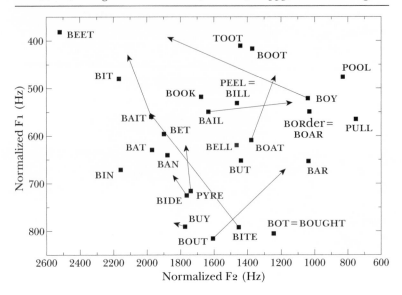

FIGURE 6.8

Matt, Younger White Male (b. 1992) from Pittsburgh

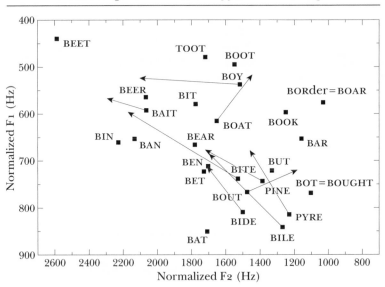

/r/, and fronting of BOOT/TOOT and BOAT nuclei. Tanesha (African American, b. 1978) shows very strong fronting of both BOOT and the nucleus of BOAT among these speakers. Tanesha also exhibits a merger of BIN and BEN, like the older speakers above. Maurice (African American, b. 1993) did not produce tokens of BEN in conversational portions of his interview, although in a word list task, he produced the words *pin* and *pen* identically and judged them to be the same as well, suggesting that he may also have a merger of these vowels. Maurice and Tanesha additionally show heavy glide-weakening on BIDE, while Jessica (white, b. 1991) and Matt (white, b. 1992) do not.

To summarize, both African Americans and whites in this sample exhibit some features of Midland/Pittsburgh dialect, specifically merging BOT and BOUGHT and fronting BOOT and BOAT nuclei. Whites in this sample show slightly more fronting of the latter than the African American speakers. For BOAT nuclei, the mean normalized F2 is 1549 Hz for whites and 1475 Hz for African Americans. A larger difference is found for BOOT, with a mean F2 of 1722 Hz for whites and 1431 Hz for African Americans. As mentioned above, however, Tanesha shows strong fronting of both BOOT and BOAT nuclei. It is possible that there is an interaction of gender with age and ethnicity, which will be a task of a future study. Clearly, the social distribution of back vowel fronting in Pittsburgh is a site for subsequent research. In regions where whites are found to be in the lead of BOOT and BOAT fronting (see Thomas 2007), these changes are relatively new in these dialect areas. In the Midland dialect, on the other hand, the fronting of BOAT is an independent feature of the area and is not generally the focus of social attention as it may be in other regions. Therefore, an analysis of back vowel fronting among African Americans in Pittsburgh will be particularly important in ascertaining alignment to the regional phonological system in the local African American community.

A comment should be made here about the speakers' realization of the "Pittsburgh Chain Shift" (Labov, Ash, and Boberg 2006). As discussed above, this pull chain shift involves the lowering of BUT by local white speakers (Kiesling and Johnstone 2007). It should be noted that a slight difference exists between the two ethnic groups: white speakers have a slightly lower BUT vowel than African Americans in this sample, leading us to hypothesize that the change is further advanced in the white community, with the African Americans taking part in the change, but at a slower pace. The mean normalized F1 for whites is 708 Hz, and 687 Hz for African Americans. Further examination of BUT is another topic for future research in the region. Because this shift is driven by the merger of BOT and BOUGHT, which African Americans share with whites, we might expect BUT-lowering to be taking place among both ethnic groups, but the details remain to be determined.

In tandem with the features of local speech that these African Americans share with whites, the speakers maintain a phonology somewhat distinct from their white counterparts, with recognized features of AAE. On the whole, the African American speakers show a BIN-BEN merger; each of the white speakers, on the other hand, maintains a clear distinction between BIN and BEN. Additionally, all of the African Americans show weakened or monophthongal BIDE glides. The white speakers also show some weakening of the glide in this vowel, as Hankey (1972) noted almost 40 years ago; however, none of these white speakers approach the monophthongal pronunciation common to AAE (Bailey and Thomas 1998; Rickford 1999) and white Southern speech (see Thomas 2001). If there has been a reversal of this feature (in other words, if earlier white western Pennsylvania speakers showed BIDE weakening but have now reverted to fuller gliding), it may be possible to attribute this reversal to the association of BIDE-monophthongization with Southern and/or African American speech (Preston 1989). This in some ways parallels findings in New York City (Coggshall and Becker 2010 [this volume]), in which younger white speakers are moving away from stereotypical features of the local dialect (raised BOUGHT and the short-a split), while African Americans show some alignment to this regional system. In the following section, I turn to an analysis of the stereotypical monophthongal BOUT to determine whether African Americans also share this characteristic or whether the ethnic groups diverge on this feature of local phonology.

BOUT-GLIDING

Figures 6.9–6.14 present a comparison of BOUT-gliding among the 32 African American and white speakers in this sample, who ranged from 14 to 87 years of age at the time of the interview. Women and men in the older generations (born before 1945) are depicted in figures 6.9 and 6.10, followed by those in the middle age range (born 1946–83), and then the younger speakers (born after 1983) in figure 6.13 and 6.14. In each graph, African American speakers are plotted with a filled symbol indicating the nucleus, and white speakers are plotted with an unfilled symbol marking the nucleus.

Among these older speakers, there is a marked difference between the ethnic groups. The white speakers exhibit very little BOUT-gliding, while the African American speakers produce much fuller diphthongs. There is variation in the length of the glide among African Americans—some speakers produce glides that are weakened (e.g., Esther, Booker, and Rodney), though none of these speakers approaches a monophthongal pronunciation. This glide-weakening may be a result of linguistic processes, such as a tendency for weakening in open syllables (Thomas 2003). Additionally, as Thomas (2001) notes, in connected speech in this region the glide of BOUT tends to reach only the height of BOUGHT, rather than the height of BOOT. I discuss the social and linguistic factors involved in BOUT glide-weakening among Pittsburgh AAE in more detail elsewhere (Eberhardt 2009). The main point here is that the difference between the ethnic groups in this age group is pronounced, with white speakers' BOUT characteristic and stereotypical of Pittsburgh speech and African Americans avoiding this pronunciation altogether. The same pattern is found—albeit in a weakened form—among men and women in the middle generation, as shown in figures 6.11 and 6.12, with whites producing much shorter glides overall than African Americans. In the younger generation, however (figures 6.13 and 6.14), less of a difference between the groups is apparent. Thus, the pronounced ethnic dichotomy is resolved not by the AAE speakers converging on the local pattern, but by the white speakers converging on a more general national pattern.

FIGURE 6.9

BOUT-Gliding in the Older Females, Based on Normalized Means

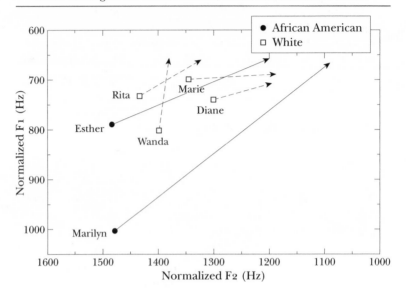

FIGURE 6.10

BOUT-Gliding in the Older Males, Based on Normalized Means

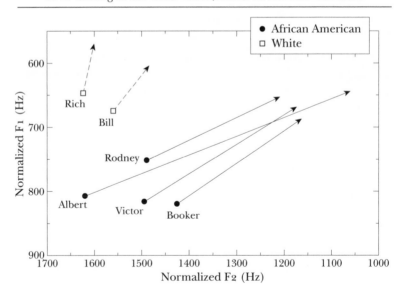

FIGURE 6.11

BOUT-Gliding in the Middle-Aged Females, Based on Normalized Means

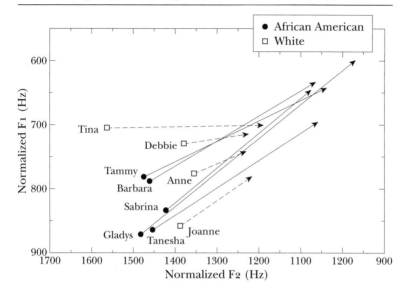

FIGURE 6.12

BOUT-Gliding in the Middle-Aged Males, Based on Normalized Means

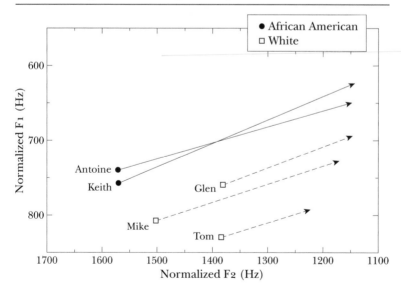

FIGURE 6.13

BOUT-Gliding in the Younger Females, Based on Normalized Means

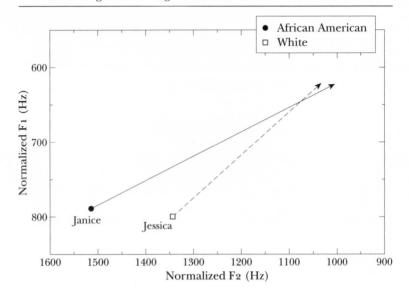

FIGURE 6.14

BOUT-Gliding in the Younger Males, Based on Normalized Means

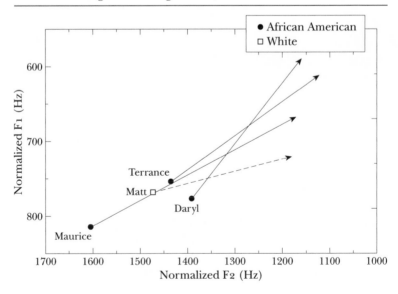

The younger speakers in figures 6.13 and 6.14 show more similarities between African Americans and whites than do older speakers in the city. The glides of the white speakers lend support to previous claims that this stereotypical pronunciation of BOUT is receding in Pittsburgh (Kiesling and Wisnosky 2003). Between the two younger women, no difference is apparent. The youngest male white speaker does show a somewhat shorter glide than the female in this age group, which suggests that the feature may be receding more slowly among men in the city (Johnstone, Bhasin, and Wittkofski 2002; Kiesling and Wisnosky 2003).

The figures above illustrate that, across the generations, African Americans show more differentiation between the nucleus and glide in BOUT than do whites, a finding that supports claims advanced by previous works on BOUT-gliding in Pittsburgh AAE (McElhinny 1993, 1999; Johnstone, Bhasin, and Wittkofski 2002; Gooden and Eberhardt 2007).

Considering these results quantitatively, we find that not only does race appear to be an important factor affecting the amount of gliding in BOUT, but it also proves to be statistically significant. For each speaker, the amount of diphthongization was determined by calculating the Euclidean distance (see Fabricius 2007; Hay and Maclagan forthcoming; Watts, Fabricius, and Kendall forthcoming), which "unites the two coordinates represented by F1 and F2 into a single polar representation, which captures the two-dimensionality of the (F1, F2) space in a single quantified relative position" (Fabricius 2007, 304). In other words, Euclidean distance eliminates the need to examine F1 and F2 planes separately to determine the extent of glide weakening or glide-loss, as has been done in previous studies (Anderson 2003; Fridland 2003b). Euclidean distance was calculated using the following formula:

$$\text{Distance} = \sqrt{(F1_{nuc} - F1_{gl})^2 + (F2_{nuc} - F2_{gl})^2}$$

The mean Euclidean distance for African Americans was 438.558 Hz, while for whites it was just over half that distance, at 248.275 Hz. In a regression analysis with Euclidean distance as the dependent variable (see table 6.2), ethnicity proved to be a significant factor, indicating that African Americans have almost 200 Hz

TABLE 6.2
Coefficients for BOUT-Gliding

	Coefficient	p
All Speakers	288.113	
Ethnicity	183.464	< .0005
Age	–0.742	.084
African Americans	438.989	
Age	–0.010	.986
Whites	366.710	
Age	–2.205	.001

more gliding on the BOUT diphthong than their white counter-parts. Additionally, when the ethnic groups are examined separately, age is selected as significant for white speakers, but not for African Americans. In other words, there appears to be a change in progress occurring among white speakers, but not for African Americans, since BOUT-monophthongization was never a feature of this community's speech pattern. Thus, age is not selected as significant for African American speakers. For white speakers, results indicate that as age decreases, the Euclidean distance increases by over 2 Hz per year, amounting to a gain of about 55 Hz every 25 years. This result lends support to previous analyses that suggested that BOUT-monophthongization may be receding among whites in Pittsburgh (Kiesling and Wisnosky 2003). The results for BOUT gliding are summarized in table 6.2.[2] These findings confirm the patterns seen in the figures above: African Americans in Pittsburgh do not show monophthongization of the glide in BOUT, while the youngest white speakers reintroduce the glide.

Now let us discuss tokens in which the vowel is followed by a liquid. In such environments, both African Americans and white speakers have a strong tendency to monophthongize (Eberhardt 2009), particularly when the vowel is followed by /l/, in words like *towel*. Further, there is no evidence to date that monophthongization of HOUR and HOWL is receding in white speech as it appears to be in other environments, reflecting a patterned symmetry with the BITE-BILE continuum. Apparently, the stigma is not attached to monophthongization in this environment. The relative importance of phonological patterning and stigma remains to be resolved. Certainly, structural factors may also be at work here, making HOUR and HOWL prone to monophthongization (see Veatch 1991; McElhinny 1993), calling for work in the future to disentangle the social and linguistic variables surrounding this diphthong.

TOWARD A SOCIAL EXPLANATION

Descriptions of individual vowel systems reveal that African Americans in Pittsburgh show convergence with the local system, while simultaneously aligning to specific supraregional AAE features, a pattern that is seen in African American communities across the United States (see, e.g., Childs and Mallinson 2004 and other chapters in this volume). The analysis of BOUT-gliding has shown, on the other hand, a sharp division between the ethnic groups. Although BOUT-monophthongization does appear to be receding in white Pittsburgh speech, the feature can be still be characterized as a salient ethnolinguistic marker (Labov 1972) in the city. First of all, African Americans in Pittsburgh point to monophthongal BOUT as a marker of white speech in the region (Eberhardt 2009), explicitly recognizing its significance as a marker of both whiteness and localness, and simultaneously distancing themselves from such identities. Secondly, even if future research further confirms that this feature is being lost in Pittsburgh speech, the perception of monophthongal BOUT as indexical of local (white) speech may remain for years to come. Wells (1982) discusses representations of a dialect far outliving actual use of the features themselves.[3] For the time being, the feature remains a central piece of local ideology about ways of speaking and will likely remain an important component in the construction of ethnic identity by African Americans in the region.

Why do we see alignment of the phonological systems of whites and African Americans with respect to some local features, but not others? It may be tempting to conclude that the explanation for the presence or absence of local features in regional varieties of AAE lies in the salience of the linguistic features under consideration.

For example, the merger of BOT and BOUGHT is below the level of awareness in Pittsburgh and is not brought into discussions or performances of local speech, while BOUT-monophthongization, as a linguistic stereotype, is highly salient and closely connected to local speech and indeed is emblematic of it. This explanation, however, would be overly simplistic, not least because it fails to incorporate many linguistic features that fall somewhere in between on a continuum of salience, such as back vowel fronting. Furthermore, salient regional features sometimes do appear in African American speech: Coggshall and Becker (2010 [this volume]), for example, demonstrate the alignment of African Americans to the pronunciation of BOUGHT that has long been a stereotype of New York City speech even though African Americans have been local community members in Pittsburgh as well as New York City since before the Great Migration. Thus, rather than reducing the explanation to a discussion of salience, a more fruitful tactic is to attempt a more nuanced analysis of the social meanings of particular linguistic features at the local level.

As mentioned above, there are other factors surrounding these features of Pittsburgh speech that may enrich the explanation, but that cannot be understood without discussion. It is not purely the salience of monophthongal BOUT that accounts for its absence in AAE in the city. This salience is paired with the social meanings of the feature for local African Americans, as strongly indexical of white speech in Pittsburgh. However, we may be seeing convergence in the phonological systems of whites and African Americans with respect to this feature due to its recession in white speech, rather than a change in local AAE phonology, so in this particular case, parallel discussions with white speakers would prove interesting.

Conversely, while the lack of salience of the BOT-BOUGHT merger likely contributed to its spread to African American speech in the city, we also must consider that mergers have a strong tendency to spread (Labov 1994), as evidenced by the sweep of the BOT-BOUGHT merger currently taking place across North America (Labov, Ash, and Boberg 2006). The contact that African Americans and whites had at the turn of the twentieth century, as discussed above, thus created the conditions for this feature to become part of the phonological system of African Americans as well.

Other characteristics of the local dialect in Pittsburgh deserve equally detailed explanations, whether they appear in African American speech in the region or prove to be largely absent. For example, if the fronting of BOAT nuclei is confirmed among a larger sample of African Americans, it may have a similar explanation as does the presence of the BOT-BOUGHT merger in Pittsburgh African American speech. If, as Thomas (2001) suggests, fronting of BOAT nuclei was indeed an established feature of regional speech before the twentieth century, it may have also spread to AAE during this extended period of contact between the ethnic groups. In several other communities that exhibit BOAT-fronting, African Americans have been found to share in this frontward movement (Thomas 1989; Wolfram and Thomas 2002; Fridland 2003a; Fridland and Bartlett 2006; Durian, Dodsworth, and Schumacher 2010 [this volume]). The same is true for the fronting of BOOT, which has been found in AAE in other regions as well (Anderson 2003; Fridland and Bartlett 2006). Because these other communities may show BOAT-fronting as part of the Southern Shift (Thomas 2007), analysis of BOAT in AAE in other Midland areas will be greatly informative in assessing the motivations for this movement in more Northern AAE varieties. Thus, a study devoted to the fronting of the nuclei of BOAT and BOOT in a larger sample of Pittsburgh speakers from both ethnic backgrounds is clearly needed to better assess its status in the area.

This chapter set out to provide a description of the vowel systems of African Americans and whites in Pittsburgh and to determine both their similarities and their differences. Overall, we find that African Americans and whites show alignment in some key features of Pittsburgh/Midland phonology, but simultaneously exhibit some crucial distinctions both by maintenance of supraregional features (like the BIN-BEN merger and BIDE monophthongization) and by stigmatizing and avoiding some local features (like BOUT monophthongization).

As other studies have found, then, Pittsburgh African Americans select from a host of available linguistic resources, both those that are associated with regionality and those marked for ethnicity. While there are features of supraregional AAE present among the African American speakers included here, this should not be taken to indicate that the same supraregional features will be present in AAE everywhere. To the contrary, an important finding of recent studies of regional AAE is that the selection of features of what has been described as supraregional AAE varies from one community to the next (see, e.g., Coggshall and Becker 2010 [this volume]). Thomas (2007) has pointed out that features associated with AAE, like absence of postvocalic /r/, vary drastically from one African American community to the next. As scholars continue to focus on AAE as it relates to the local communities in which speakers live, we can also look forward to more information about the distribution of features of AAE across the linguistic landscape.

Additionally, this study has identified areas in need of further attention. In particular, an expanded study of the fronting of BOOT and BOAT nuclei in Pittsburgh speech is needed to determine the extent of the fronting among both ethnic groups and to tease apart what factors contribute to its fronting, if this pattern is confirmed with a larger sample of speakers. An expanded study of BUT-lowering is additionally needed. This study joins the others in this volume in pointing to the need for continued analysis of regional varieties of AAE, which will allow for more comparison across varieties and ultimately enable a description to emerge based not on sociolinguistic myths, but as a product of the "exacting empirical scrutiny" (Wolfram 2007) of AAE that is long overdue.

NOTES

I would like to thank Trista Pennington for the collection of a portion of the data, and Shelome Gooden for contributions to a previous stage of this project. In addition, Scott Kiesling and Barbara Johnstone have provided not only some of the data, but also continuous guidance and support. Many thanks also to Malcah Yaeger-Dror and Erik Thomas for their many helpful answers and comments on this chapter. Finally, I thank the National Science Foundation for grants that supported a portion of the fieldwork presented here (BCS-0417657 and BCS-0417684, awarded to Barbara Johnstone and Scott Kiesling, and BCS-0745455, awarded to me).

1. The index of dissimilarity is a measure that indicates what percentage of people from one race would need to move to another neighborhood in order for there to be racial balance. In other words, in Pittsburgh, 67% of whites would have to move to another neighborhood in order for there to be even distribution of African Americans and whites in all neighborhoods.
2. I include only age and ethnicity here, since social class and gender are beyond the scope of this paper.
3. Thanks to Gerard van Herk for suggesting this example from Wells's (1982) *Accents of English*.

REFERENCES

Anderson, Bridget L. 2002. "Dialect Leveling and /ai/ Monophthongization among African American Detroiters." *Journal of Sociolinguistics* 6: 86–98.

———. 2003. "An Acoustic Study of Southeastern Michigan Appalachian and African-American Southern Migrant Vowel Systems." Ph.D. diss., Univ. of Michigan.

Bailey, Guy, and Erik Thomas. 1998. "Some Aspects of African-American Vernacular English Phonology." In *African-American English: Structure, History and Use*, ed. Salikoko S. Mufwene, John R. Rickford, Guy Bailey, and John Baugh, 85–109. London: Routledge.

Baldwin, Leland D. 1937. *Pittsburgh: The Story of a City*. Pittsburgh, Pa.: Univ. of Pittsburgh Press.

Bernstein, Cynthia. 1993. "Measuring Social Causes of Phonological Variation in Texas." *American Speech* 68: 227–40.

Bodnar, John, Roger Simon, and Michael P. Weber. 1982. *Lives of Their Own: Blacks, Italians, and Poles in Pittsburgh, 1900–1960*. Urbana: Univ. of Illinois Press.

Boersma, Paul, and David Weenink. 2007. *Praat: Doing Phonetics by Computer*. Ver. 4.5.12. http://www.fon.hum.uva.nl/praat/.

Childs, Becky, and Christine Mallinson. 2004. "African American English in Appalachia: Dialect Accommodation and Substrate Influence." *English World-Wide* 25: 27–50.

City of Pittsburgh. 2000. "Neighborhood Census Data 2000." http://www
    .city.pittsburgh.pa.us/cp/html/census_map.html.
Coggshall, Elizabeth L., and Kara Becker. 2010. "The Vowel Phonologies
    of African American and White New York City Residents." In Yaeger-
    Dror and Thomas, 101–28.
Dickerson, Dennis C. 1986. *Out of the Crucible: Black Steelworkers in Western
    Pennsylvania, 1875–1980.* Albany: State Univ. of New York Press.
Durian, David, Robin Dodsworth, and Jennifer Schumacher. 2010. "Con-
    vergence in Blue-Collar Columbus, Ohio, African American and
    White Vowel Systems?" In Yaeger-Dror and Thomas, 161–90.
Eberhardt, Maeve. 2008. "The Low-Back Merger in the Steel City: African
    American English in Pittsburgh." *American Speech* 83: 284–311.
———. 2009. "Identities and Local Speech in Pittsburgh: A Study of
    Regional African American English." Ph.D. diss., Univ. of Pittsburgh.
    Available at http://etd.library.pitt.edu/ETD/available/etd-04212009-
    085859/unrestricted/Eberhardt_2009.pdf.
Epstein, Abraham. 1969. *The Negro Migrant in Pittsburgh.* New York: Arno.
Fabricius, Anne. 2007. "Variation and Change in the TRAP and STRUT Vow-
    els of RP: A Real Time Comparison of Five Acoustic Data Sets." *Journal
    of the International Phonetic Association* 37: 293–320.
Fought, Carmen. 2002. "Ethnicity." In *The Handbook of Language Variation
    and Change,* ed. J. K. Chambers, Peter Trudgill, and Natalie Schilling-
    Estes, 444–72. Malden, Mass.: Blackwell.
Fridland, Valerie. 2003a. "Network Strength and the Realization of the
    Southern Vowel Shift among African-Americans in Memphis, Tennes-
    see." *American Speech* 78: 3–30.
———. 2003b. "'Tie, Tied and Tight': The Expansion of /ai/ Monoph-
    thongization in African-American and European-American Speech in
    Memphis, Tennessee." *Journal of Sociolinguistics* 7: 279–98.
Fridland, Valerie, and Kathy Bartlett. 2006. "The Social and Linguistic
    Conditioning of Back Vowel Fronting across Ethnic Groups in Mem-
    phis, Tennessee." *English Language and Linguistics* 10: 1–22.
Fullilove, Mindy Thompson. 2004. *Root Shock: How Tearing Up City Neigh-
    borhoods Hurts America, and What We Can Do about It.* New York: One
    World Books.
Gagnon, Christina L. 1999. "Language Attitudes in Pittsburgh: 'Pittsbur-
    ghese' versus Standard English." M.A. thesis, Univ. of Pittsburgh.
Glasco, Laurence. 1989. "Double Burden: The Black Experience in Pitts-
    burgh." In *City at the Point: Essays on the Social History of Pittsburgh,* ed.
    Samuel P. Hays, 69–110. Pittsburgh, Pa.: Univ. of Pittsburgh Press.

————. 1996. "Pittsburgh." In *Encyclopedia of African-American Culture and History*, ed. Jack Salzman, David Lionel Smith, and Cornel West, 4: 2157–59. New York: Macmillan.

————. 2006. "Pittsburgh, Pennsylvania." In *Encyclopedia of the Great Black Migration*, ed. Steven A. Reich, 672–76. Westport, Conn.: Greenwood.

Gooden, Shelome, and Maeve Eberhardt. 2007. "Local Identity and Ethnicity in Pittsburgh AAVE." In "Selected Papers from NWAV 35," ed. Toni Cook and Keelan Evanini, 81–95. *University of Pennsylvania Working Papers in Linguistics* 13.2.

Hankey, Clyde T. 1972. "Notes on West Penn-Ohio Phonology." In *Studies in Linguistics in Honor of Raven I. McDavid, Jr.*, ed. Lawrence M. Davis, 49–61. University: Univ. of Alabama Press.

Hay, Jennifer, and Margaret Maclagan. Forthcoming. "Social and Phonetic Conditioners on the Frequency and Degree of 'Intrusive /r/' in New Zealand English." In *Methods in Sociophonetics*, ed. Dennis Preston and Nancy Niedzielski. New York: Mouton de Gruyter.

Herold, Ruth. 1990. "Mechanisms of Merger: The Implementation and Distribution of the Low Back Merger in Eastern Pennsylvania." Ph.D. diss., Univ. of Pennsylvania.

Hinshaw, John. 2002. *Steel and Steelworkers: Race and Class Struggle in Twentieth-Century Pittsburgh.* Albany: State Univ. of New York Press.

Johnstone, Barbara, Neeta Bhasin, and Denise Wittkofski. 2002. "'Dahntahn' Pittsburgh: Monophthongal /aw/ and Representations of Localness in Southwestern Pennsylvania." *American Speech* 77: 148–66.

Johnstone, Barbara, and Scott Kiesling. 2008. "Pittsburgh Speech and Society." http://english.cmu.edu/pittsburghspeech/index.html.

Kiesling, Scott F., and Barbara Johnstone. 2007. "More on the Pittsburgh Chain Shift." Paper presented at the 36th conference on New Ways of Analyzing Variation (NWAV 36), Philadelphia, Oct. 11–14.

Kiesling, Scott F., and Marc Wisnosky. 2003. "Competing Norms, Heritage Prestige, and /aw/-Monophthongization in Pittsburgh." Unpublished MS. Available at http://www.pitt.edu/~kiesling/kiesling-wisnosky-aw.pdf.

Kurath, Hans, and Raven I. McDavid, Jr. 1961. *The Pronunciation of English in the Atlantic States: Based upon the Collections of the Linguistic Atlas of the Eastern United States.* Ann Arbor: Univ. of Michigan Press.

Labov, William. 1972. *Sociolinguistic Patterns.* Philadelphia: Univ. of Pennsylvania Press.

————. 1984. "Field Methods of the Project in Linguistic Change and Variation." In *Language in Use: Readings in Sociolinguistics*, ed. John Baugh and Joel Sherzer, 28–53. Englewood Cliffs, N.J.: Prentice-Hall.

————. 1991. "The Three Dialects of English." In *New Ways of Analyzing Sound Change*, ed. Penelope Eckert, 1–44. San Diego: Academic Press.

————. 1994. *Principles of Linguistic Change*. Vol. 1, *Internal Factors*. Malden, Mass.: Blackwell.

Labov, William, Sharon Ash, and Charles Boberg. 2006. *The Atlas of North American English: Phonetics, Phonology, and Sound Change*. Berlin: Mouton de Gruyter.

Lewis Mumford Center. 2004. "Metropolitan Racial and Ethnic Change." http://mumford.albany.edu/census/WholePop/CitySegdata/365100oCity.htm.

Logan, John. 2001. "Ethnic Diversity Grows, Neighborhood Integration Lags Behind." Lewis Mumford Center. http://mumford.albany.edu/census/WholePop/WPreport/MumfordReport.pdf.

Lubove, Roy. 1969. *Twentieth Century Pittsburgh: Government, Business, and Environmental Change*. New York: Wiley.

Mallinson, Christine, and Walt Wolfram. 2002. "Dialect Accommodation in a Bi-ethnic Mountain Enclave Community: More Evidence on the Development of African American English." *Language in Society* 31: 743–75.

McElhinny, Bonnie. 1993. "We All Wear the Blue: Language, Gender and Police Work." Ph.D. diss., Stanford Univ.

————. 1999. "More on the Third Dialect of English: Linguistic Constraints on the Use of Three Phonological Variables in Pittsburgh." *Language Variation and Change* 11: 171–95.

Nguyen, Jennifer Griffith. 2005. "Real-Time Changes in Social Stratification: Status and Gender in Trajectories of Change for AAE Variables." In "Papers from NWAV 34," ed. Michael L. Friesner and Maya Ravindranath, 159–71. *University of Pennsylvania Working Papers in Linguistics* 12.2.

Preston, Dennis R. 1989. *Perceptual Dialectology: Nonlinguists' Views of Areal Linguistics*. Dordrecht: Foris.

Rickford, John R. 1999. *African American Vernacular English: Features, Evolution, Educational Implications*. Malden, Mass.: Blackwell.

Thomas, Erik R. 1989. "Vowel Changes in Columbus, Ohio." *Journal of English Linguistics* 22: 205–15.

————. 2001. *An Acoustic Analysis of Variation in New World English*. Publication of the American Dialect Society 85. Durham, N.C.: Duke Univ. Press.

————. 2003. "Secrets Revealed by Southern Vowel Shifting." *American Speech* 78: 150–70.

————. 2007. "Phonological and Phonetic Characteristics of African American Vernacular English." *Language and Linguistics Compass* 1: 450–75.

Thomas, Erik, and Tyler Kendall. 2007. *NORM: The Vowel Normalization and Plotting Suite*. Version 1.0. Available at http://ncslaap.lib.ncsu.edu/tools/norm/.

U.S. Census Bureau. 2009. "State and County QuickFacts: Pittsburgh (city), Pennsylvania." http://quickfacts.census.gov/qfd/states/42/4261000.html.

Veatch, Thomas Clark. 1991. "English Vowels: Their Surface Phonology and Phonetic Implementation in Vernacular Dialects." Ph.D. diss., Univ. of Pennsylvania.

Watts, Dominic, Anne Fabricius, and Tyler Kendall. Forthcoming. "More on Vowels: Plotting and Normalization." In *Sociophonetics: A Student's Guide*, ed. Marianna DiPaolo and Malcah Yaeger-Dror. New York: Routledge.

Wells, J. C. 1982. *Accents of English*. 3 vols. Cambridge: Cambridge Univ. Press.

Wetmore, Thomas H. 1959. *The Low-Central and Low-Back Vowels in the English of the Eastern United States*. Publication of the American Dialect Society 32. University: Univ. of Alabama Press.

Wolfram, Walt. 2007. "Sociolinguistic Folklore in the Study of African American English." *Language and Linguistics Compass* 1: 292–313.

Wolfram, Walt, and Erik R. Thomas. 2002. *The Development of African American English*. Oxford: Blackwell.

Yaeger-Dror, Malcah, and Erik R. Thomas, eds. 2010. *African American English Speakers and Their Participation in Local Sound Changes: A Comparative Study*. Publication of the American Dialect Society 94. Durham, N.C.: Duke Univ. Press.

THE URBAN MIDWEST

7. CONVERGENCE IN BLUE-COLLAR COLUMBUS, OHIO, AFRICAN AMERICAN AND WHITE VOWEL SYSTEMS?

DAVID DURIAN   ROBIN DODSWORTH
Ohio State University   *North Carolina State University*

JENNIFER SCHUMACHER
Ohio State University

THE TYPES AND EXTENT of regional phonetic and phonological variation in African American English (AAE) are largely unknown and understudied, despite sociolinguists' detailed knowledge of AAE morphosyntax (Bailey and Thomas 1998). Systematic comparative studies of regional AAVE varieties also remain rare (though see Thomas 2001, 2007b; Labov, Ash, and Boberg 2006). Additionally, there are relatively few instrumental comparisons of AAE to local predominant varieties (but see Bailey and Thomas 1998; Wolfram and Thomas 2002; Fridland and Bartlett 2006). Because of the relative lack of research in this area, these questions remain open: (1) What are the phonetic similarities and differences among regional AAE varieties? (2) In what ways do regional AAE varieties compare phonetically with corresponding local and regional varieties? As Fought (2006, 60) notes, if regional differentiation of AAE follows the patterns of other English dialects, then there should be greater variability in phonetic features than in morphosyntactic ones.

Columbus, Ohio, a metropolis located in the heart of the North American Midland, provides an informative context for exploring the relationship between ethnicity and vocalic variation. As of the 2000 U.S. Census, Columbus has a population of 711,470 residents in the Columbus Metropolitan Statistical Area. Among the population, 24.5% are African American and 67.9% are white

(U.S. Census Bureau 2000). In the urban core, there is frequent contact between blue-collar whites and blue-collar African Americans because of migration patterns among both ethnicities during the late nineteenth century and twentieth century. As discussed in Murphy (1970) and Bryant (1983), a significant number of African Americans moved to the southern and eastern areas of the urban core of Columbus to pursue industrial jobs in factories following the Civil War and again in the post–World War I and World War II periods. Some migrated directly from the South (in particular, Virginia, North Carolina, South Carolina, Georgia, Kentucky, Tennessee, Alabama, and West Virginia), while others moved first to Eastern cities such as Philadelphia and Pittsburgh and later resettled in Columbus. In most cases, African Americans migrated to areas in the urban core, where they found themselves in daily contact with recent white migrants of predominantly Upper Southern, Lower Northern, and Appalachian backgrounds, as well as long-time Columbus residents, whose families had begun settling in the Columbus area in the early 1800s (Lentz 2003).

Until the 1970s, most African Americans in Columbus were working class as a result of Columbus being a predominantly "separate but equal" community, essentially since the founding of Columbus in 1812 (Jacobs 1994). Since the end of the Civil War, the "separate but equal" policy led to decades of discrimination in hiring practices by local businesses, as well as housing segregation, resulting from restrictive deed covenants and the displacement of members of the African American community during the 1960s due to the construction of Interstates 70 and 71 (Oriedo 1982; Burgess 1994). These factors prevented African Americans from obtaining higher skilled labor positions in the community, either physically, due to geographic distance, or socially, due to job accessibility limitations.

During the late 1960s, however, the situation began to change as a result of the passage of the Civil Rights Act of 1968, which put an end to the enforcement of overt housing and employment discrimination practices in the community (Jacobs 1994). In conjunction with these changes, the Columbus public schools underwent changes from a "separate but equal" system to one that was, at first, voluntarily desegregated, in the late 1960s, to one that was later court-ordered to desegregate via the use of busing, in 1979. This policy was in effect until 1995, when the Columbus public schools ended the formal use of busing as a means of desegregation (Foster 1997).

These changes notwithstanding, racial segregation continues to have a significant impact on the sociogeographic makeup of Columbus. Based on 1990 U.S. Census data, Columbus had a Taeuber dissimilarity index score of 63.0 (Harrison and Weinberg 1992).[1] As a result, the African American population remains predominantly blue collar and living in areas closely surrounding the urban core, and contact among many blue-collar whites and African Americans continues to occur in areas closest to the core, most intensely on the southeast and east sides. These areas, which include the portions of Columbus from which our informants were drawn, are indicated in figure 7.1.

The dialect features of blue-collar urban Columbus speech that have emerged as a result of this contact are a complex mixture of Northern and Southern features. Thomas's (2001) instrumental reanalyses of data collected for the *DARE* (1985–) dialect survey, along with his (1989b) primarily impressionistic analyses of blue-collar white and African American speech, reveal much about the continued development of these dialect patterns in the region during the late nineteenth century and early to mid-twentieth century. During this period, the predominant vernacular in Columbus included features typically associated with the Southern Shift, such as the frontward movement of the nuclei of BOUT,[2] BOAT, BOOK, TOOT, and BOOT, and North Midland (Lower North) features, such as *r*-fulness, the backing of BOT, and the merger of BORder and BOAR.

Less diachronic information about Columbus AAE is available. Thomas (1989b) posits that features traditionally assumed to be most strongly affiliated with supraregional AAE norms—such as *r*-lessness, glide-weakening of BUY and BIDE (similar to the pattern found in Southern speech), and the tendency for BOUT, BOAT, and BOOT to remain back—were a strong element of blue-collar AAE in Columbus in the late nineteenth and early twentieth century but

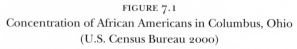

FIGURE 7.1

Concentration of African Americans in Columbus, Ohio
(U.S. Census Bureau 2000)

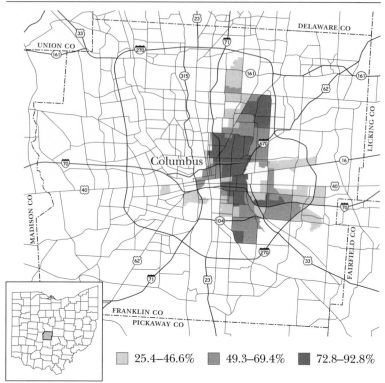

declined during the second half of the twentieth century. Based on data collected in 1985 from blue-collar African Americans born after 1965, Thomas not only reported the decreased presence of these features, but also provided evidence that Columbus African American speakers have begun to realize a partial merger of BOT-BOUGHT before /t/ and the frontward movement of the nuclei of BOUT, BOAT, BOOT, and TOOT. He argued that African American vowel systems in Columbus appear to be showing some convergence with local white norms, like other recently studied communities such as Hyde County, North Carolina (Wolfram and Thomas

2002), Texana, North Carolina (Childs, Mallinson, and Carpenter 2010 [this volume]), Pittsburgh (Eberhardt 2010 [this volume]), and Memphis, Tennessee (Fridland 2003; Fridland and Bartlett 2006). This marks the differences between groups in contrast to the nonconvergence noted earlier in other communities, such as Springville and Silsbee, Texas (Bailey and Thomas 1998), Philadelphia (Graff, Labov, and Harris 1986), and Wilmington, North Carolina (Thomas 1989a). Although Thomas's data were collected at only one timepoint, the assumption that earlier AAE speakers may have displayed more Southern or older supra-regional AAE features is consistent with the historical migration patterns of African American residents in Columbus. However, as more extensive data were unavailable to him, many of his conclusions remain open to further exploration.

More recent studies of sociolinguistic variation in Columbus, both in the suburbs and in the urban center, have focused on the variable fronting and lowering of the nucleus of the BOAT class, a feature central to Thomas's convergence argument. In these studies, BOAT-fronting has been found among white speakers and appears to be led by young white females. For example, Durian (2008a) found that young females led in the fronting of both BOAT and BOUT nuclei among white-collar white Columbusites; Dodsworth (2005) found similar results for BOAT in the white-collar Columbus suburb of Worthington, as did Thomas (1996) in the blue-collar exurb of Johnstown.

Thomas (1989b) found that, among blue-collar speakers, females led in the fronting of BOAT, with the most extreme fronting among white females. No single linguistic environment significantly conditioned BOAT nucleus-fronting except that following liquids disfavored it, especially among whites; however, centralization before /l/ occurred at a 44% rate among African Americans. From this evidence, Thomas argued that the African Americans' centralization of the nucleus of BOAT resulted from contact with blue-collar whites and that the centralization was generalized to include pre-/l/ position.

In this context, we address the following questions concerning the relationship between AAE and the predominant vernacular as spoken by blue-collar residents living in the urban core of Columbus. First, what do Columbus AAE vowel spaces look like today, and how do they compare with those of blue-collar whites in Columbus? Second, considering the centrality of BOAT to Thomas's argument for convergence, is there apparent-time evidence that Columbus AAE is shifting toward participation in BOAT-fronting? Third, how does systematic vocalic variation in Columbus AAE compare to that in other regional AAE varieties?

METHODOLOGY

Data were collected from four distinct populations. The first set was collected in 1992 for a project focusing on morphosyntactic and phonological variation among blue-collar African Americans living on the southeast side of Columbus. Fifty-four African Americans were originally recorded, though the current study focuses on a subset of 14 born between 1942 and 1977. Samples consisted of conversational speech, and all field-workers and participants were African American and within-group members of a family and their closest neighbors (see Weldon 1994; McGuire 2003; and Durian 2008b for more details on this study). Individual vowel plots for four speakers are presented in the next section, while BOAT data from all 14 are presented in the section after that.

The second set of recordings was obtained from four blue-collar white speakers born between 1950 and 1980 from the Buckeye Corpus (Pitt et al. 2007), a collection of 40 one-on-one sociolinguistic interviews conducted by white researchers at the Ohio State University in 2000. The data from these four speakers appear in the individual vowel plots section as well as the BOAT comparison. A third set of recordings, largely of read speech, was made available by Erik R. Thomas from his corpus of speakers born between 1946 and 1964 and now living in Johnstown, Ohio, an exurb of Columbus (see Thomas 1996 for more details on this study). These recordings were made in 1994 with nine blue-collar whites who grew up in Columbus and are used in the BOAT analysis presented. In addition, a white male speaker, born circa 1984, and a white female speaker, born circa 1977, recorded in 2007 and 2008 via hour-long sociolinguistic interviews by the first author, are also included in the analysis of BOAT.

All blue-collar African American informants were recorded interacting with other blue-collar African American informants by an African American field-worker, and all tokens were extracted from conversational speech. For the white informants, the speakers recorded for the Buckeye Corpus and by David Durian specifically for this project were interviewed by white interviewers, and all tokens from these interviews were extracted from conversational speech. For the Thomas (1996) study speakers, data were elicited from white speakers by a white field-worker, and all tokens were extracted from a mix of word list, reading passage, and conversational speech environments.[3]

All white informants were selected because they were raised or currently live in sections of the urban core in which the socioeconomic status, as well as the contact situation between African Americans and whites, was similar to that found in southeastern Columbus (where a relatively high percentage of blue-collar whites and African Americans live in close quarters to each other). The occupation level of adult informants was also used to ensure speakers were representative of blue-collar speech.

Sex, birth date, race, locale in which speakers were raised (if known),[4] and occupation of all 29 speakers (14 African Americans and 15 European Americans) are provided in table 7.1. Interviewer characteristics (including sex and race), the date of the recording session with the speaker, and the type of speech elicited from the speaker during each type of recording session are also listed in table 7.1.

For the individual speaker vowel plots, classes appearing in small capital letters represent the mean value of ten tokens, while those appearing in < > notation represent the mean value of three to eight tokens, except for the BOAT class.[5] Token selections for these classes were limited to no more than 3 repetitions of the same lexical item. For BOAT, 15 tokens per speaker were extracted, with no more than 4 repetitions of the same lexical item. The mean value for the 15 tokens of BOAT is plotted in the individual as well

TABLE 7.1

Demographic Characteristics of the Speaker Sample Population

#	Sex	Birthdate	Speaker Race	Speaker Location	Occupation	Interviewer Sex	Interviewer Race	Date of Interview	Speech Style
1	F	c1950	AA	SE Side	warehouse office mgr	F	AA	1992	Casual
2	F	c1950	W	Short N	nurse	M	W	2000	Casual Int
3	F	c1969	AA	SE Side	student	F	AA	1992	Casual
4	F	c1976	W	NE Side	homemaker	F	W	2000	Casual Int
5	M	c1957	AA	SE Side	car rental service mgr	F	AA	1992	Casual
6	M	c1959	W	E Side	HVAC worker	M	W	2000	Casual Int
7	M	c1975	AA	SE Side	student				Casual
8	M	c1980	W	NE Side	landscaper	F	W	2000	Casual Int
9	F	c1945	AA	SE Side	cashier	F	AA	1992	Casual
10	F	c1947	AA	SE Side	warehouse worker	F	AA	1992	Casual
11	F	c1952	AA	SE Side	warehouse worker	F	AA	1992	Casual
12	F	c1952	AA	SE Side	warehouse worker	F	AA	1992	Casual
13	F	c1954	AA	SE Side	receptionist	F	AA	1992	Casual
14	F	c1953	W	N Side	house cleaner	M	W	1994	Read
15	F	c1960	W	S Side	factory worker	M	W	1994	Read
16	F	c1960	W	NE Side	homemaker	M	W	1994	Read
17	F	c1976	AA	SE Side	student	F	AA	1992	Casual
18	F	c1977	W	W Side	teacher's aide	M	W	2007	Casual Int
19	M	c1942	AA	SE Side	exterminator	F	W	1992	Read
20	M	c1951	W	NE Side	fire truck builder	M	W	1994	Read
21	M	c1955	W	Short N	trucker co. employee	M	W	1994	Read
22	M	c1956	W	N Side	sales rep	M	W	1994	Read
23	M	c1957	W	N Side	baker	M	W	1994	Read
24	M	c1958	W	NE Side	car painter	M	W	1994	Read
25	M	c1958	W	N Side	mason	M	W	1994	Read
26	M	c1976	AA	SE Side	high school student	F	AA	1992	Casual
27	M	c1977	AA	SE Side	student	F	AA	1992	Casual
28	M	c1977	AA	SE Side	student	F	AA	1992	Casual
29	M	c1984	W	E Side	waiter	M	W	2008	Casual Int

as group plots. On average, speakers each contributed roughly 20–30 minutes of speech, generally with more from the one-on-one interviews and less from the group interviews. For all vowel classes analyzed, tokens occurring in environments with a preceding or following liquid or a following nasal were excluded (with the exception of BAR and BOAR). All data were analyzed acoustically in Praat (Boersma and Weenick 2006), using a variable window of 10–14 LPC coefficients depending on the quality of the token. Initial measurements were taken by all three authors and an additional researcher, aided by a custom-made formant extraction script in Praat, with adjustments made by hand when necessary. The data were checked for inter-rater reliability across measurements following the initial coding.

Traditional monophthongs, BIT, BET, BAT, BOT, BOUGHT, BOOK, BAR, and BOAR are plotted with a measurement of the steady state taken at the 50% point of the vowel's duration. Vowels that are commonly treated as diphthongs, BEET, BAIT, BIDE, BITE, BOUT, BOAT, BOOT, and TOOT, are plotted using measurements taken at 20% and 80% to represent the nucleus and offglide, with arrowheads marking the offglide. TOOT is treated as a separate class from BOOT because preceding alveo-palatals and alveolars ordinarily induce fronting of /uw/ (Labov, Ash, and Boberg 2006), while BAR and BOAR are treated separately from BOT and BOUGHT to provide a more detailed picture of the back portion of the speaker vowel spaces. BIDE is also treated as a separate class from BITE, given the tendency for voiced segments following /ai/ to induce shortening of the offglide in central Ohio. In our data, the BOAR and BORder classes are treated as a singular merged category.

PRESENT-DAY BLUE-COLLAR COLUMBUS VOWEL SYSTEM VARIATION

For the comparative plots presented in the following section, data were normalized using the Lobanov (1971) z-score formula, after the raw Hertz values were first transformed into Bark using the formula provided in Traunmüller (1990). The data were first transformed to Bark in an effort to increase compatibility between the general vowel plots and the BOAT specific analysis, which were normalized using the mean Z3 implementation of the Bark Difference Metric (Thomas and Kendall 2007). Following normalization, the data were then scaled to Hertz-like values across all eight speakers for display purposes using the formulas provided by Thomas and Kendall (2007).

Speaker vowel plots are grouped so that one African American speaker and one white speaker of the same gender and relative age appear in the same plot. Figure 7.2 illustrates the vowel system for speaker 1, an older African American female, and speaker 2, an older European American female. The center of the word represents the vowel nucleus. Offglides are denoted by lines moving away from the nucleus and ending in an arrowhead to show their terminus. Although it is not noted explicitly in the figures, most speakers show an apparent near-merger of the BOT and BOUGHT classes, at least before /t/. However, for several speakers, our data have a high concentration of lexical items with word-final /t/, so our

FIGURE 7.2

Speakers 1 and 2, Older Blue-Collar Females from Columbus

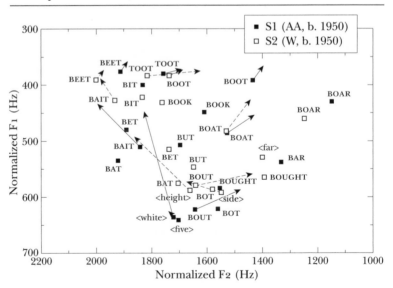

findings may be somewhat skewed by this environment. It should also be noted that in the plots in this section, more conservative blue-collar white speaker vowel systems are displayed for our speakers in each age group, as these are the speakers with whom the blue-collar African American speakers in our data show the strongest signs of convergence. This is most clearly demonstrated in the context of the BOAT specific analysis that follows.

Our plots show that all speakers have an essentially monophthongal BEET, with slight lowering among only some African American women (as in figure 7.3). However, our data suggest that this lowering is largely diminishing across ethnicity as well as age. The BAIT class also reflects some nuclear lowering, but only among African American speakers, and appears to be reversing, as our young speakers (speakers 3 and 7) show no signs of lowering compared with the older female African American (speaker 1). This contrasts with Thomas's earlier findings, in which BAIT-lowering was found to some extent among both European Americans and African Americans.

FIGURE 7.3

Speakers 3 and 4, Younger Blue-Collar Females from Columbus

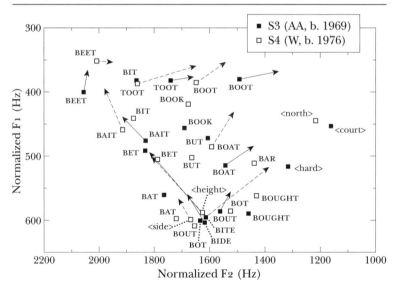

BIT and BET vary considerably.[6] Raising of BET is found among the younger African American male (speaker 7) and also the older African American woman (speaker 1), but it is not found among the older African American male (speaker 5), who actually shows some mild lowering, or the younger African American female (speaker 3). In contrast, no raising of BET was found among the white speakers, although some retraction of the nucleus was found among the older white woman (speaker 2). BIT also appears to be raised only among African American speakers, and raising appears for both younger African American speakers (speakers 3 and 7) and the older African American woman (speaker 1). However, raising of BIT is not found among the white speakers. Taken together, these results indicate movement away from earlier documented cases of Southern-style tensing and raising (Thomas 2001) among whites, while raising is still common among African Americans.

Another noteworthy tendency is the mild raising of BAT among some African Americans and whites. Previously, Thomas (1989b) found /æ/ to be relatively stable among both ethnic groups, with

FIGURE 7.4
Speakers 5 and 6, Older Blue-Collar Columbus Males

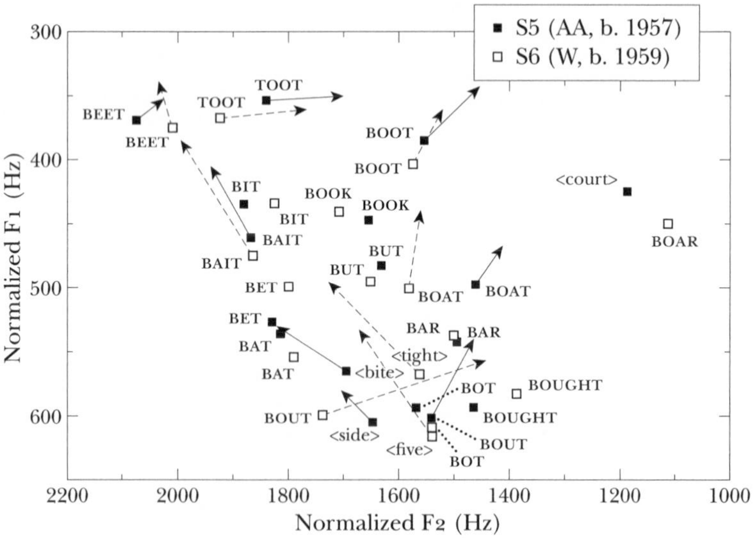

raising found only to a limited extent among whites and mainly before nasals. Our data differ from Thomas's in that we find more extensive raising in nonnasal environments among both African Americans and whites, albeit more among African Americans (speakers 1, 5, and 7) than whites (speaker 6).[7] Both of our white female speakers differ from Thomas's (1989b) whites by also show-ing some retraction. However, similar retraction has also been found in nearby Worthington and Johnstown among both young male and young female white speakers (Thomas 1996; Dodsworth 2005), suggesting the retracted variant may be acquiring new social meaning.

Our evidence for the BITE and BIDE classes is less definitive than for most other vowels because the shortness of some of the interviews made it impossible to extract enough tokens. A few gen-eral observations are possible, though. With regard to the nuclei, all the speakers show quite low nuclei for BIDE. The formant plots suggest that some of the speakers, especially the males, may show "Canadian raising"—i.e., higher nuclei for the BITE class than

FIGURE 7.5
Speakers 7 and 8, Younger Blue-Collar Columbus Males

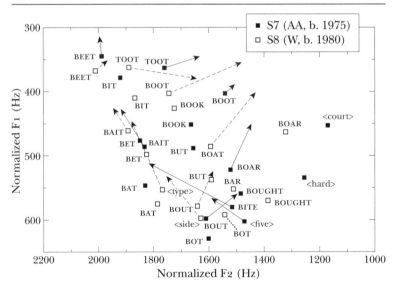

the BIDE class—but again, we lack conclusive evidence. As for the glides, the BITE class usually shows strong glides, but several speakers of both ethnicities show rather weak glides for BIDE class words, as others have found for the Midland region (e.g., Labov, Ash, and Boberg 2006).

The back vowels BOT and BOUGHT are often realized as nearly merged across class and racial groups in Columbus. As Thomas (1989b) has discussed, BOT and BOUGHT are often merged before /t/ in Columbus on a lexeme-by-lexeme basis, but African Americans appear to be resisting the merger in other environments. Our speakers show a different trend, however. The younger African American woman (speaker 3) shows only a partial merger of these classes before /t/ in our data, while the older African American woman (speaker 1) and younger African American male (speaker 7) show little evidence of partial merger even before /t/, and the older African American male has a more or less fully merged pair of classes. As Thomas has also reported, near-merger appears to be more robust among white speakers, who tend to exhibit merger before voiceless stops more frequently than African Americans. Our white speakers also differ in this respect and show this pattern only before /t/. In other environments, our plots show fronter BOUGHT for all four African American speakers relative to the white speakers, as well as fronting of BOT for speakers 3 and 7 and lowering of BOT for speakers 1 and 7. Bar and BOAR present an exception to this trend, with three white speakers showing fronter BAR and BOAR tokens relative to the African American speakers, the older white speaker constituting an exception. However, speakers of both ethnic groups show a similar degree of merger with the BORDER class (as discussed above), regardless of age or sex.

The fronting and/or lowering of BOT, taken together with the raising of BAT, BIT, and BET, are trends that might indicate that speakers 1 and 7, as well as possibly speaker 3, are participating in what Thomas (2007b) has called the African American Shift. However, it should be noted that speaker 3 has substantial BIT-raising with a somewhat lowered BEET, while speaker 1 has some degree of BET-raising with at least some degree of BAIT lowering. Hence, the Southern Shift may describe these speakers' vowel configurations better than the African American Shift, although as noted above, the lowering of BAIT appears to be receding over time. More research needs to be conducted in Columbus before such a determination can be made conclusively. In contrast, among white speakers, the retraction of BAT and BET, along with the partial merger of BOT and BOUGHT before /t/ in the vowel system of the older white woman (speaker 2), suggests that some blue-collar speakers may be showing signs of participating in what Clarke, Elms, and Youssef (1995) and Labov, Ash, and Boberg (2006) have defined as the Canadian Shift, a trend that was also found recently in Columbus by Durian (2008a) in the vowel systems of white-collar white males born after 1962.

For BOOK, most speakers in Columbus evidence some fronting as discussed in detail in Thomas (1989b) and Labov, Ash, and Boberg (2006), while blue-collar African American speakers tend strongly toward BUT-raising (speakers 1, 3, and 5). However, note that speaker 6 also appears to show a mild tendency toward raising as well, a trend previously unreported among white speakers. For BOOK, white speakers realize on average fronter and higher articulations, while African Americans' are lower and backer.

As previously documented (Thomas 1989b, 2001; Labov, Ash, and Boberg 2006; Durian 2008a), the non–low back vowels (BOAT, TOOT, and BOOT) and the diphthong BOUT appear to be undergoing fronting of the nucleus, and, to some extent, the offglides. These trends appear to be interrelated, suggesting a possible chain shift, though previous studies disagree as to whether this term can be applied to the covariant behavior exhibited in central Ohio (cf. Labov, Ash, and Boberg 2006; Thomas 2001; Durian 2008a). All speakers in figures 7.2–7.9 show nuclear fronting of the TOOT class along with varying degrees of nuclear fronting for BOOT, BOAT, and BOUT. Where groups in Columbus differ is in the extent of nuclear fronting that occurs and the impact of nuclear fronting on the offglides.

The fronting of the nucleus of TOOT coincides with glide reduction among African Americans (speakers 1, 3, and 7), whereas glides appear relatively unaffected among white speakers (see speakers 2, 4, 6, and 8). BOOT fronting appears to be a general trend among speakers of both ethnicities, with the least amount of fronting found among older African Americans. The mild fronting among younger African Americans suggests the beginning of convergence of African American norms with white norms. All eight speakers in these data realize BOOT with a back glide and five of eight realize the nucleus of BOOT lower than TOOT. White speakers clearly lead in nuclear fronting for BOOT and, to a somewhat lesser degree, for TOOT.

Thomas's (1989b) impressionistic analysis of African American and white speakers for BOUT fronting suggests that glide reduction typifies African American usage as a byproduct of nucleus-fronting. Our data are consistent with Thomas's findings, and we find that among whites BOUT realizations generally show less glide reduction but more nuclear fronting than among African Americans. In our data, African American speakers generally realize BOUT with both a lower nucleus and more reduced glide than white speakers. However, there is significant overlap between the groups for frontness of the nucleus and glides among the younger males and older females. The two young females show more differentiation, however, because the young African American woman has a retracted nucleus.

In regard to BOAT, the data in figures 7.2–7.5 and Thomas's (1989b, 2001) earlier findings suggest that blue-collar white and African American speakers both show fronting of the nucleus. The pattern is both sex-differentiated and age-graded: younger women are typically the most advanced fronters, regardless of race, although as the evidence among younger white men and women in both figures 7.3 and 7.5, as well as among the speakers plotted in the following section, suggests, the young female lead may be showing signs of diminishing among young blue-collar urban speakers. For height, white speakers, particularly younger men, have higher nuclei and glides than African American speakers, while African Americans tend toward slightly shorter glides. For frontness, the trends generally support Thomas's conclusion that BOAT-fronting exhibits convergence between African American and white varieties. However, as the next section reveals, the situation is also more complex than what figures 7.2–7.5 depict.

A DETAILED EXPLORATION OF COLUMBUS
BOAT-FRONTING

Figures 7.6–7.9 present a side-by-side comparison of African American and white variation patterns for BOAT, subdivided by age and sex, for the larger sample of 29 blue-collar speakers (14 African American and 15 white) analyzed in this study. It should be noted that only measurements obtained from the BOAT tokens themselves were used to feed the normalization calculations for the data presented in this section, as additional data from the African American speakers was not available to allow the use of additional vowel classes (such as corner vowels) in those calculations. As a result, a vowel-intrinsic method, rather than vowel-extrinsic (such as the Lobanov 1971 technique used in the full vowel systems plotted above), was used—the Bark Difference Metric (Thomas and Kendall 2007).

Because little information on the shape of the vowel space for these speakers is available as a result of using a vowel-intrinsic normalization, the results appear to show some signs of distortion. In some recordings, F3 is indistinct or poorly tracked; because the Bark Difference method relies on F3, some skewing of the results may have resulted. In particular, several speakers appear to have inappropriately skewed normalized mean values relative to their mean values in raw Hertz. These include higher nucleus F2 values in relationship to other speakers (such that they appear to have fronter nuclei than they likely have) for speakers 1 and 2 among the older women, as well as speaker 26 among the young men. Also, speaker 12 among the older women appears to have a lower nucleus F2 value (a backer nucleus), and speaker 6 among the older men has a lower nucleus F1 mean value (a higher nucleus) than he likely has.[8] Thus, the results below are best viewed as an estimate of the convergence trends found among our speakers clustered as groups, presented for the purposes of comparison with other studies collected in this volume.

To perform the normalization, the data were first transformed into Bark using the formula provided in Tranmüller (1990). Following conversion to Bark, a mean Z3 value was obtained from measurements extracted across 15 tokens of BOAT at 50% of the token's duration for each speaker to allow a speaker-specific centroid value to be established. The height dimension of all tokens' nuclei and glides were then calculated using the formula mean $Z3-Z1$, while the frontness dimension of all tokens' nuclei and glides were calculated using the formula mean $Z3-Z2$. As in the full vowel systems plotted above, values for the nuclei were extracted at 20% of the vowel's duration, while values for glides were extracted at 80% of the vowel's duration. Each symbol denotes the mean value for the nucleus across 15 tokens for a given speaker's BOAT class, and offglides are indicated by an arrowhead. Table 7.2 provides group mean values for each group in these figures.

As shown in figure 7.6, blue-collar African American women born before 1969 show a more diverse mixture of realizations for BOAT in comparison to African American female speakers born after 1969 (figure 7.7). Speakers 10 and 13 tend toward nearly monophthongal realizations, while the other four older African American women (speakers 1, 9, 11, and 12) show more diphthongal realizations, although their glides are still shorter than those of the older blue-collar white women (speakers 2, 14, 15, and 16).

The older African American women are roughly 1.2 Bark backer as a group than their white counterparts for the nucleus and roughly 0.9 Bark backer for the glide. Thus, their realizations

TABLE 7.2
Mean Values by Speaker Group, in Mean Z3 Normalized Bark

	$\mu Z3-Z1$ (nucleus)	$\mu Z3-Z1$ (nucleus)	$\mu Z3-Z1$ (offglide)	$\mu Z3-Z1$ (offglide)
Older AA Men	8.64	4.75	8.85	4.91
Older W Men	9.06	3.71	9.71	4.18
Younger AA Men	8.61	4.32	9.11	4.73
Younger W Men	9.86	3.84	10.52	4.89
Older AA Women	8.84	4.28	9.20	4.74
Older W Women	9.38	3.07	10.11	3.85
Younger AA Women	9.15	4.22	9.70	4.83
Younger W Women	9.16	3.96	10.00	4.81

FIGURE 7.6
Mean BOAT Realizations: Older African American and White Females

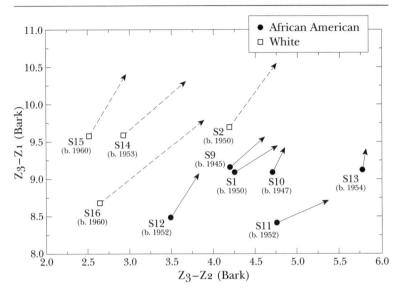

are, as a group, more central than those of white women. Older African American women also show a previously unreported trend toward higher glide F1 frequencies than their white counterparts, and two of the six also show higher nucleus F1 frequencies than the older white women.

In contrast, young women, plotted in figure 7.7, show an ethnic difference of only 0.26 Bark in the nuclear F2 mean and of only .02 Bark in the glide F2 mean. Low speaker numbers limit the strength of our conclusions, but based on the available data, it would appear that the substantial difference in BOAT fronting observed among the older speakers (figure 7.6) has been leveled among the younger generation. This convergence results most robustly from higher F2 means among the African Americans (speakers 3 and 17) for both nucleus and glide, but also from lower glide F1 means for the white speakers (speakers 4 and 18). That is, younger African American women are differentiating the nucleus and glide more than older

FIGURE 7.7

Mean BOAT Realizations: Younger African American and White Women

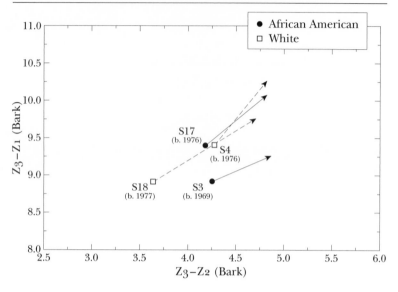

African American women, while younger white women are short-ening the glide more than older white women. Younger African American women also appear to produce higher BOAT nuclei and glides (i.e., with lower F1) than older women. Speaker 17's mean nucleus F1 and F2 values are nearly the same as speaker 4's, while speaker 3's mean nucleus F2 value is nearly the same as speaker 17's, and her mean nucleus F1 value is nearly the same as speaker 18's. The range of values among speakers of both groups for F1 also show less overall differentiation, suggesting that African American and white women's productions are converging over time for F2 and likely for F1 as well.

As shown in figure 7.8, African American men born before 1975 (speakers 5 and 19) tend toward shorter and more monoph-thongal realizations of BOAT than those of either African American men born after 1975 (figure 7.9) or any of the white men analyzed in this study. They also produce variably front-gliding or back-gliding realizations with shorter and lower glides, which the means reveal only partially. Older white men (speakers 6 and

FIGURE 7.8

Mean BOAT Realizations: Older African American and White Men

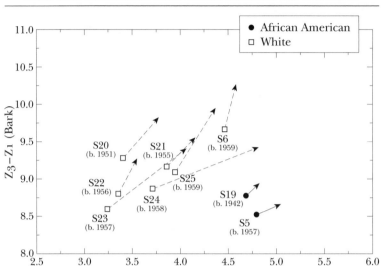

20–25), in comparison, show realizations ranging from back variants to strongly fronted ones. Like older African American women, older African American men show lower glides than older white men, although in contrast to the difference shown among some of the older African American and white women, the older African American and white men's nuclei are of comparable height.

As revealed by figure 7.9, young African American men (speakers 7, 26, 27, and 28) exhibit a similar movement toward fronter productions for both nucleus and glide, as well as more overlap in the mean of F2 for the nucleus of BOAT with their white counterparts (speakers 8 and 29). There is also a tendency toward more diphthongal forms of BOAT like those displayed by younger women. The younger white males also tend to show longer glides than the older white males, though some older males (speakers 23 and 24) show comparable glides. All four young African American males show much higher nuclear and glide F1 frequency values than the young white males. Thus, young African American males tend to resemble the more conservative of the younger white males

FIGURE 7.9

Mean BOAT Realizations: Younger African American and White Men

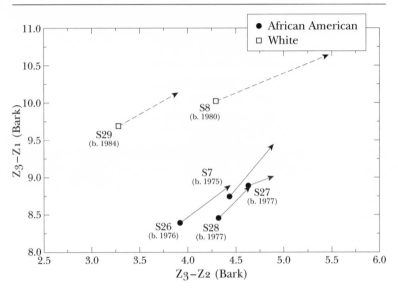

(speaker 8) for F2 of the nucleus and the less conservative of the white males (speaker 29) for F2 of the glide, but they resemble neither for F1 of either the nucleus or the glide.

In sum, our findings are consistent with those of Thomas (1989b) in showing convergence between African American and white speakers for F2 at both the nucleus and offglide of BOAT. Our data also reveal a previously unreported trend toward lowering of the glide among older African American women and younger African American men, suggesting possible divergence from white norms for height.

SOCIAL AND REGIONAL IMPLICATIONS
OF COLUMBUS VOWEL VARIATION

As the above findings reveal, blue-collar African American and white speakers show convergence along the frontness dimension for the vowels TOOT, BOOT, BOOK, BOAT, and BOUT, as well as convergence along the height dimension for TOOT and BOOT. On the other hand, they show divergence for BOUGHT, BOT, BOOK, BOAT, BOUT, BET, BIT, and possibly BUT along the height dimension, and BOUGHT and BOT along the frontness dimension. For BOAT in particular, our larger sample reveals that the trends suggested by the individual plots generally reflect variation within Columbus for speakers born after 1940. The status of BAT is unclear because of the range of realizations shown by our white speakers, while that of BEET and BAIT is unclear because of conflicting patterns among African Americans. For blue-collar African Americans, taken together, the raising of BAT, BET, and BIT and the fronting of BOT may indicate that some speakers are participating in the African American Shift, although the data are inconclusive because our older African American female speaker shows BAIT lowering and our younger African American female shows BEET lowering, which may instead represent the Southern Shift.

Within the context of the Columbus speech community, the convergent trends may be motivated by some of the social patterns discussed above. First, there has been longstanding contact between the groups within most areas from which speakers were sampled in this study because of the historical migration patterns discussed above. Second, continued contact has been fostered between groups because the socioeconomic profile of these areas has remained low over time. Third, most of the speakers born after 1969 of both races attended high school with court-ordered desegregation and busing leading to increased contact between the races throughout Columbus public schools. Considering the increase in "face time" fostered by school desegregation, it seems plausible that this extra exposure would promote convergence for TOOT, BOOT, BOOK, BOAT, and BOUT among our youngest speakers. This is demonstrated in particular by the growing similarity in the back vowel subsystem over time, not only in our study, but also in Thomas's (1989b) study of high school–aged teens, which was conducted during the height of desegregation in Columbus schools in the 1980s.

Nevertheless, developments in white speech may be leading to new ethnic differences. For instance, BET and BAT appear to be undergoing the Western and Canadian tendency toward retraction among some of our white female informants. This movement is not occurring among the African Americans, who, if anything, appear to be intensifying the raising of BET and possibly BAT and still show latent evidence of BAIT and BEET lowering. Thus, divergence for these classes appears to be a result of changes from earlier community speech norms not only among the African American speakers, but also among the white speakers. Clearly, the interrelationship of these social and linguistic factors is a complex matter, and one that requires additional research targeting each factor specifically.

With respect to alignment with regional dialect norms, our data appear to confirm that Columbus vowel systems among speakers of both ethnic groups are typified by the North/South transitional flavor that Thomas's earlier studies (1989b, 2001) would lead us to expect.

However, the patterns of BET and BAT retraction show a stronger Western dialect alignment element among our white speakers than has been noted in previous research (e.g., Thomas 1989b, 2001; Labov, Ash, and Boberg 2006), with the exception of Durian (2008a). In addition, the tendency of our speakers to realize only a partial merger of BOT and BOUGHT before /t/ differs from Thomas's (1989b) earlier results as well.

With regard to the relationship of Columbus blue-collar African American speech to African American speech elsewhere, it would appear that, over time, the stronger trend toward increased fronting of the nuclei of back upgliding vowels in Columbus AAE is similar to what has been found recently in certain other communities, namely Hyde County, North Carolina (Wolfram and Thomas 2002), Texana, North Carolina (Childs, Mallinson, and Carpenter 2010 [this volume]), Pittsburgh (Eberhardt 2010 [this volume]), and Memphis, Tennessee (Fridland 2003; Fridland and Bartlett 2006). These communities also show convergence with local white speech norms for TOOT, BOOT, BOOK, and BOAT. The range and mean values for BOAT among our 14 speakers show strong parallels with vowel plot data or results discussed in those studies. Our plots likewise show clear parallels with patterns noted for TOOT, BOOT, and BOOK in those communities, although the trends are generally less robust in terms of the maximal degree of frontness exhibited by speakers than in the North Carolina communities. Hence, it is perhaps unsurprising to find similar patterns in Columbus, since historically, these vowels have also shown Southern Shift tendencies in central Ohio (though perhaps from western Pennsylvania influence instead of from the South proper, hence the similarity as well with Pittsburgh). Additionally, aside from Pittsburgh, these communities show the reversal of the front vowel subsystem classes BET and BAIT, although BAIT-lowering appears to be on the decline in Memphis among younger speakers, a development that renders Memphis more similar overall to the present-day Columbus speech community than to the North Carolina communities.

The trends found among our African American speakers for the front vowels, particularly the raising of BAT, BET, and BIT, also resemble those found in Memphis by Fridland and Bartlett (2006), as well as in a variety of locales (including Brooklyn, New York; Austin, Texas; and Cleveland Heights, Ohio) by Thomas (2001, 2007a). The raising behavior of these classes in those areas, along with covariant fronting and/or lowering of BOT, constitute the core evidence Thomas (2007b) used to argue for the African American Shift as a supraregional feature of AAE. However, as previously noted, our speakers' alignment with this putative AAE norm cannot be confirmed definitively in our data set because it is at present unclear from the mixed results in our study whether African Americans instead display the Southern Shift.

Beyond these patterns, as noted earlier, BUT-raising among African Americans in Columbus appears to align with supraregional AAE norms, while the divergence in the height of BOOK, BOAT, and BOUT may be unique to Columbus AAE, as this trend has not been reported in other communities in which African American speakers evidence fronting (e.g., Wolfram and Thomas 2002; Fridland 2003; Childs, Mallinson, and Carpenter 2010 [this volume]). The reason African American speakers show such trends requires more extensive research, though it seems possible they may index racial identity, since frontness no longer differentiates African American and white speakers in Columbus robustly.

CONCLUSIONS

In terms of the social motivations underlying interrelationships in ethnic vowel variation in Columbus, our study has raised as many questions as it answers. Rather than attempting to disentangle these issues, given constraints of space, we provided instead only a descriptive analysis of the vowel systems in order to contribute to the broader investigation of local AAE convergence to/divergence from predominant regional varieties as well as supraregional AAE norms.

Four additions to this analysis would allow more confident comparisons between local predominant and AAE vernaculars and across regional AAE varieties. First, a greater number of speakers could confirm the patterns of age-grading suggested by our data. Second, as Wolfram and Thomas (2002) observe, an adequate investigation of vocalic variation in any community would consider more thoroughly the identity-based motivations underlying language maintenance and change. Third, more studies investigating the occurrence of the African American Shift in communities across the United States are required so that the ramifications of the shift as it affects Columbus AAE vowel systems can be better understood.

Finally, there is the matter of the normalization technique (Bark Difference Metric) utilized in our analysis of BOAT. As discussed in that section, the technique was utilized because of a lack of available data from some of the African American speakers to permit the use of a vowel-extrinsic method. This would likely have improved the quality of the results, as vowel-extrinsic methods have been shown in a recent comparative analysis of normalization techniques (Adank, Smits, and van Hout 2004) to perform better than vowel-intrinsic techniques. In particular, the Bark Difference Metric appears to be quite sensitive to fluctuations in F3, and if the data have poorly formed or indistinct F3, as in the case of at least some of our African American recordings, the effectiveness of the technique appears to be strongly impacted.

NOTES

We wish to thank Bridget Smith for her significant contribution in the analysis of data as well as content suggestions appearing in this chapter. We also thank Erik R. Thomas for comments and the contribution of speakers from his 1990s study of Johnstown, Ohio. In addition, we thank Donald Winford, Cynthia Clopper, Mary Beckman, and Malcah Yaeger-Dror for comments that strengthened our analysis.

1. A Taeuber index score of 100 indicates complete segregation (a completely uneven distribution of minorities), whereas a score of 0 indicates complete integration (a completely even and uniform distribution of minorities) of residents in a community. In other words, the higher the score, the greater the level of residential segregation.

2. Note that throughout this discussion, vowel classes are marked using a modified version of the notation for word classes provided by Wells (1982).

3. For these reasons, Thomas's (1996) results can be compared only tentatively with the other studies' in this volume.

4. With regard to speakers for whom we were unable to sufficiently determine this information, the location in which the informant currently lives is listed instead. These speakers include 1, 7, 10, 15–18, and 23.

5. A second exception is that, for speaker 7, only 1 token of the BOOT class (*food*) is plotted, while 10 tokens of the lexeme *move* are plotted for speaker 8. Hence, in their plots, we use <food> and <move> to refer to their mean values for BOOT.

6. Although not plotted here due to low frequency counts in our African American data, our impressionistic analysis of BIN and BEN tokens among our white and African American speakers reveals that speakers of both ethnicities frequently substitute the BIT for the BET vowel before nasals. This trend is most pronounced among African American speakers, a finding which agrees with Thomas's (1989b) earlier observations.

7. Although not instrumentally analyzed due to audio quality issues in the African American data, impressionistic analysis of BAN tokens among our European American and African American speakers reveals similar raising trends to those found in Thomas's (1989b) study.

8. This assessment is based on a comparison of the placement of BOAT among speakers for whom we did have full vowel system data rather

than only BOAT data, using the mean Z3 method versus the placement of BOAT for the speakers, using both the Lobanov (1971) and Nearey (1978) "log mean" methods.

REFERENCES

Adank, Patti, Roel Smits, and Roeland van Hout. 2004. "A Comparison of Vowel Normalization Procedures for Language Variation Research." *Journal of the Acoustical Society of America* 116: 3099–107.

Bailey, Guy, and Erik Thomas. 1998. "Some Aspects of African-American Vernacular English Phonology." In *African-American English: Structure, History, and Use*, ed. Salikoko S. Mufwene, John R. Rickford, Guy Bailey, and John Baugh, 85–109. London: Routledge.

Boersma, Paul, and David Weenink. 2006. Praat: Doing Phonetics by Computer. Version 4.4.30. http://www.praat.org/.

Bryant, Vinnie Vanessa. 1983. "Columbus, Ohio, and the Great Migration." M.A. thesis, Ohio State Univ.

Burgess, Patricia. 1994. *Planning for the Private Interest: Land Use Controls and Residential Patterns in Columbus, OH, 1900–1970*. Columbus: Ohio State Univ. Press.

Childs, Becky, Christine Mallinson, and Jeannine Carpenter. 2010. "Vowel Phonology and Ethnicity in North Carolina." In Yaeger-Dror and Thomas, 23–47.

Clarke, Sandra, Ford Elms, and Amani Youssef. 1995. "The Third Dialect of English: Some Canadian Evidence." *Language Variation and Change* 7: 209–28.

DARE. Dictionary of American Regional English. 1985–. Ed. Frederic G. Cassidy and Joan Houston Hall. 4 vols. to date. Cambridge, Mass.: Belknap of Harvard Univ. Press.

Dodsworth, Robin M. 2005. "Linguistic Variation and Sociological Consciousness." Ph.D. diss., Ohio State Univ.

Durian, David. 2008a. "A New Perspective on Vowel Variation throughout the 20th Century in Columbus, OH." Paper presented at the 37th annual conference on New Ways of Analyzing Variation (NWAV 37), Houston, Texas, Nov. 6–9.

———. 2008b. "The Vocalization of /l/ in Urban Blue Collar Columbus, OH African American Vernacular English: A Quantitative Sociophonetic Analysis." *Ohio State Working Papers in Linguistics* 58: 30–51.

Eberhardt, Maeve. 2010. "African American and White Vowel Systems in Pittsburgh." In Yaeger-Dror and Thomas, 129–57.

Foster, Paul N. 1997. "'Which September': Segregation, Busing, and Reseg-
regation in the Columbus Public Schools, 1944–1996." B.A. honors
thesis, Harvard Univ.

Fought, Carmen. 2006. *Language and Ethnicity.* Cambridge: Cambridge
Univ. Press.

Fridland, Valerie. 2003. "Network Strength and the Realization of the
Southern Vowel Shift among African Americans in Memphis, Tennessee." *American Speech* 78: 3–30.

Fridland, Valerie, and Kathy Bartlett. 2006. "The Social and Linguistic
Conditioning of Back Vowel Fronting across Ethnic Groups in Memphis, Tennessee." *English Language and Linguistics* 10: 1–22.

Graff, David, William Labov, and Wendell A. Harris. 1986. "Testing Lis-
teners' Reactions to Phonological Markers of Ethnic Identity: A New
Method for Sociolinguistic Research." In *Diachrony and Diversity*, ed.
David Sankoff, 45–58. Amsterdam: Benjamins.

Harrison, Roderick J., and Daniel H. Weinberg. 1992. *Racial and Ethnic Residential Segregation in 1990.* Washington, D.C.: U.S. Census Bureau.

Jacobs, Gregory S. 1994. "Getting around *Brown*: Desegregation, Develop-
ment, and the Columbus Public Schools, 1954–1994." M.A. thesis,
Ohio State Univ. Available at http://etd.ohiolink.edu/send-pdf.cgi/
Jacobs%20Gregory%20Scott.pdf?acc_num=osu1220536463.

Labov, William, Sharon Ash, and Charles Boberg. 2006. *The Atlas of North
American English: Phonetics, Phonology, and Sound Change.* Berlin: Mouton de Gruyter.

Lobanov, B. M. 1971. "Classification of Russian Vowels Spoken by Different Speakers." *Journal of the Acoustical Society of America* 49: 606–8.

Lentz, Ed. 2003. *Columbus: The Story of a City.* Charleston, S.C.: Arcadia.

McGuire, Grant. 2003. "The Realization of Interdental Fricatives in Columbus, OH, AAVE." Paper presented at the Montreal-Ottawa-Toronto
Phonology Workshop, Toronto, Feb. 7–9.

Murphy, Melvin L. 1970. "The Columbus Urban League: A History, 1917–
1967." Ph.D. diss., Ohio State Univ.

Nearey, Terrance Michael. 1978. *Phonetic Feature Systems for Vowels.* Bloom-
ington: Indiana Univ. Linguistics Club.

Oriedo, Evelyn. 1982. "African American Business Development: Its
Impact on the Economic Status of the African American Community
in Columbus, OH." M.A. thesis, Ohio State Univ.

Pitt, Mark A., Laura Dilley, Keith Johnson, Scott Kiesling, William Ray-
mond, Elizabeth Hume, and Eric Fosler-Lussier. 2007. *Buckeye Corpus
of Conversational Speech.* 2nd release. Columbus: Dept. of Psychology,
Ohio State Univ. Available at http://www.buckeyecorpus.osu.edu/.

Thomas, Erik R. 1989a. "The Implications of /o/ Fronting in Wilmington, North Carolina." *American Speech* 64: 327–33.

———. 1989b. "Vowel Changes in Columbus, Ohio." *Journal of English Linguistics* 22: 205–15.

———. 1996. "A Comparison of Variation Patterns of Variables among Sixth Graders in an Ohio Community." In *Focus on the USA*, ed. Edgar W. Schneider, 149–68. Amsterdam: Benjamins.

———. 2001. *An Acoustic Analysis of Vowel Variation in New World English.* Publication of the American Dialect Society 85. Durham, N.C.: Duke Univ. Press.

———. 2007a. "Conclusions: Symposium on Vowel Phonology and Ethnicity." Paper presented at the annual meeting of the Linguistic Society of America, Anaheim, Calif., Jan. 4–7.

———. 2007b. "Phonological and Phonetic Characteristics of African American Vernacular English." *Language and Linguistics Compass* 1: 450–75.

Thomas, Erik R., and Tyler S. Kendall. 2007. NORM: The Vowel Normalization and Plotting Suite. Available at http://ncslaap.lib.ncsu.edu/tools/norm/.

Traunmüller, Hartmut. 1990. "Analytical Expressions for the Tonotopic Sensory Scale." *Journal of the Acoustical Society of America* 88: 97–100.

Weldon, Tracey. 1994. "Variability in Negation in African American Vernacular English." *Language Variation and Change* 6: 359–97.

Wells, J. C. 1982. *Accents of English.* 3 vols. Cambridge: Cambridge Univ. Press.

Wolfram, Walt, and Erik R. Thomas. 2002. *The Development of African American English.* Oxford: Blackwell.

U.S. Census Bureau. 2000. "State and County QuickFacts: Columbus (city), Ohio." http://quickfacts.census.gov/qfd/states/39/3918000.html.

Yaeger-Dror, Malcah, and Erik R. Thomas, eds. 2010. *African American English Speakers and Their Participation in Local Sound Changes: A Comparative Study.* Publication of the American Dialect Society 94. Durham, N.C.: Duke Univ. Press.

8. THE VOWEL PHONOLOGY OF URBAN SOUTHEASTERN WISCONSIN

THOMAS C. PURNELL

University of Wisconsin–Madison

THE UPPER MIDWEST is currently a hotbed of vowel changes.[1] Vowel space restructurings include the Northern Cities Shift (NCS), Canadian Raising, and prevelar raising. Additionally, the Midland dialect reaches up into southwestern Wisconsin and contrasts with the Inland North dialect in northern Wisconsin and the upper peninsula of Michigan. Given these vowel changes observed in the upper Midwest, we should wonder whether it is reasonable to expect vowel changes and dialect patterns to occur more widely among all speech communities in the region. This chapter explores whether or not vowel space restructuring in the predominant local vernacular of southeastern Wisconsin is also found in the vowel space of African Americans. Additionally, the role of accommodation will be examined.

This study compares the vowel spaces of African Americans with those of whites of the same background. All of the speakers have strong ties to the area. All speakers have been educated in predominantly white universities within the region, but the African American English (AAE) speakers vary in their past contact with whites. First we will examine the general lack of contact between racial groups in Milwaukee to contextualize the observable variation across speakers.

This study, like the others reported in this volume, provides new insights into the complexity of personal identity revealed in verbal behavior. Evidence from this analysis includes the participation and nonparticipation by African American speakers in what we will refer to as "pan–African American English" and local white patterns. Generally, the vowel spaces of black speakers deviate from pan-AAE patterns particularly with respect to diphthongization as a marker of contact across ethnic groups. I conclude both that the AAE speakers accommodate to the predominant vernacular in the area and that as a group they maintain specific pan-AAE socio-phonetic features not shared by whites in the community, with the amount of accommodation correlated with the amount of inter-racial contacts speakers have had.

DEMOGRAPHIC AND MIGRATION PATTERNS OF AFRICAN AMERICANS

Since this chapter reports a sampling of the linguistic behavior of speakers from the general southeastern Wisconsin geographic region, it is important to understand the demographic and migration patterns of the region. The linguistic region of southeastern Wisconsin consists of a triangular-shaped area encompassing Madison and Janesville in the west, the lower Fox Valley in the northeast, and Racine County in the southeast.[2] At the cultural center of this region is the city of Milwaukee, which contrasts with the closest large metropolitan centers of Minneapolis and Chicago as a regional center. The total population of the city of Milwaukee is 596,974, and the total population for the expanded Milwaukee-Racine census area is approaching 1.7 million people (U.S. Census Bureau 2000). Outside of Menominee County (and reservation) in the northern part of the state, Milwaukee County has the highest percentage of minority residents (34%), and fully half of the residents of the city of Milwaukee are nonwhite (U.S. Census Bureau 2000). Specifically with respect to African Americans, census data indicate that Milwaukee County is 25.7% African American, while Racine County to the south is 10.6% African American. Over 75.9% of the African Americans in the state of Wisconsin live in Milwaukee County.

The first wave of immigrants to the area were by and large German (Ostergren and Vale 1997). The initial migration of African Americans into Milwaukee took place between 1916 and 1930, increasing the number of African Americans from under 5,000 to over 10,000 (U.S. Census Bureau 1961). Migration into the state brought residents from Mississippi and Tennessee, followed (in terms of numbers of residents) by Alabama, Georgia, and Arkansas (McHugh 1987). Subsequent migrants came via other urban centers, such as Indianapolis and Chicago, to work in factories in Beloit and Milwaukee. Approximately 12,000 African Americans were listed in the 1940 U.S. Census (U.S. Census Bureau 1961). However, the bulk of African American immigration occurred after the Great Migration. Continued migration during World War II and the postwar eras, as well as the development of African American neighborhoods, increased this number to 74,500 by 1960, according to the census taken that year. In 2000, the Milwaukee-Racine census area had a black population of 254,810 residents (U.S. Census Bureau 2000).

Given that portions of the state like Milwaukee were seen as progressive due to black suffrage in the 1840s (e.g., *Gillespie v. Palmer* in 1856, which reinforced black voting rights) and the antislavery movement in the 1850s and 1860s, the low immigration rate during and after the Great Migration, and even up to the 1960s, is remarkable. By the time of the 1960 increase noted above, over 54% of counties had fewer than 10 black residents (U.S. Census Bureau 2000).

Moreover, the current effects of racial segregation in Milwaukee were enforced in the 1940s by real-estate compacts not to sell or rent to black residents outside the region of Milwaukee outlined by W. North, W. Juneau, N. 3rd, and N. 12th streets (Trotter 1985; Ranney 1995). These compacts, not overturned until 1951 (Ranney 1995), established the core black sector of Milwaukee from which the community has spread primarily in a northwestern direction (figure 8.1, census tracts with more than 5% African American residents are shaded). In the late 1950s Irwin Rinder and others on the Intercollegiate Council on Intergroup Relations in Milwaukee wrote the following summary of their study on the housing situation for blacks living in Milwaukee.

At the present time, most Negroes must locate within the portions of the city already opened and available to "nonwhites." This means that the movement of Negroes and other racial minorities into an area coincides with the withdrawal of white persons out of it. [Rinder 1955, 48]

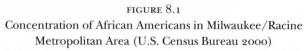

FIGURE 8.1

Concentration of African Americans in Milwaukee/Racine
Metropolitan Area (U.S. Census Bureau 2000)

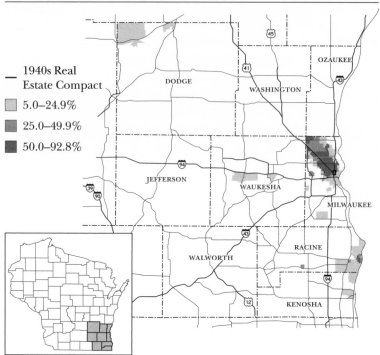

Little has changed over the years in terms of the racial segregation in Milwaukee; African Americans have by and large remained
in the same geographic location and have not diffused throughout
the city or spread in any significant way throughout the surrounding counties. It is worth noting, however, that the speakers examined in the present study are all young college-educated speakers,
who cannot be directly compared with the Columbus blue-collar
workers (Durian, Dodsworth, and Schumacher 2010 [this vol-
ume]), or the speakers from the Lower East Side of Manhattan and
the South Bronx, most of whom are blue collar as well (Coggshall
and Becker 2010 [this volume]).

VOWEL PATTERNS

The predominant local vernacular spoken in Wisconsin (henceforth, Wisconsin Vernacular English [WVE]) is most often discussed within the context of dialect regions spanning the state, in particular the Inland North and Midland dialects (Labov, Ash, and Boberg 2006), with certain local idiosyncracies. Vowels of WVE in this portion of the state are generally considered to be engaged in the Northern Cities Shift (Labov, Ash, and Boberg 2006). Table 8.1 summarizes the WVE vowel distinctions.

When discussing the /æ/ vowel in the Inland North, Labov, Ash, and Boberg (2006, 122) state that "the entire short-*a* class is raised and fronted." This generalization, as it applies to southeastern Wisconsin, may refer only to the nucleus of the vowel, of contextual variation (raising: _n > _d > _g) within the short-*a* class of vowels in the Northern Cities Shift region (2006, 181, column 2), and of prevelar raising: _g > _d (2006, 181, column 1). BAN raising is fairly common (Labov, Ash, and Boberg 2006, 174–75), while breaking or diphthongization of BAD and raising of BAG add to the complexity of the realizations of the /æ/ vowel.

The most striking aspect of WVE is the prevelar raising of /æ/ to /eɪ/ or /ɛ/ before a voiced velar plosive coda consonant so that *haggle* and *Hegel* may rhyme, as may *bag* and *beg* (Zeller 1997; Labov, Ash, and Boberg 2006; Bauer and Parker 2008; Purnell 2008; Purnell and Salmons forthcoming). Labov, Ash, and Boberg (2006) identify this process as occurring outside southeastern Wisconsin but within the Inland North and Canada. Both Zeller (1997) and I (Purnell 2008) observe prevelar raising in southeastern Wisconsin as well. Labov, Ash, and Boberg label this prevelar raising as a "merger," but based on the differences between the BAG and BEG trajectories, Bauer and Parker (2008) question this assumption. Often BAG and BAN are more raised than other /æ/ vowel words, with BAG often higher than BAN. Labov, Ash, and Boberg (2006, 177) describe how diphthongization frequently accompanies the raising of /æ/ vowels. The diphthongization occurs as a mid steady-state followed by a low steady-state ([eæ]), except for BAG (the [_g] context) and probably [_ŋ], where up-gliding may occur. BAD ([_d]) seems to undergo diphthongization more than other con-

texts BACK, TAP, and TAB might not be diphthongized through raising the vowel head. BAT can resemble either an unraised BACK or
a raised BAD. When speakers display a raised nonnasal /æ/ vowel
nucleus in southeastern Wisconsin, their /ɛ/ vowel often occurs at
or below the nucleus of /æ/ but not as far as the vowel's glide.

Movement among other vowels in the NCS is not as pronounced
in southeastern Wisconsin as it elsewhere in the NCS region. BOT
may shift slightly forward, but not as far forward toward BACK.
BOUGHT can drop down and forward toward BOT. Labov, Ash, and
Boberg (2006, 65) suggest that fronting of BOT "protects" the BOT-
BOUGHT distinction in southeastern Wisconsin. While the low back
merger is generally not observed in southeastern Wisconsin, the
BOUGHT and BOT word classes have been observed to overlap for
some speakers from Milwaukee. As in other parts of the north, /ɪ/
and /ɛ/ may lower, especially before [l] (BILL) and as part of the
NCS (BIT, BET).

Back vowels generally remain stable. Labov, Ash, and Boberg
(2006, 154, 156) observed that BOOT and BOAT in the Inland North
are not fronting. BOOT and BOAT are often diphthongized. Peterson and Barney (1952), however, noticed that nuclei of BAIT and
BOAT were apparently monophthongal in this area (55 years ago).

Since this study compares the local middle-class African American English (henceforth Wisconsin African American English
[WAAE]) with the speech of other middle-class long-term residents, it is important to review vowel patterns representative of a
pan-AAE variety that might contrast with the white patterns mentioned above. This discussion will follow chapter 22 of Labov, Ash,
and Boberg (2006), based largely on Thomas (2001, 2007). Overall, the claim is that pan-AAE patterns reflect more conservative
Southern patterns with the exception of the BIN-BEN merger and
the possibility of advanced fronting of BUT and BOOK nuclei. One
of the key features of conservative Southern speech, less fronted
BOOT and BOAT vowels, may be relevant in the Deep South but is
largely irrelevant here, where the predominant local vernacular
generally does not front these vowels.

Other evidence—Graff, Labov, and Harris (1986), Gordon
(2000), and Thomas (2001, 2007)—suggests that Northern AAE
does not take part in innovative local vowel changes, but recently,

authors in the present volume and elsewhere (Thomas 1989; Henderson 1996; Jones 2003; Carpenter and Hilliard 2005) have been finding some accommodation to regional dialects. Let us refer to the two possibilities for Milwaukee AAE speakers as the Isolate and Convergent Hypotheses. The differences between the two outcomes are seen on table 8.1. Thomas (2001) notes that BAD, BAT, and so on might raise in AAE to BET, although it would be difficult to distinguish speakers participating in this raising from those participating in an NCS-like shift. Similarly, BOT and BOUGHT do not

TABLE 8.1

Comparison of Vowel Characteristics Realized by an Isolate
or Convergent Dialect within the Context of Southeastern Wisconsin

Keyword	Pan-AAE (Isolate)	Predominant Local Vernacular (Convergent)
BAIT	F1 < 600 toward BET, F2 < 1800	F1 > 550, F2 > 1880
BET	F1 nearing BAIT	F1 at or below BAD nucleus, F2 not as peripheral as BAD
BAT	low front monophthong	either low monophthong or raised diphthong
BAN	raised	raised
BAG	low, front	nearing BET or BAIT, may diphthongize
BAD	low, front	raised nucleus, diphthong
BOT	F2 < 1443	F2 > 1443
BITE	no raised nucleus or glide reduction	along Lake Mich., F1 < 770, F2 < 1550
BIDE	no raised nucleus, glide reduction	nucleus lower than BITE, F2 difference > 60, shorter offglide
BOUT	nucleus back of center, F1 raised; glide shortened below BOUGHT	nucleus F2 < 1550, glide at or above BOUGHT
BOUGHT	variable back upglide	some fronting, F2 > 1255
BOAT	F1 > 620, no fronting	F1 < 620, no fronting, F2 < 1550
BOOK	some fronting, F2 > 1550	no fronting
BUT	some fronting, F2 > 1550	no fronting
BOOT	some fronting, F2 > 1550	no fronting

merge in either dialect. Certain diphthongs would be distinctive: in the isolate mode, BIDE should exhibit an open nucleus and glide weakening (Thomas 2001), while in the convergent mode, there would be raising of the nucleus but no reduction in the glide. Similarly, the isolate mode of BOUT should have an open and fronted nucleus and glide weakening, while the convergent vowel nucleus might be somewhat raised, but the glide would not be weakened. As table 8.1 shows, the isolate mode includes: perhaps a raised and fronted /ɛ/ with concomitant lowering of /eɪ/ as in BET and BAIT; raising of BAT and so on to BET; monophthongization or glide weakening of /aɪ/ before a voiced obstruent in BIDE; a lack of an /ɹ/-like pronunciation in postvocalic /Vɹ/ or rhotic vowels /ɚ, ɝ/; and generally fronting of BUT, BOOK, and BOOT, but not BOAT. See table 8.1 for a comparison. With the exception of BAR, VR sequences will not be discussed in table 8.1 or in this chapter.

METHODOLOGY

SUBJECTS. Nine middle-class African Americans and 9 equivalent whites who are native speakers of this region's English were recorded for this study (tables 8.2 and 8.3).[3] All speakers were educated at

TABLE 8.2
African American Subjects

	Gender	Birth Year	Age	Dialect City	Interviewer
Group 1 (lowest contact)					
WAAE001	M	1985	22	Racine	AA
WAAE002	F	1986	21	Milwaukee	AA
WAAE003	F	1988	19	Milwaukee	AA
Group 2					
WAAE007	F	1978	23	Milwaukee	W
WAAE008	F	1980	22	Milwaukee	W
WAAE009	F	1977	24	Milwaukee	W
Group 3 (highest contact)					
WAAE004	F	1985	22	Milwaukee	W
WAAE005	F	1983	19	Milwaukee	W
WAAE006	F	1981	21	Wauwatosa	W

TABLE 8.3
White Subjects

	Gender	Birth Year	Age	Dialect City	Interviewer
WVE001	F	1989	18	Watertown	W
WVE002	M	1988	19	Fox Point	W
WVE003	F	1988	19	Grafton	W
WVE004	F	1976	25	Kenosha	W
WVE005	F	1977	24	Wauwatosa	W
WVE006	F	1981	21	Fox Point	W
WVE007	F	1987	19	Fox Point	W
WVE008	F	1984	22	Milwaukee	W
WVE009	F	1984	22	Jackson	W

predominantly white universities in Wisconsin and raised in urban areas in southeastern Wisconsin, generally within the broader Milwaukee-Racine combined census area. Each subject was recorded using various styles of elicitation such as free conversation, word list and sentence reading, picture naming, and telling the story from the picture book *Frog Where are You?* by Mercer Meyer (1969). None of the African American subjects, with perhaps the exception of one, would be heard as white.

Examination of the nine WAAE speakers revealed that certain social contact characteristics—geography, family, and interviewer ethnicity—separated the speakers into three equal subgroups. This distinction is consistent with findings by Deser (1990, cited in Thomas 2001), who found linguistic accommodation based on black-white contact. The first two subgroups are those speakers from the north side of Milwaukee which, as noted above, represents the residential area of most blacks in the city (and state). This group is further divided by those speakers recorded speaking to a peer (a college-aged female African American English speaker also from the north side of Milwaukee) from those speakers recorded speaking to an outsider (a middle-aged white male speaker raised elsewhere). The third group of speakers was also interviewed by the same white male interviewer. What distinguishes this last group of speakers is that they have had greater contact with the white speech community, having grown up in multiracial families, living

TABLE 8.4
Numbers of Speakers from Each Group

Interviewee	Interviewer Gender	Interviewee Female	Interviewee Male
1. AA Low Contact	F	2	1
2. AA Low Contact	M	3	0
3. AA High Contact	M	3	0
4. White	M	2	1

outside the north side community, or having attended predominantly white schools even before college. This three-way division of subjects is shown in table 8.2. Because each set of WAAE subjects was reduced to three subjects, three white speakers from the WVE set were selected for comparison based on gender or age. Table 8.4 shows the final division of each group for a more careful examination of individual vowel space features.

Speakers' contact experience and discourse setting maximize the likelihood of finding differences in speech patterns (Deser 1990). The first group of WAAE speakers should display an increased number of pan-AAE patterns, because we would expect a WAAE peer to elicit more AAE-insider speech patterns. The second group of WAAE speakers, interviewed by the white male professor, might therefore speak more formally and accommodate more toward WVE speech patterns. Although the speakers of group 3 are also talking to an outsider, because of their past experiences with white speakers, they might show more code-switching or demonstrate more conformity of speech than the group not having that same level of interracial experience. Given the focus on accommodation, the fact that women are said to accommodate more read-

TABLE 8.5
Vowels under Particular Focus for This Analysis

Pan AAE

    BAIT, BEAR, BEAT, BIDE, BILE, BAR, BIT, BITE, BOAT, BOY, BOOT, BOUT, BUT, BOOK

Wisconsin

    BACK, BAD, BAG, BAN, BAT, BET, BOT, BOUGHT, TAP

ily (e.g., Labov 2001, chap. 11) led to a choice of predominantly female speakers, as tables 8.2 and 8.3 highlight.

From these interviews, I chose appropriate vowels to analyze. Their vowels were analyzed acoustically, following the same protocol used for other studies in this volume: vowels were analyzed with Praat following a strict protocol to permit comparison among the studies. Attempts were made to use a minimum of five tokens of each vowel from the conversation. When the number of tokens for that word class was below five, the token set was supplemented by samples taken from sentences, word lists, picture naming, and storytelling. The phonological classes of most interest are found on table 8.5.

ACOUSTIC ANALYSIS. The first three formants for every target vowel were measured at two points using a combination of Matlab and TF32 (Milenkovic 2005). The two points represent the nucleus and glide of the vowel (Andruski and Nearey 1992; Assmann and Katz 2000). Identification of the measurement points occurred when the first three formants either moved the least or reached a maximum or minimum. The nucleus and glide of all vowels are shown. In order to compare vowels within an individual speaker's vowel space, these measurements were recorded in Hertz, normalized using Labov's Telsur G method (Labov, Ash, and Boberg 2006), and plotted using NORM (Kendall and Thomas 2009), as were the measurements for other studies in this volume.

The goal of this chapter is to identify the distribution of vowels among various members of the African American and white speech communities in the greater Milwaukee region. Given the low numbers of speakers in each group and the fact that only one speaker in 9 was male, comments will be limited to means for each vowel and descriptions of vowel spaces on an individual basis. Our expectations echo much of the discussion that has ensued in the literature about divergence and convergence (e.g., Labov 1987; Rickford 1999). One might expect that given the low density of African Americans overall in Wisconsin and that the speakers investigated are connected to predominantly white universities, the African American speakers would display norms much closer to the regional variety in line with Deser (1990). Results of this study indicate that a number of pan-AAE features are preserved in the African American speakers from southeastern Wisconsin, while others are more influenced by the degree of contact speakers have had with speakers of the predominant local vernacular, WVE.

RESULTS

Overall, the picture emerging from the present data is that African American speakers in southeastern Wisconsin have a mixed vowel system; that is, some vowels display pan-AAE and others do not. Below we will examine the acoustic characteristics of the isolate and convergent patterns (table 8.1). The backdrop for examining the target vowels are the vowels of white speakers. Figures 8.2–8.4 show the vowel plots for the control speakers: WVE002, WVE007, and WVE009. The vowel plot for WVE002 demonstrates that individual middle-class speakers may not present the archetypical NCS

FIGURE 8.2

WVE002, White Male (b. 1988) from Fox Point

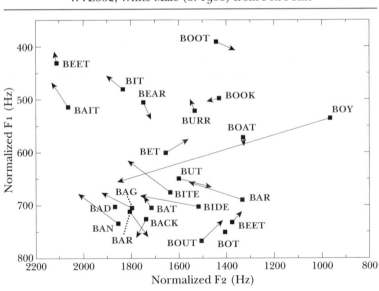

FIGURE 8.3
WVE007, White Female (b. 1987) from Fox Point

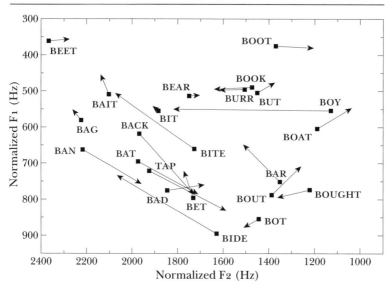

FIGURE 8.4
WVE009, White Female (b. 1984) from Jackson

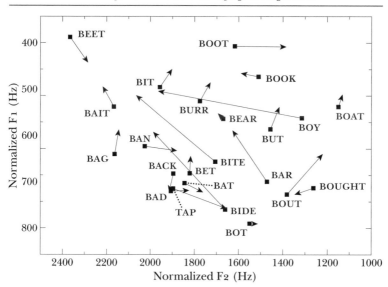

vowel that we expect, based on Labov, Ash and Boberg (2006). Note, however, that WVE002 is the only male in the control group, and we might expect his vowels to be less innovative than those of the females in his cohort. In the other two speakers' vowel space plots, we can see the more general southeastern Wisconsin vowel system pattern: BAG with an upward trajectory, BAG nucleus at or above BAN nucleus, BAN raised above other /æ/ vowels, lowering of BET, and raising of BITE's nucleus. BOUT is either raised among the WVE speakers (e.g., WVE007, WVE009) or lower (WVE002). In all cases, the glide of BOUT is at or above BOUGHT.

The vowel plots for the African American speakers are shown in figures 8.5–8.13. Although it is argued that each group has certain particularities in the vowel space, we can observe a number of shared features before moving into the differences. With the exception of WAAE002, BAIT and BOAT are diphthongs, as they are for all of the WVE speakers. Second, BOUGHT is generally between BOT and BOAT. Third, BOOK and BUT are generally not very fronted except for WAAE002 and WAAE003, whose BOOK appears some-

FIGURE 8.5

WAAE001, African American Male (b. 1985) from Racine

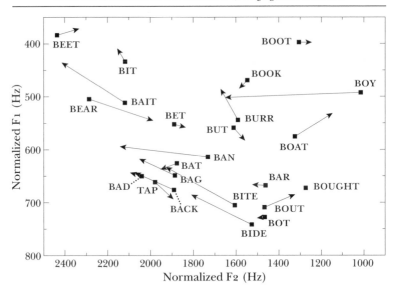

FIGURE 8.6

WAAE002, African American Female (b. 1986) from Milwaukee

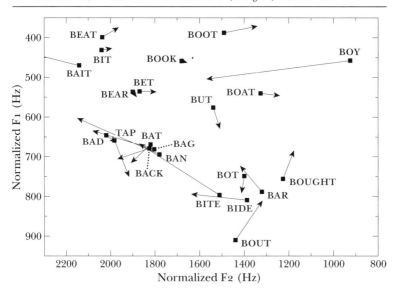

FIGURE 8.7

WAAE003, African American Female (b. 1988) from Milwaukee

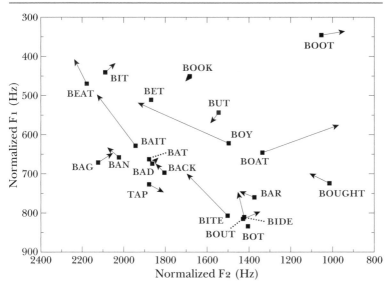

what advanced. Now let us compare these speakers with three different groups of speakers from the African American community:

GROUP 1. Recall that this group of three test speakers, shown on table 2, has arguably the least motivation for accommodating to the predominant local vernacular, given that they grew up in Milwaukee and may have had less overall contact with white speakers than the other two groups, not to mention that they are interacting with an in-group interviewer, while all the others are interacting with a member of the larger stereotypically "dominant" group. The vowel plots for these speakers are shown in figures 8.5–8.7.

For the group, two vowels of particular note are the nuclei of BITE and BIDE, as well as the nucleus of BAR. First, while the three white speakers had centralized BITE but not BIDE, these three speakers have less difference in F1, which correlates with voicing of the following consonant. Comparing just the two female speakers in both groups, the difference between the F1 nucleus means for BITE and BIDE is 13 and 4 Hz, for WAAE002 and WAAE003, respectively. The same measure for WVE007 and WVE009, respectively, is 235 and 102 Hz. Second, while the three white speakers have no significant difference in the glides when the following consonant is voiced or voiceless, the three African American speakers follow a more Southern pattern, with reduced glides before a voiced obstruent. The difference between the lengths of BITE and BIDE trajectories for WVE007 and WVE009 is 88 and 21 Hz, whereas for WAAE002 and WAAE03 it is 135 and 151 Hz, respectively. Third, the three white speakers have backed BAR nuclei ($\bar{x}$ = 1335, 1350, and 1472 Hz, resp.), with a longish transition to the /ɹ/ ($\bar{x}$ Euclidean distance = 229, 188, and 188 Hz, resp.) giving the appearance of diphthongization. In contrast, the three African American speakers in group 1 also have F2 below 1500 ($\bar{x}$ = 1463, 1327, and 1372 Hz, resp.). The fact that the white speakers, like those analyzed in Chicago (McCarthy 2008), have a backed nucleus rather than a classic NCS nucleus permits less of a possible contrast between the groups.

GROUP 2. This group is treated separately from group 1 because the interviewer for this group was not of the same speech community. As we can see in figures 8.8–8.10, there are some shared features

FIGURE 8.8
WAAE007, African American Female (b. 1978) from Milwaukee

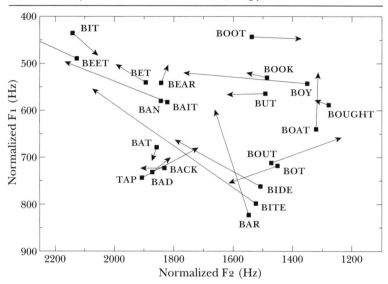

FIGURE 8.9
WAAE008, African American Female (b. 1980) from Milwaukee

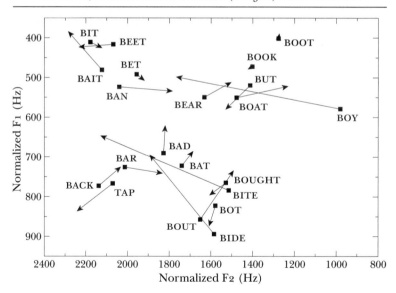

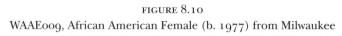

FIGURE 8.10
WAAE009, African American Female (b. 1977) from Milwaukee

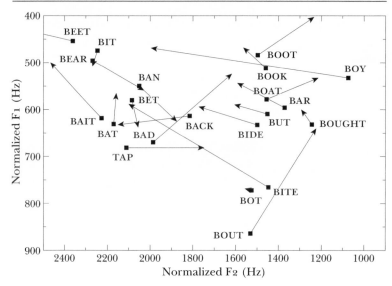

with group 1. Additionally, two speakers in this group (WAAE008 and WAAE009) and one speaker in group 1 (WAAE003) display a more typical AAE pattern of BET being at or above the nucleus of BAIT and BIT being higher in the vowel space than the nucleus of BEET, rather than having the lowered nuclei for BET and BIT that are common in the NCS area. The role of BET here is important since BET is often lower for NCS speakers (Eckert 2000; Labov, Ash, and Boberg 2006) and higher for Southern Shift speakers (Labov, Ash, and Boberg 2006; see, however, Baranowski 2007 and Wroblewski, Strand, and Dubois 2010 [this volume]). The mean F1 for the nucleus of BET for the white speakers is 601, 796, and 681 Hz, respectively, while for the group 2 speakers the mean F1 for BET is 545, 498, and 579, respectively.

Regarding glide trajectories, only one white speaker had an F2 for a BITE or BIDE nucleus lower than 1550 Hz, while only one group 2 speaker had F2 over 1550 Hz. For all group 2 speakers, the glides are considerably longer before the voiceless stop (by 299, 265, and 398 Hz, resp.); this can also be attributed to the influence of AAE. Additionally, the glide of BOUT is more consistent with the local white speakers' ($\bar{x}$F1 × $\bar{x}$F2: 767 × 1507, 787 × 1386, and 727 × 1382 Hz, resp.) than with any evidence from Thomas (2001, 2007) for African American speakers. Compare with group 2 speakers: $\bar{x}$F1 × $\bar{x}$F2: 718 × 1486, 868 × 1672, and 862 × 1528 Hz, respectively.

The word classes of BAN, BOUGHT, and BAR highlight the complex relation of this set of speakers with the predominant local vernacular. BAN is raised above the other /æ/ vowels, as it would be for either an isolate or a convergent vowel phonology. This is shared by both pan-AAE speakers and NCS speakers and is not a diagnostic vowel. The difference in mean F1 between BAN and BAD is 153, 169, and 120 Hz, respectively, for the group 2 speakers. The same comparison for the two female white speakers is 113 and 97 Hz, respectively. Two of the three speakers have unlowered or unfronted BOUGHT nuclei ($\bar{x}$F1 × $\bar{x}$F2: 594 × 1292, 775 × 1548, and 630 × 1242 Hz, resp.), which is also not a feature of the predominant local vernacular (compare to white: $\bar{x}$F1 × $\bar{x}$F2: 732 × 1378, 774 × 1221, and 713 × 1262 Hz, resp.). On the other hand, one speaker has fronted nuclei for BAR (WAAE008, $\bar{x}$ = 2037 Hz), which is consistent with neither a pan-AAE nor a predominant local vernacular depicted in figures 8.2–8.4 and the evidence of McCarthy (2008); only one speaker has the backed nucleus that one might expect (WAAE009, $\bar{x}$ = 1367 Hz).

GROUP 3. This "high contact" group from table 8.2 differs from group 1 not only in that the elicitation was conducted by a white, but also, more importantly, each of the speakers had more contact with whites either from having lived outside Milwaukee (WAAE006) or from having one parent who is white (WAAE004, WAAE005), leading us to expect greater convergence toward the local phonology. Moreover, WAAE005 attended a language immersion school and spent a year in Europe during high school. The first thing to note about this group's plots in figures 8.11–8.13 is that the glide of BIDE is higher than the other groups'. Since the glide of BITE for all speakers of the three groups is higher than the glide in BIDE we can see that for this group the glide extends the highest. Moreover, nuclei of BET for group 3 speakers (WAAE004 $\bar{x}$F1 = 600 Hz,

FIGURE 8.11

WAAE004, African American Female (b. 1985) from Milwaukee

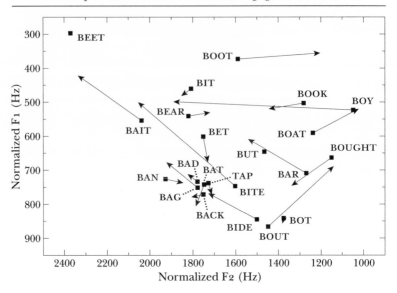

FIGURE 8.12

WAAE005, African American Female (b. 1983) from Milwaukee

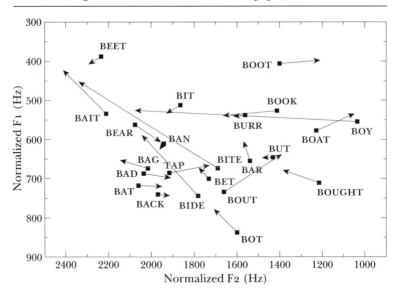

FIGURE 8.13

WAAE006, African American Female (b. 1981) from Wauwatosa

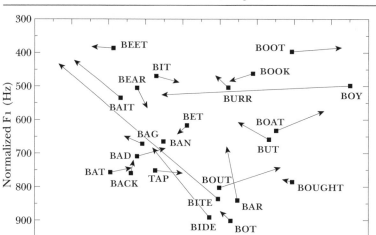

WAAE005 $\bar{x}$F1 = 681 Hz, WAAE006 $\bar{x}$F1 = 599 Hz) also conform to the NCS patterns used locally: nuclei are lowering. This is in contrast with the BET raisers in the other two groups (closest of the other groups was 579 Hz). Finally, BAR nuclei appear closer to the 1500-Hz line, which Labov, Ash and Boberg (2006) consider the central divider, although they do not pass it (group 1: 1463, 1328, 1372 Hz; group 2: 1563, 2037, 1367 Hz; and group 3: 1267, 1499, 1461 Hz).

DISCUSSION

This chapter has presented evidence from a carefully organized sample of vowels from southeastern Wisconsin speakers. The sample was selected to maximize the possibility of finding dialect accommodation (Purnell 2009). Examination of the vowel plots demonstrates not only the similarities and differences between the groups of speakers, but more importantly that increased social con-

TABLE 6

Comparisons of Select Features by WAAE Subject

Speakers	01	02	03	07	08	09	04	05	06
BET lowering	–	?	–	–	–	–	–	+	?
BAN raising	–	–	+	+	+	+	+	+	+
BAG raising	–	–	+					+	+
Canadian raising	–	–	–	–	?		+	+	–
BIDE	cent.	cent.	cent.	back	cent.	back.	cent.	for.	for.
BAR (<1500)	+	+	+	–	–	+	+	+	+
BOOT, BOAT (<1400)	–	–	–	BOOT	BOAT	+	+	–	–
BOOK, BUT (>1400)	+	+	+	+	+	+	+	+	+
BOUT tail < BOUGHT	–	–	–	at	at	at	at	above	above

tact with members of outside groups influences vowel nucleus position and the Euclidean distance of the glide. Table 8.6 lists patterns that are found in the three groups of WAAE speakers. First, African American speakers in southeastern Wisconsin appear to retain features akin to pan-AAE or the Southern Shift involving BET, BAIT, BIT, and BEET, whether or not they accommodate to an outsider. Second, African Americans in southeastern Wisconsin display diphthongization in contrast with Southern dialects. Moreover, /aɪ/ diphthongization is gradient and influenced by past exposure to whites (group 3) or by the white interviewer (groups 2 and 3). The similarity of pushing the glide higher up in the vowel space is observable for both groups. This might be attributable to the white interviewer. Nevertheless, the /aɪ/ glides are exaggeratedly high for group 3, that is, above even the white location. Note also that the Euclidean distance of the glide from the nucleus for BOOT, and for PULL and BAR to a lesser extent, suggests some degree of accommodation by African American speakers of a local white feature. This finding agrees with Deser (1990), who observed a covariation of content and diphthongization.

This study presents clear evidence that the greater the motivation for accommodation to the predominant local vernacular norm, the more extensive the restructuring of the vowel space. The research paradigm of the present study afforded two ways for African Americans to accommodate to whites. First, they could accommodate in the interview process. Indeed, we find that the vowel space of group 1, who were interviewed by another black speaker, should stand in contrast to the other two groups. The second type of accommodation we hypothesized could arise from extended dialect-development exposure that took place prior to the interview process. Our expectation was that group 3, whose speakers had more extensive white contact, would be distinct from groups 1 and 2. We observe that variable accommodation in group 3 is realized in the raised nucleus and glide of BITE, BIDE, and BOUT, and diphthongization and an increased /æ/-/ɛ/ interaction (especially BET lowering).

These findings call for further research. The first area to pursue in order to understand the vagaries of African American speech is to better understand whether the observed diphthongization covaries with accommodation of African American to white speech or whether it is a middle-class African American speech feature. In the upper Midwest, a wider sample from the city core and periphery or between Milwaukee or Racine and Madison, or recording the same speaker in different interview settings, may provide more insight into the nexus of social class and accommodation in a speaker's vowel space. Second, large cross-regional studies like those in the present volume will further our understanding of how African American speech communities or communities of practice are self-defined. No effort was made in the present study to have subjects self-define their identity, the strength of their identity, or past practice of interaction with members of other groups. Consequently, the typical study on AAE absent the context of similar studies cannot provide clarity regarding variation in geographic-specific African American identities. Finally, studies such as those included in this volume should generate discussion among sociophoneticians as to what impact the Great Migration has on individual studies of specific speech communities. Our field of inquiry should expect that the pressures to accommodate are distinct across the range of locales from a non–Great Migration community (e.g., many Southern communities), to an intermediate Great Migration city (e.g.,

Indianapolis), or a post–Great Migration locale (e.g., Milwaukee) or a returning–Great Migration locale (e.g., Atlanta). Milwaukee specifically, and southeastern Wisconsin in general, present a distinct sociohistorical milieu. Here, African Americans appear to balance identities through the conveyance of a historical connection with the South by using a partial remnant of vowel features. At the same time, these speakers distance themselves from a Northern white identity by not participating in vowel space restructurings.

NOTES

I wish to thank Jessica Dickerson for help in data collection along with Blake Rodgers, Eric Raimy, Joe Salmons, Erik Thomas, and Malcah Yaeger-Dror for discussing portions of this chapter with me. A portion of this work was funded by the University of Wisconsin–Madison Graduate School.

1. For this chapter, the upper Midwest includes Wisconsin, Minnesota, and Michigan's upper peninsula. The Association for Institutional Research in the Upper Midwest considers North Dakota, South Dakota, Illinois, and Michigan part of the upper Midwest in addition what is used here, although it is noted that the narrow geographic distribution is the most common one.

2. Although Kenosha is south of Racine, it is often considered as an extension of the greater Chicago metropolitan area, as is the case for the 2000 U.S. Census.

3. The subjects were recruited through the friend-of-a-friend method but were not asked to self-identify as African Americans or blacks.

REFERENCES

Andruski, Jean E., and Terrance M. Nearey. 1992. "On the Sufficiency of Compound Target Specification of Isolated Vowels and Vowels in /bVb/ Syllables." *Journal of the Acoustical Society of America* 91: 390–410.

Assmann, Peter F., and William F. Katz. 2000. "Time-Varying Spectral Change in the Vowels of Children and Adults." *Journal of the Acoustical Society of America* 108: 1856–66.

Baranowski, Maciej. 2007. *Phonological Variation and Change in the Dialect of Charleston, South Carolina.* Publication of the American Dialect Society 92. Durham, N.C.: Duke Univ. Press.

Bauer, Matt, and Frank Parker. 2008. "/æ/-Raising in Wisconsin English." *American Speech* 83: 403–31.

Carpenter, Jeannine, and Sarah Hilliard. 2005. "Shifting Parameters of Individual and Group Variation: African American English on Roanoke Island." *Journal of English Linguistics* 33: 161–84.

Coggshall, Elizabeth L., and Kara Becker. 2010. "The Vowel Phonologies of African American and White New York City Residents." In Yaeger-Dror and Thomas, 101–28.

Deser, Toni. 1990. "Dialect Transmission and Variation: An Acoustic Analysis of Vowels in Six Urban Detroit Families." Ph.D. diss., Boston Univ.

Durian, David, Robin Dodsworth, and Jennifer Schumacher. 2010. "Convergence in Blue-Collar Columbus, Ohio, African American and White Vowel Systems?" In Yaeger-Dror and Thomas, 161–90.

Eckert, Penelope. 2000. *Linguistic Variation as Social Practice: The Linguistic Construction of Identity in Belten High.* Malden, Mass.: Blackwell.

Gordon, Matthew J. 2000. "Phonological Correlates of Ethnic Identity: Evidence of Divergence?" *American Speech* 75: 115–36.

Graff, David, William Labov, and Wendell A. Harris. 1986. "Testing Listeners' Reactions to Phonological Markers of Ethnic Identity: A New Method for Sociolinguistic Research." In *Diversity and Diachrony*, ed. David Sankoff, 45–58. Amsterdam: Benjamins.

Henderson, Anita. 1996. "The Short 'a' Pattern of Philadelphia among African American Speakers." In "(N)WAVES and MEANS: A Selection of Papers from NWAVE 24," ed. Miriam Meyerhoff, 127–40. *University of Pennsylvania Working Papers in Linguistics* 3.1.

Jones, Jamila. 2003. "African Americans in Lansing and the Northern Cities Vowel Shift: Language Contact and Accommodation." Ph.D. diss., Michigan State Univ.

Kendall, Tyler, and Erik Thomas. 2009. Vowels: Vowel Manipulation, Normalization, and Plotting in R. R package. Version 1.0-2. Available at http://ncslaap.lib.ncsu.edu/tools/norm.

Labov, William. 1987. "Are Black and White Vernaculars Diverging?" *American Speech* 62: 5–12.

———. 2001. *Principles of Linguistic Change.* Vol. 2, *Social Factors.* Oxford: Blackwell.

Labov, William, Sharon Ash, and Charles Boberg. 2006. *The Atlas of North American English: Phonetics, Phonology, and Sound Change.* Berlin: Mouton de Gruyter.

McCarthy, Corinne. 2008. "The Northern Cities Shift in Real- and Apparent-Time: Evidence from Chicago." Paper presented at the 37th annual conference on New Ways of Analyzing Variation (NWAV 37), Houston, Texas, Nov. 6–9.

McHugh, Kevin E. 1987. "Black Migration Reversal in the United States." *Geographical Review* 77: 171–82.

Meyer, Mercer. 1969. *Frog, Where Are You?* New York: Dial.

Milenkovic, Paul. 2005. TF32: Time-Frequency Analysis for 32-Bit Windows. Available at http://userpages.chorus.net/cspeech/index.html.

Ostergren, Robert C., and Thomas R. Vale. 1997. *Wisconsin Land and Life.* Madison: Univ. of Wisconsin Press.

Peterson, Gordon E., and Harold L. Barney. 1952. "Control Methods Used in a Study of the Vowels." *Journal of the Acoustical Society of America* 24: 175–84.

Purnell, Thomas C. 2008. "Prevelar Raising and Phonetic Conditioning: Role of Labial and Anterior Tongue Gestures." *American Speech* 83: 373–402.

———. 2009. "Convergence and Contact in Milwaukee: Evidence from Select African American and White Vowel Space Features." *Journal of Language and Social Psychology* 28: 408–27.

Purnell, Thomas C., and Joseph C. Salmons. Forthcoming. "Coherence over Time and Space in Sound Change." In memorial volume for Sergei Starostin, ed. Vitaly Shevoroshkin and Harald Sverdrup. Copenhagen: Underskoven.

Ranney, Joseph A. 1995. "Wisconsin's Legal History: Part 13—Looking Further than the Skin: A History of Wisconsin Civil Rights Law." *Wisconsin Lawyer* 68.7: 20–23, 52–53. Available at http://www.wisbar.org/AM/Template.cfm?Section=Wisconsin_s_legal_history&TEMPLATE=/CM/ContentDisplay.cfm&CONTENTID=35860.

Rickford, John R. 1999. *African American Vernacular English: Features, Evolution, Educational Implications.* Malden, Mass.: Blackwell.

Rinder, Irwin D. 1955. *The Housing of Negroes in Milwaukee, 1955.* Milwaukee, Wis.: Intercollegiate Council on Intergroup Relations.

Thomas, Erik R. 1989. "Vowel Changes in Columbus, Ohio." *Journal of English Linguistics* 22: 205–15.

————. 2001. *An Acoustic Analysis of Vowel Variation in New World English.* Publication of the American Dialect Society 85. Durham, N.C.: Duke Univ. Press.

————. 2007. "Phonological and Phonetic Characteristics of African American Vernacular English." *Language and Linguistics Compass* 1: 450–75.

Trotter, Joe William, Jr. 1985. *Black Milwaukee: The Making of an Industrial Proletariat, 1915–1945.* Urbana: Univ. of Illinois Press.

U.S. Census Bureau. 1961. *Census of Population: 1960.* Vol. 1, part 51, Wisconsin. Washington, D.C.: GPO.

————. 2000. Summary File 1. http://www.census.gov/Press-Release/www/2001/sumfile1.html.

Wroblewski, Michael, Thea Strand, and Sylvie Dubois. 2010. "Mapping a Dialect 'Mixtury': Vowel Phonology of African American and White Men in Rural Southern Louisiana." In Yaeger-Dror and Thomas, 48–72.

Yaeger-Dror, Malcah, and Erik R. Thomas, eds. 2010. *African American English Speakers and Their Participation in Local Sound Changes: A Comparative Study.* Publication of the American Dialect Society 94. Durham, N.C.: Duke Univ. Press.

Zeller, Christine. 1997. "The Investigation of a Sound Change in Progress: /æ/ to /e/ in Midwestern American English." *Journal of English Linguistics* 25: 142–55.

INDEX

/ɑ/, 9. *See also* BOT; BAR
accommodation. *See* speech accommodation
Adams, Carol M., 2, 4
Adank, Patti, 186
/æ/, 9. *See also* BAT; BAD; BACK; BAG; BAN
African American English (AAE), 1, 80,
  101–2, 114; origins, 3; in North
  Carolina, 23–43; in Louisiana, 48–69;
  in Roswell, Ga., 75–97; in New York
  City, 101–25; in Pittsburgh, 129–53;
  in Columbus, 161–88; in Milwaukee,
  191–214
African American shift, 103, 117, 118,
  174–75, 183, 185, 186
/aɪ/, 9. *See also* BIDE; BITE; PILE; PINE; PYRE
Alabama, 162, 193. *See also* Anniston
Albany, N.Y., 109
Alim, H. Samy, 6
Anderson, Bridget L., 7, 24, 42, 79, 119,
  129, 147, 151
Andres, Claire, 65, 79
Andruski, Jean E., 201
Anglicist position, 3
Anniston, Ala., 13
Appalachia, 5; Beech Bottom, N.C., 34–37;
  Texana, N.C., 37–41
Appalachian English, 35, 39, 42
Arkansas, 193
Ash, Sharon, 2, 59, 60, 62, 65, 66, 68, 79, 85,
  87, 101, 102, 107, 108, 112, 113, 130,
  131, 132, 135, 141, 150, 161, 169, 174,
  175, 184, 195, 196, 201, 204, 208, 211
Asian Americans, 2, 6, 105; Chinese Ameri-
  cans, 108, 111
Assmann, Peter F., 201
Atlanta, Georgia, 10, 24, 76, 81, 84, 85, 88,
  92, 93, 97
Atlas of North American English, 107
/aʊ/, 9. *See also* BOUT; HOUR; HOWL; BOUGH
Auer, Peter, 6
Austin, Texas, 185
Babbitt, E. H., 109

backing: in Southern Shift, 23; in North
  Carolina, 30; in Roswell, Ga., 80, 84, 87;
  New York City, 107, 108, 110; in Columbus, 163, 175
BACK: in Milwaukee, 195–96
BAD: raising in New York City, 107, 109–12,
  120–24; breaking or diphthongization in
  Milwaukee, 195–97, 200, 209
BAIL-BELL merger: in New York City, 103,
  116, 122–24; in Pittsburgh, 136
Bailey, Guy, 2, 3, 4, 38, 79, 80, 88, 91, 96,
  102, 106, 112, 116, 118, 125, 129, 132,
  137, 142, 161, 165,
BAIT, 4, 7, 10; in Roanoke Island, N.C., 30;
  in Hyde County, N.C., 32; in Louisiana,
  51, 53, 57, 59–62, 65; reversal with BET
  in Roswell, Ga., 80–81, 85–88, 92–93,
  95; in New York City, 120; in Columbus,
  169, 171, 174–75, 184–85; in Milwau-
  kee, 196, 198, 204, 208, 212
BAIT-BET reversal, 5; in Louisiana, 65; in
  Roswell, Ga., 80–81, 85–88, 92–93, 95
Baldwin, Leland D., 129, 130
BAN: in Louisiana, 64–65; in New York City,
  107, 109–12, 120–23; in Pittsburgh, 137;
  in Columbus, 187; in Northern Cities
  Shift, 195
Bankston, Carl L., III, 48, 51
Baranowski, Maciej, 62, 65, 208
Barney, Harold L., 196
Barry, Betsy, 24
Bartlett, Kathy, 5, 7, 11, 62, 151, 161, 165,
  184, 185
Bassett, Marvin H., 2, 4
BAT: in NCS, 12; in Louisiana, 57, 60, 64–65;
  in New York City, 103, 109–12, 117,
  121, 123–24; in Pittsburgh, 137; in
  Columbus, 169, 172, 174–75, 183–85; in
  Wisconsin, 196
Bauer, Matt, 195
Baugh, John, 6, 125